Feeding 9 billion

The contribution of new genetic technologies to global food production

Peter Evans

David Bennett and Richard Jennings

Feeding 9 billion

The contribution of new genetic
technologies to global food production

Lead editor: Peter Evans
Editors: Dr David Bennett and Dr Richard C. Jennings

Feeding 9 billion is based on *Successful Agricultural Innovation in Emerging Economies: New Genetic Technologies for Global Food Production* published by Cambridge University Press in 2013, with the publisher's permission.

Contributors to *Successful Agricultural Innovation in Emerging Economies: New Genetic Technologies for Global Food Production* include: Dr Alfredo Aguilar; Professor Klaus Ammann; Dr Tina Barsby; Professor Sir David Baulcombe FRS; Dr Roger Beachy; Jack Bobo; Graham Brookes; Samuel Burckhardt; Dr Claudia Canales Holzeis; Mark F. Cantley; Dr Eugenio J. Cap; Dr Danuta Cichocka; Professor Sir Gordon Conway FRS; Dr Adrian Dubock; Professor Jim M. Dunwell; Dr Ioannis Economidis; Professor George Gaskell; Professor Ian Graham; Dr Julian Gray; Professor Jonathan Gressel; Professor Sir Brian Heap CBE FRS; T.J.V. Higgins; Jens Högel; Professor Drew L. Kershen; Professor Christopher J. Leaver CBE FRS FRSE; Professor Lu Bao-rong; Dr Diran Makinde; Carel du Marchie Sarvaas; Nathalie Moll; Professor Larry Murdock; Dr Martin Porter; Tim Radford; Professor Wayne Powell; Professor Chavali Kameswara Rao; Professor Pamela Ronald; Piet Schenkelaars; Idah Sithole-Niang; Dr Sally Stares; Dr Eduardo J. Trigo; Dr Piero Venturi; Katy Wilson.

This publication was made possible through the support of grants from the John Templeton Foundation.

ISBN 978-0-9563387-8-5

Published in 2014 by Banson, 27 Devonshire Road, Cambridge CB1 2BH, UK

Citation: Evans, P., Bennett, D. and Jennings, R.C. (eds) 2014. *Feeding 9 Billion.* Banson.

Text editors: Helen de Mattos, Bart Ullstein
Design and layout: Banson
Cover image: Romastudio/Dreamstime.com
Print: The Lavenham Press, UK

Peter Evans has more than 30 years experience hosting a weekly science magazine programme for BBC Radio 4, authored 11 books, been commissioning editor for two major publishing houses and given media and communications training to members of many scientific research organisations.

Dr David Bennett is a Senior Member of St Edmund's College, Cambridge, UK.

He has a PhD in biochemical genetics and an MA in science policy studies with long-term experience of the relations between science, industry, government, education, law, the public and the media. He works with the European Commission, government departments, companies, universities, public-interest organisations and the media, and has lived in the UK, USA, Australia and The Netherlands.

Dr Richard C. Jennings is an Affiliated Research Scholar at the University of Cambridge, UK. His research interests are in the ethics of science and technology. He pioneered the university's teaching of ethics in science and continues to run graduate ethics workshops. He has developed, with others, a framework for assessing ethical issues in new technologies.

FOREWORD

World population is forecast to grow from 7 billion to 9 billion by 2050. One in eight people – some 827 million – are already hungry, and food production must increase by 70–100 per cent during this period. No single solution will resolve the problem, but the new genetic technologies of plant breeding developed during the last 30 years can do much to increase agricultural efficiencies and save people from hunger in a sustainable manner, particularly in African nations where the need is greatest.

Advanced molecular plant breeding based on genomics, marker-assisted screening, phenotype analysis, computer modelling and, when necessary, genetic modification (GM), have greatly accelerated the breeding process. Substantial efforts in basic scientific research and agricultural practice over the last 30 years have yielded dramatic results, particularly in North America, South America and a number of other emerging economies, as the new technologies have spread worldwide. This has contributed to:

- higher yields;
- resistance to pests, diseases, drought and soil salinisation;
- lower energy consumption and pesticide use and a reduction in soil damage thanks to low-till agriculture;
- enhanced nutritional quality;
- increased efficiency of nutrient uptake and water use.

The latest advances can help meet demands on world farming by rapidly incorporating traits from the immense genetic variability of wild relatives into established crops, combining many genes to enhance desirable traits and tailoring existing crops to meet new environmental challenges, for example from climate change. They can reduce the time and costs taken to improve research on neglected local crop varieties and so-called orphan crops found in emerging economies. And they can be used to domesticate new crops from semi-wild plants, providing practical and economically feasible new crops.

The problems and challenges now lie in the implementation of these impressive scientific advances where they are desperately needed. And this is the issue that has not so far received adequate attention or support.

This book owes its origins to its parent volume, *Successful Agricultural Innovation in Emerging Economies: New Genetic Technologies for Global Food Production*, published by Cambridge University Press in 2013 and edited by David Bennett and Richard Jennings. The parent book was published because of the need to address the many environmental, technical, political, legal and ethical issues involved in implementing the new biotechnologies. The need to put these scientific advances into practice to feed the 9 billion mouths was already widely recognised, yet there was still no source of information for a much wider, non-specialised readership on how this may be effected. The parent book was thus compiled as a series of essays for those wishing to understand the key issues in depth. It was an attempt by experienced people – who have through a good part of their lives worked in the sciences involved and on the policies and practices surrounding them – to explain and promote these advances in the developed and emerging worlds.

The present book provides a collected, reliable and succinct account of those same issues in a more accessible format. Its various chapters explore the issues from different angles, but all of them deal expressly with the successful implementation of the new plant genetic sciences in emerging economies in the context of inter-related key social, ethical, political, regulatory and trade matters. Its aim is to contribute to global efforts to "feed 9 billion", so its main focus is on food crops, but it also includes information on some non-food crops – such as cotton – because the issues surrounding them are similar to those of crops grown for food. It is a resource for students in many disciplines undertaking courses, in-service training, workshops, extension work and similar activities worldwide, whether in developed or emerging economies.

We would like to express our sincere gratitude, both to Cambridge University Press for permitting material in *Successful Agricultural Innovation in Emerging Economies: New Genetic Technologies for Global Food Production* to provide the basis for this book, and to the John Templeton Foundation for support in writing the parent volume, and for funding the writing and production of the present book. Without their considerable support, this would not have been possible.

David Bennett and Richard Jennings

CONTENTS

INTRODUCTION

FOOD PRODUCTION AND SECURITY – CHALLENGES AND SOLUTIONS

worryingly rapid game of leapfrog is taking place on a global scale. The world's population, currently more than 7 billion, is predicted to reach 9 billion by 2050. Already, one in every eight people on our planet goes to bed hungry. So, in order to close this pressing resource gap, food output will have to increase in the coming decades by at least 70–100 per cent. How can production keep pace with this tug of war between supply and demand?

To meet the needs of the world's ever growing population, food output will have to increase by 70–100 per cent in the coming decades.

There is no simple answer, as analysts ranging from Thomas Malthus in 1798 with *An Essay on the Principle of Population* to Paul Ehrlich with *The Population Bomb* in 1968 have amply demonstrated. The much-discussed 1972 book *The Limits to Growth*, commissioned by the Club of Rome, used computer modelling to explore the tension between unchecked population growth and the capacity for technology to increase the availability of resources, which is relatively limited.

A complex problem

Clearly, improved crop technologies and farming practices are crucial to securing adequate food production. But it is not simply a matter of encouraging or empowering farmers to generate more calories from their land. Other considerations come into play alongside simple yield.

Aspects of sustainability including greenhouse gas emissions, soil erosion, water availability and depletion together with deleterious impacts on other aspects of the Earth system, especially biodiversity, all have to be taken into account when computing the arithmetic of supply and demand. And, of course, any new technologies must deliver a discernible benefit to the farmer: without prospects for improvement there can be no investment in sustainability.

A further complication is the geographical location of the growing population. Eighty per cent of the increase to 9 billion people in 2050 will take place in the developing and transition countries of China, India, Africa, Southeast Asia and South America, with the majority living in cities. The next 40 years will see the population of Africa double, placing immense strains on arable land, so that each hectare will need to feed five people compared to just two in 1960.

Looking long term

In the face of climate change through fossil-fuel use and the intensification of agriculture, which further drives up greenhouse gas emissions and atmospheric carbon dioxide (CO_2) levels, food producers will be hard-pressed to keep abreast of their targets. Water availability is expected to decline and pests and pathogens to increase, with an impact on both food production and post-harvest losses, but urbanisation will pursue its course and dietary requirements will continue to rise, with a concomitant demand for meat.

Today, all these factors can, more or less, be coped with, particularly if efforts are made to reduce food waste on both the supply and the demand sides of the equation. Existing food stocks are also adequate to respond to the acute hunger associated with civil unrest or adverse climatic influences. In the long term, however, these chronic problems will need to be overcome by measures designed to promote so-called sustainable intensification. This means growing more from less in order both to meet current needs and to improve the ability of future generations to meet their own dietary requirements while looking after the planet on which they live.

Revolutionary science

A crucial factor in meeting these goals will undoubtedly lie in maintaining what has been a genuine revolution in plant science. Humankind has been breeding crops for about 10,000 years by selecting seeds or cuttings from plants with desirable characteristics. More recently, scientists have accumulated an ever deepening understanding of the information encoded within the genes of plants, as well as those of the pests and pathogens that attack them.

We have entered the era of "-omics" technologies – such as genomics (the study of genomes) and proteomics (the study of proteins) – which are revealing the intricacies of genetic structures and their relationship with how plants function. Researchers are drawing on bioinformatics and computer modelling to integrate this knowledge, supported by the use of appropriate chemicals and farming practices.

We now have an unprecedented ability to produce more robust and productive crops, either through sophisticated molecular breeding methods based on our new powers of observation and selection, or by directly and specifically changing a plant's genetic composition and function.

Around 1.3 billion tonnes of food, about a third of all production, is wasted every year – at a cost of US$ 750 billion.

Crop yields in selected regions, 1961–2012

Tonnes per hectare

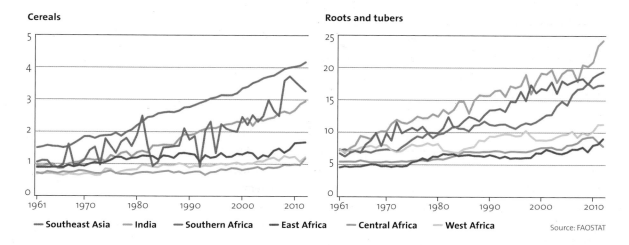

Cereals

Roots and tubers

Southeast Asia — India — Southern Africa — East Africa — Central Africa — West Africa

Source: FAOSTAT

Southern Africa was the only part of the continent to enjoy the benefits of the Green Revolution during the second half of the 20th century.

Through all these techniques and technologies we can be reasonably confident of meeting the food production challenge. That, at least, is the hope, provided that a number of other important components fall into place. What are these?

Policy matters

Science and technological innovation cannot operate in a vacuum. Their implementation takes us into tricky areas of policy. Take Africa, where the population is expected to double, from 1 billion to 2 billion, by 2050. Unlike other developing regions such as Asia and Latin America, Africa has failed to enjoy significant uplifts in food security and productivity: indeed, with the exception of Southern Africa, crop yields in Sub-Saharan Africa have largely stood still over the past 50 years or so when compared with the impact of the Green Revolution in India and Southeast Asia.

Expanding production by increasing the land available would be costly in both environmental and economic terms, so the continent is likely to suffer ever more intense pressure to produce more food from the same – or even less – agricultural land. Nor will improved farming technologies – such as irrigation systems or mechanisation – be sufficient to meet such huge demands.

Even in those regions where pressures are fewer than in Africa, and scientific innovations are more likely to make an impact, there are political hurdles to overcome. Genetically modified (GM) foods have been eaten for many years in the USA, yet in Europe they are persistently regarded by many people as unsafe, unnatural and not particularly beneficial. The public remains so sceptical about them that politicians have been reluctant to press their case until recently, in spite of the scientific and economic arguments in their favour. They see no advantage in adopting policies that will attract more votes "against" than "for".

There is a tangle of social, political, industrial and scientific complexities here that needs to be unravelled if decision makers, within and outside government, are to convert our new knowledge in plant science into widely acceptable practice.

Socio-political, legal and ethical issues

Major technological changes have, throughout history, met with opposition, debate and downright hostility, not necessarily on rational grounds but because they tug firmly at people's hearts and minds. In truth, scientific and technological innovations can often be judged quite irrationally: historically, there are many examples of this – famously, the 1865 Red Flag Act in England, which stipulated that a person with a red flag had to walk in front of railway engines.

Nonetheless, surveys of public opinion such as the European Commission's Euro-barometer suggest that, in general, public attitudes to science and its offerings are positive and that scientists are trusted to explain the impacts on society of what they are doing in the laboratory. So far so good. On the other hand, when it comes to the acceptability or otherwise of novel scientific enterprises such as GM foods, it is not a simple cost/benefit equation with perceived advantages being weighed against perceived disadvantages. Viewpoints vary. What may be seen as an advantage to one individual or nation may be regarded as the complete opposite by other people living in quite different circumstances in different parts of the world.

When evaluating GM, in particular, a bewildering number of players have points to make: the environmentalists, the biotechnology – or biotech – sciences and industry, the media, philosophers and ethicists, and economists. Each group has its well-argued position, its passionate advocacy, its prejudices and weaknesses. At no point is it easy to take a black and white stand for or against such subtleties.

One key aim of this book is to present the range of available technologies, the arguments and counterarguments, so that we can all make up our own minds. But this must surely build upon sound evidence-based science.

Public confidence in science and technology

Responses to the question *"Do you think that the overall influence of science and technology on society is positive or negative?"*

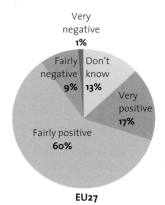

Very negative
1%

Fairly negative
9%

Don't know
13%

Very positive
17%

Fairly positive
60%

EU27

Source: European Commission, 2013

Structure and content

This book is designed to cover our current knowledge of novel crop technologies in the context of global food production and demand by splitting a complex topic into four main sections.

- *Plant science and food security*, which ranges over population growth and the benefits of innovatory crop science for food security; the economic, agricultural and environmental impacts of biotech crops; and some of the general techniques being deployed in emerging economies.
- *New agricultural genetics across the emerging world* – a series of detailed analyses of transformative agricultural practices in Africa, South America, China and India, along with case studies of particular crops and their impact in particular contexts.
- *Policy factors* that shape the enablement and regulation of crops developed through the new genetics, biotechnology research for innovation and sustainability, and matters of international trade.
- *The social, legal, ethical and political implications of GM crops* and other biotech innovations in agriculture.

Each section consists of a series of chapters illustrated with case studies and graphics. At the head of each chapter is a summary of the key ideas, and at the end of every section comes a brief list of suggested discussion, essay or research topics for individual or class follow-up, as well as guidance on further reading and useful websites.

Given the wide-ranging nature of the issues discussed here, every effort has been made to keep scientific – and other – technicalities to a minimum in terms of language and concepts. A glossary is provided for further reference (page 193).

SECTION ONE

THE IMPACT OF INNOVATORY PLANT SCIENCE ON FOOD SECURITY

The world may well be on the way to securing its food supply in the face of a peaking global population that begins to feel the first major effects of man-made climate change.

This section outlines the background to the challenges of food security and describes a diverse range of appropriate technologies based on current knowledge and progress in plant science. These technologies aid sustainable production, improve the nutritional quality of crops and help to reduce levels of food waste both pre- and post-harvest. There is no one-size-fits-all, no single silver-bullet solution, but a range of biotechnologies with advantages in specific contexts.

Innovation to promote food security can take place at different levels. Crop technologies may be traditional, intermediate or conventional, or so-called new platform. A traditional approach might be, for example, a community-developed method of irrigation. A conventional category of innovation is the development of hybrid African/Asian species of rice through tissue culture, which is frequently used for reproducing plants of the same variety, or the new generation of agrochemicals that directly enhance the defences of plants to pathogens rather than targeting the pathogens themselves. Intermediate is somewhere between the two – part local knowledge, part modern methods – for example the use of companion cropping, such as planting an insect-repellent species in the vicinity of a valuable food crop to protect it from pests.

The recent category of new-platform technologies includes "new genetics", drawing on our growing knowledge of DNA sequence data – the precise ordering of the four bases adenine, guanine, cytosine and thymine in a strand of DNA. And it is now possible not just to describe the sequence of genes within a plant but to go one stage further and link sequences in a plant's genome to its particular characteristics, referred to as "traits". This means that breeders can produce more precisely tailored crops – both major ones and minor locally grown ones – based on knowledge of the appropriate genetic sequences. They can also look forward to transferring desired traits such as yield, pest resistance and drought resistance between varieties using genetic modification (GM) technology – enhancing one crop through the genes of another or its wild relatives. A further exciting development in genomic sequencing is that it offers the prospect of predicting the performance of new varieties.

In all this discussion of plant technologies, the farmer is not overlooked. Modern biotechnology is often regarded as the exclusive province of multinational corporations whose interests go against those of small farmers and less developed countries. This is not always so, however, as these chapters illustrate. Big agricultural business may need to focus on big targets that can be reached in many regions and over very large areas of land, using industrialised agricultural systems to produce such major crops as rice or maize. But biotechnology in general, and GM in particular, may prove to be most beneficial when used alongside traditional or intermediate technology and with local – often staple – but hitherto largely neglected orphan crops such as banana, pigeon pea, cowpea, sorghum, cassava and plantain, amongst many others. A hundred of these crops have been listed by the African Orphan Crops Consortium, which aims to sequence their genomes.

Orphan crops: "A group of crops that are vital to the economy of developing countries due to their suitability to the agro-ecology and socio-economic conditions, but [which] remain largely unimproved."
Africa Technology Development Forum, 2009

If a framework can be found to establish this integration, the world may well be on the way to securing its food supply in the face of a peaking global population that begins to feel the first major effects of man-made climate change.

1

HOW TO MATCH SUPPLY TO DEMAND
HOW TO MATCH SUPPLY TO DEMAND
Harnessing plant science for food security

KEY THEMES

- Interaction between food supply, demand, yield and sustainability.
- Revolutionary tools and methods of modern plant science.
- Radical innovations that could transform future agriculture.

Two lines of attack

Global food security needs a two-pronged attack: reducing demand for food along with increasing sustainable crop production. Both will be necessary if recent developments in plant science are to be harnessed optimally. Technological innovations will be most effective if rolled out as integrated components of agricultural systems, as the case studies in this chapter illustrate.

As far as demand is concerned, food security would clearly benefit from a slowing of population growth, improved food distribution mechanisms, reduced consumption of meat from grain-fed animals, and minimising the immense waste that currently takes place both before and after harvest. With comprehensive measures to address these issues, the challenge of increasing crop production would obviously be lessened.

Unfortunately, however, there is little cause for optimism that the demand side of the equation can be tackled. The United Nations Millennium Development Goal of halving the *proportion* of undernourished people between 1990 and 2015, for example, is not so far from being realised, but the World Food Summit target of halving the *number* of hungry is a long way behind schedule (Figure 1.1), largely

Figure 1.1 State of the world's food insecurity, 1990–2013

The number of food-insecure people in the world, 827 million in 2013, has fallen in recent decades, but not fast enough to meet the 2015 World Food Summit target.

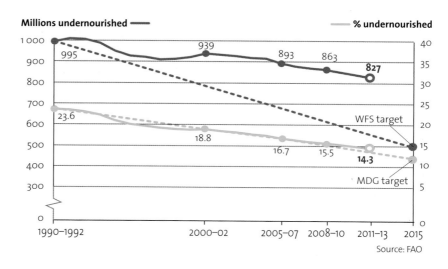

Source: FAO

due to population growth. We have, instead, to look to the other side of the coin – that of increasing supply through improvements in production.

In doing so, it is vital to take into account problems of sustainability and increasing yield. Current production is not always based on sustainable practices. Indeed, crops at present occupy around 12 per cent of the land surface of the Earth, which has colossal implications for the environment – depleting natural resources, degrading ecosystems, polluting groundwater through pesticide and fertiliser use, and damaging the atmosphere by driving up levels of nitrous oxide, a potent greenhouse gas. Future climate change will undoubtedly make matters worse by changing rainfall patterns and increasing desertification, and by subjecting crops to the stress of extremes of temperature and flooding.

Researchers have made quite spectacular progress in understanding plant biology down to the level of individual molecules.

This means that strategies for meeting future needs have to embrace increases in yields while deploying more sustainable production methods than those currently in use. A further complication is that there are few regions where more land will be available for cultivation without adversely affecting the environment: only existing agricultural land can be used effectively.

Crop yields in regions with industrialised crop production systems can exceed 10 tonnes per hectare, but output is constantly limited by environmental and sustainability considerations. There is regional variability as well. Whereas parts of Central and South America and much of Asia benefited from the first Green Revolution, yields in Sub-Saharan Africa have largely stagnated. Had the continent increased agricultural yields by just 1 or 2 tonnes per hectare, there would have been dramatic improvement to both local and global output.

The role of plant science

There are various ways of improving output, not all of them involving new technology. Subsidising the cost of fertilisers and pesticides is one example. The focus here, though, is on the contribution of technological innovation.

The term "revolution" is often and justifiably applied to modern plant science in which genetics plays a major role. Researchers have, over the past couple of decades, made quite spectacular progress in understanding plant biology down to the level of the individual molecules that constitute the genetic machinery. This has led to powerful new tools for improving crops, both by manipulating their genomes and by enhancing conventional breeding methods.

Among these tools is the ability to generate sequence data for DNA or RNA to the point of cataloguing the entire genome of organisms: all their genetic information and their whole transcriptome – all the different types of RNA molecules in their cells. What is more, this can now be done quite quickly and cheaply. Today, the challenge is not so much to generate data as to make sense of it through computational analysis – and science can now use powerful bioinformatics programs to slice, analyse and interpret these large datasets.

Cellular imaging, too, has taken big strides forward. Today's advanced microscopy systems produce far better images than simple microscopes. Plant tissue can be penetrated deeper, and far more data can be made available for computational analysis than was possible only a few years ago. This means that subtle changes in sub-cellular structures far below the limits of detection of normal light microscopes can be directly monitored: the effects of genes and the proteins they code for can now be seen in action.

Chemical analysis of the composition and characteristics of plant extracts has also become more sophisticated using the tools of mass spectrometry. Today it is possible to monitor previously uncharacterised proteins or other components of plant cells at critical transition points, such as during development or in response to external stimuli. Again, microscopic biological processes can be tracked as they actually happen.

Golden Rice, rice genetically engineered to biosynthesise beta-carotene, could save lives in places where there is a shortage of dietary vitamin A – estimated to cause the death of around 670,000 children under five every year.

How do these extraordinary advances in plant science translate into improved crop production? The three case studies on the following pages illustrate how the new science links not only with modern biotechnology, including genetic modification (GM), but also with more classical approaches such as organic and other low-input methods.

The coming of age of genetic modification

Gene cloning, genetic mapping and advanced DNA sequencing have all become everyday automated reality in the genetic revolution of the past few decades. All have profound repercussions for the future of agriculture.

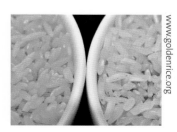

www.goldenrice.org

- Genetic modification has several advantages over conventional cross-breeding techniques. For one thing, crossing one plant with another and then selecting the most appropriate progeny often necessitates repeated procedures: backcrossing a plant with its parent a number of times in order to achieve a variety that possesses the desired trait. For another, it obviates

CASE STUDY Push-pull systems in East Africa

Insecticides to control pests and the diseases they carry can undoubtedly be effective in eliminating unwanted insects. But they often have the disadvantage of being indiscriminate, targeting insects other than the pest. Insect-resistant varieties of some crops do exist, but not necessarily the ones a farmer needs or can afford.

An alternative strategy is based on the use of plants which produce chemicals that can powerfully affect the behaviour of insect pests. These signalling chemicals – semiochemicals – influence mating or feeding behaviour, as attractants or repellents. One successful application of this approach is the control of stem-borer moths that attack maize in East Africa, based on a push-pull strategy sometimes referred to as companion cropping.

It works like this: a maize field is surrounded by a border of forage grass – *Pennisetum purpureum* – which provides the "pull" by being more attractive than maize to stem-borer moths seeking a site for laying their eggs. It also generates a gum-like substance that kills the pest when the moth larvae enter the grass stem. This constitutes a first line of defence.

In addition, rows of maize are intercropped, or interplanted, with rows of the forage legume silverleaf (*Desmodium uncinatum*), which releases semiochemicals that repel the stem-borer moth from the maize: the "push" mechanism.

An added bonus is that silverleaf also fixes atmospheric nitrogen in root nodules, thus enhancing crop nutrition. Not only that, it is also toxic to another weed plant – the parasitic African witchweed or *Striga* – which is capable of wiping out whole maize crops if left unchecked.

Practicalities: pros and cons
There are considerable advantages to a push-pull strategy. Because it controls but does not eliminate a pest, there is little selection pressure on the offending insect to develop insecticide resistance. This makes it a more environmentally sustainable and possibly durable method than pesticide use.

However, this is still a relatively unadopted technology and is not seen to be broadly applicable or effective in Africa. Nor has it enjoyed wide application in intensive or larger-scale industrial agriculture – for three reasons:

1 Companion cropping, even when apparently working well, gives lower yields than crops cultivated intensively using fertilisers. It is therefore economically unattractive, though this will probably change over time with rising fuel costs and an incentive to use less energy.
2 The costs of the agricultural engineering and machinery necessary for companion cropping arrangements are also high, although this too could change as farmers learn more about optimising their resources.
3 There is some way to go in understanding the basic science of how plants and pests interact.

The better our understanding, the more precisely, cost-effectively and sustainably will farmers be able to adopt push-pull methods.

CASE STUDY Priming for defence

Crop protection chemicals, for all their obvious advantages, have a few limitations. They can be useful against insects and fungi, but are ineffective on bacteria or viruses. They are also prohibitively costly for, say, subsistence farmers. They can have unintended adverse effects on the environment or farmers and people living nearby. And many pests and pathogens acquire resistance to them.

One alternative chemical strategy being explored by plant scientists is to target not the pest itself but the inbuilt defence machinery of the threatened plant.

Plants can draw on a defensive mechanism known as systemic acquired resistance (SAR). If infected by one pathogen they become resistant to a second invader, in the following manner. Once a pathogen attacks a plant it triggers a long-distance signal that stimulates defensive responses away from the invasion site. Specifically, the signal switches on a set of genes that code for proteins with anti-microbial properties which combat the pathogen.

Likewise, there is another kind of defensive mechanism – induced systemic resistance (ISR) – that can be activated when beneficial microorganisms colonise plant roots. Again, a signal is sent through the plant's vascular system to trigger immunity in the parts of the plant growing above ground.

Both SAR and ISR have been shown by researchers to be effective against a broad range of virulent plant pathogens. How then can this knowledge be used? The theory is that synthetic chemicals that mimic plants' signalling molecules could be applied to exploit these inbuilt defence systems by inducing a "memory" mechanism that would persist, with no need for further chemical applications. These mimics would have broad-spectrum effectiveness because the defensive mechanism they induce is not specific to any particular pathogen: a genuinely multi-purpose protection.

That, at least, is the theory. To date, these priming compounds have not been widely used in the field as they need to be applied ahead of infection and new technologies for monitoring and detection would have to be developed. Furthermore, the experimental compounds that have been tested vary in their performance.

Despite these limitations, the priming technique is a promising and durable alternative to pesticide-based methods. The consensus is that it justifies more investment in research to identify suitable compounds.

linkage drag, whereby the crossing procedures result in the introduction of other, linked genes that adversely affect the selected crop. With GM, the gene that determines the desired trait is transferred more quickly and precisely with no unwanted linked genes finding their way into the recipient plant.

Figure 1.2 Genome sequencing for a desired characteristic

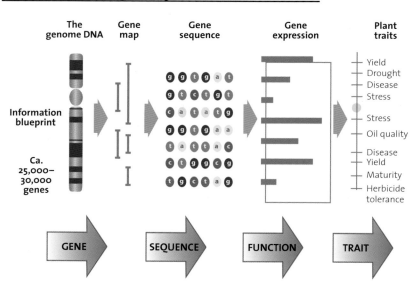

Conventional plant breeding has been very successful but historically it has been an imprecise art. The new molecular technologies, including genome sequencing – which identifies the precise order of the four bases adenine, guanine, cytosine and thymine in a strand of DNA – are changing this. The scientific basis of all crop improvement is the identification of the genes that encode and regulate specific traits of benefit to the farmer.

- Using GM to transfer genes between plants has the advantage that a gene can be inserted into several varieties suited to different localities with different agricultural conditions.

- Genetic techniques directly manipulating an organism's genome using biotechnology will become more flexible and useful than they have been to date. The first generation of GM crops mostly used genes transferred from bacteria – an enzyme called 5-enolpyruvoylshikimate-3-phosphate (EPSP) synthase, which conveys herbicide tolerance, and Cry (standing for crystalline) proteins for insect resistance. Herbicide tolerance and insect resistance were derived from bacterial genes and virus resistance from viral genes. That is changing. Now that genes associated with desirable traits can be isolated as stretches of DNA, genetic manipulation can be used to transfer genes from a crop or crop relative into the target plant using standard transfer techniques. One example of such a transgene is the fungal-disease-resistant potato developed by transferring a fungal-blight-resistance gene from a wild potato relative into a commercial agricultural potato.

- The ability to sequence the genome that contains genes of interest, although likely to be hundreds of genes, not just one or two – those conferring improved yield for example – also finds applications in conventional plant breeding. Breeding programmes designed to develop desired crop traits and characteristics may be speeded up and costs reduced. In addition, our continuously developing knowledge will make it possible to breed crops with traits for yield and drought resistance that are regulated by a multiplicity of genes, not just one.

Future grand challenges

The case studies in this chapter illustrate how current science and the novel technologies it drives could contribute to sustainable crop production, with yields that are adequate to meet a growing demand. However, while radical in themselves, these advances are really no more than valuable refinements to existing crop production technology and farming practices. Looking to the future, far more fundamental innovations could change agriculture beyond recognition. For this to happen, three challenges need to be met:

- Cereals and other crops that today are annuals will need to become perennials. (It has been suggested that humans may in fact have originally chosen annual varieties because they could be selectively bred quickly by saving the seeds of desired plants each year.) With perennial varieties, the

CASE STUDY New kid on the block – homologous gene targeting

Recent research has resulted in a novel approach to crop improvement: homologous gene targeting. In essence, this is a way of targeting changes to plant genomes to create useful mutations with properties such as toxin production for protection against pests or enhanced crop growth and development.

The science underpinning targeted modification of genomes turns on the discovery of a set of enzymes called transcription factors, which copy genetic information encoded in DNA to messenger molecules – RNA – as the first step in synthesising more proteins within the plant cell. These transcription factors – TAL effectors – control whether genes are switched on or off at specific sites along the DNA molecule.

TAL effectors can be used as a route of entry for DNA from outside sources modified to incorporate specific mutations with beneficial effects, such as the ability of a plant to become resistant to a specific pathogen. They allow these desired mutations to enter the recipient genome at a precisely determined point such that they become totally incorporated within the host plant's genetic machinery.

Once plants have been exposed to this newly acquired DNA, the targeted modifications can be propagated as part of the genetic material of a new and improved variety.

These technologies have only recently been developed and are yet to be shown to be a feasible way forward in practice.

Figure 1.3 Commercial genetically modified crops worldwide, 2013

Million hectares

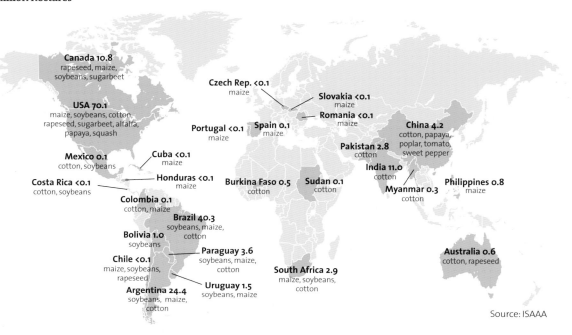

Canada 10.8
rapeseed, maize,
soybeans, sugarbeet

Czech Rep. <0.1
maize

Slovakia <0.1
maize

Romania <0.1
maize

USA 70.1
maize, soybeans, cotton,
rapeseed, sugarbeet, alfalfa,
papaya, squash

Portugal <0.1
maize

Spain 0.1
maize

China 4.2
cotton, papaya,
poplar, tomato,
sweet pepper

Pakistan 2.8
cotton

Mexico 0.1
cotton, soybeans

Cuba <0.1
maize

India 11.0
cotton

Costa Rica <0.1
cotton, soybeans

Honduras <0.1
maize

Burkina Faso 0.5
cotton

Sudan 0.1
cotton

Myanmar 0.3
cotton

Philippines 0.8
maize

Colombia 0.1
cotton, maize

Brazil 40.3
soybeans, maize,
cotton

Bolivia 1.0
soybeans

Paraguay 3.6
soybeans, maize,
cotton

Australia 0.6
cotton, rapeseed

Chile <0.1
maize, soybeans,
rapeseed

Uruguay 1.5
soybeans, maize

South Africa 2.9
maize, soybeans,
cotton

Argentina 24.4
soybeans, maize,
cotton

Source: ISAAA

aerial part of the crop would be cut, or allowed to die back, but its root systems would remain undisturbed to grow again and produce above-ground leaves and seed in subsequent years. Conventional breeding would struggle to achieve perennialisation, but gene transfer techniques that carry the trait of perennialisation from wild crop relatives could well deliver this benefit. The impact of perennial grains and other crops in both developing and developed countries would be game-changing because replanting every year would no longer be necessary. Breeding of new varieties would still be needed, however, both to combat evolving pests and pathogens that become resistant and to adapt to changing climatic conditions.

- Photosynthesis needs to improve in efficiency. In photosynthesis, the basis for all life on this planet, plants make organic compounds from carbon dioxide (CO_2) and water using the energy from sunlight. They do so in a complex sequence of biochemical events involving a number of metabolic pathways. In some major crops such as wheat and rice photosynthesis can be wasteful, with non-productive and energy-consuming processes impairing CO_2 uptake and fixation efficiency. But in other plants this limitation has been overcome by an alternative pathway coming into play

In 2013, some 18 million farmers across 27 countries grew genetically modified crops over more than 170 million hectares.

At the global level, productivity increased steadily during the second half of the 20th century while the area of cropland under cultivation rose by only 10 per cent. This was thanks to four major areas of innovation:

- mechanisation and irrigation;
- synthetic fertilisers;
- pesticides and fungicides;
- plant breeding and genetics.

Figure 1.4 Twentieth century innovation: can it happen again?

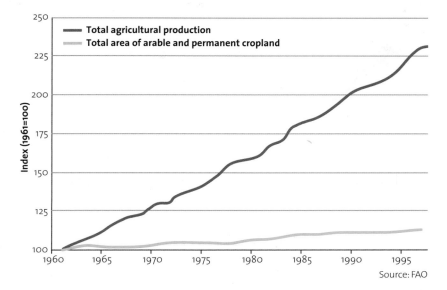

Source: FAO

to act as a metabolic shunt, or shortcut. If an artificial version of this could be designed through genetic engineering, crops might benefit from a photosynthetic pathway that could greatly enhance their productivity. Again, basic research could lead to such a radical improvement.

- The final grand challenge is to improve food crops other than wheat, rice and maize which, today, account for more than half of global calorie consumption. Major crop yields have increased sevenfold since the beginning of the 20th century as a result of spectacular improvements in farming methods: mechanisation and irrigation together with the use of crop protection chemicals and synthetic fertilisers coupled with plant breeding and genetics – the Green Revolution. Could something similar be achieved for those hitherto neglected, orphan or underused crops such as sorghum, cowpea or millet, which are the staple food of many millions of people in developing countries but have enjoyed little attention until recently? Here, surely, is an open goal for basic science in the century ahead.

FEEDING A TEEMING PLANET
Global population growth, food security and future farming

The broad sweep of history

What are the trends in population growth – past, present and future – and how do these interact with agricultural production and food security? What factors influence these trends?

The broad picture shows a world population of between 1 million and 10 million people at the dawn of agriculture some 10,000–15,000 years ago, growing to 300 million about 2,000 years ago (Figure 2.1), thence doubling to 600 million in the early part of the 17th century. As the 20th century opened, the total had reached 1.5 billion, climbing rapidly to today's 7 billion or thereabouts.

A key take-off point (Figure 2.2) came in around 1950 when the curve turned dramatically upwards as less developed regions began to enjoy marked reductions in death rates: within 50 years there were to be two and a half times as many people on the planet.

KEY THEMES

- Past, present and future links between population and production.
- Measuring hunger.
- Constraints on agricultural output.
- Production improvement strategies.

Figure 2.1 Global human population growth over the last 2,000 years

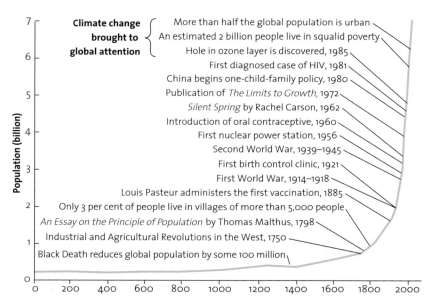

The plague that swept along the Silk Route and reached its peak in Europe in the mid-14th century, killing some 30–60 per cent of the region's population, was the last major event to cause a drop in global human numbers. No further population checks have affected the upward trend of the graph.

Source: Wordpress, 2011

While the population of Europe, North America and Oceania is expected to remain largely stable, significant growth is forecast for both Africa and Asia.

Figure 2.2 Population growth by region, 1950–2050

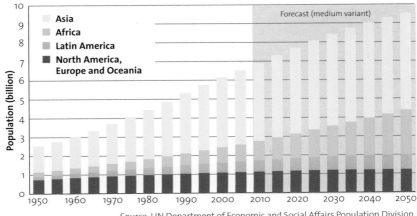

Source: UN Department of Economic and Social Affairs Population Division

The rapid uplift in the population after 1950 was, in many countries, accompanied by a corresponding increase in agricultural production, with more land being given over to crops which, themselves, were being improved through better farming practices and genetic enhancement. The Food and Agriculture Organization of the United Nations (FAO) recorded a rise in production of around 150 per cent over the last five decades.

Not all regions enjoyed such increases, though. While China and India saw grain production surging upwards – not only in terms of total production but also per head of their populations, particularly so in China – no such progress occurred elsewhere, notably Sub-Saharan Africa.

The Global Hunger Index

The unequal distribution of improvements in agricultural production means that, today, three-quarters of the world's population live in the developing world where poverty is concentrated: 1 billion people have to live on less than US\$ 2 a day, some 827 million of whom are hungry. In fact, every hour of every day, more than 1,000 people die from hunger-related causes.

What do we mean by hunger? The best-known measure is the Global Hunger Index (GHI), which combines three equally weighted indicators:

- undernourishment – that is, insufficient calorie intake to meet dietary energy requirements;

Figure 2.3 Food Price Index, 1961–2013

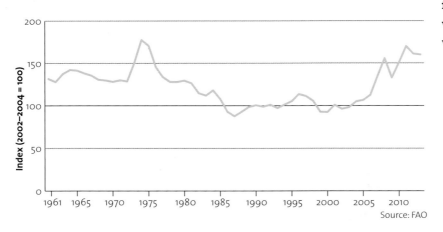

Source: FAO

Recent spikes in world food prices highlighted the vulnerability of those living with food insecurity.

- underweight – low weight for age, wasting and stunted growth in children under five years;
- child mortality – death rates in children under five, reflecting inadequate diet in terms of both calories and micronutrients such as vitamins, iron and iodine, and unhealthy living conditions for mothers and children.

Although the GHI shows some recent progress in reducing hunger, the number of hungry people remains high. One factor contributing to this is the volatility and sudden rapid surges – spikes – of global food prices (Figure 2.3).

Population in the 22nd century

Looking to the long term, the United Nations Department of Economic and Social Affairs foresees a global population of around 9 billion in 2050, veering to anything between the current 7 billion and more than 25 billion by 2100, depending on fertility rates – the numbers of children born per woman of reproductive age. Figure 2.4 shows the link between projected fertility rates and population size in the decades ahead.

The role of urbanisation

In 2010, the numbers of people living in towns and cities across the world overtook those in the countryside for the first time in history. This dramatic shift has been speeding up over the past 40 years, partly due to agricultural mechanisation, with the result that the proportion of people employed in agriculture has fallen severely, despite the overall growth in population.

In 2010, the numbers of people living in towns and cities across the world overtook those in the countryside for the first time in history.

The United Nations projects a world population of 9.3 billion in 2050, a 27.5 per cent increase from today. Forecasts for 2100 vary widely, from 7 billion to more than 25 billion.

Figure 2.4 Projected world population based on variable fertility rates

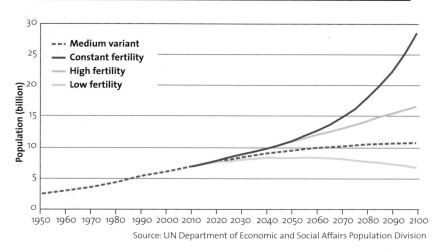

Source: UN Department of Economic and Social Affairs Population Division

Currently, about 3.2 billion of us are urban and require 2.4 billion tonnes of food each year. In addition, an important consequence of economic development and urbanisation is that consumption patterns change towards higher-value foods: sugar, vegetable oil and livestock products (dairy, meat and eggs), and fish. As far as livestock products are concerned, milk consumption has almost doubled since the 1960s, meat consumption has tripled and that of eggs has risen fivefold.

Factors that limit agricultural production

Access to appropriate land

This is the most fundamental constraint on production and has, in recent years, been influenced a good deal by various global crises: in finance, the environment, energy and food. This in turn has driven land deals made by a number of Middle Eastern and Asian governments – which are finance-rich and resource-poor – in areas of the world that are resource-rich and finance-poor, such as Africa and South America. These transactions, aimed at securing the future food and energy requirements of one group of countries, but often to the detriment of another, has led to a move by organisations such as the World Bank, the United Nations – including the FAO – and other socially aware bodies to regulate such land deals.

Water

If enough farming land is available, water becomes the next most important limiting factor on output. Some 70 per cent of all water use on the planet is in agriculture. Here, the future is both bright and bleak, depending on which regions we consider.

As a consequence of climate change, water availability – in rivers, lakes, reservoirs and aquifers as well as in soils – is predicted to decline in Africa, the Near and Middle East and northeastern China, which are already water-scarce and experiencing increasing desertification. Australia and most countries in the Americas, however, are forecast to have enough water to generate the calories needed by their populations. Understandably, regional conflicts and increased economic and environmental migration are also predicted as these disparities in access to water become more acute and obvious.

Climate change

Global warming and the related phenomenon of increased carbon dioxide (CO_2) levels and other greenhouse gases in the atmosphere – such as methane from agriculture – will have a number of effects on agriculture: some problematic, some not.

For example, 95 per cent of all plant species are so-called C3 plants (relating to how they fix carbon during photosynthesis), and these will probably enjoy increased yields. On the other hand, some specific crops such as wheat and rice will be adversely affected by the forecast temperature rises of 1–3 °C and will give lower yields. Another impact with potentially negative consequences will be a proliferation of soil-borne pathogen populations in warmer weather.

Strategies for enhancing production

Novel crops

Historically, agricultural development has turned on increasing the output of a relatively small number of crops, particularly cereals. This has undoubtedly been beneficial, saving countless lives in Asia, for example, during the Green Revolution of the 20th century. However, some experts argue that there has been too much emphasis on grain production at the expense of valuable but underused crops such as nutrient-rich pulses, fruits and vegetables. The Crops for the Future initiative is an attempt to redress this imbalance by giving underused crops their own organisation to drive research and development.

It is a sobering thought that, today, just 12 species of plant – barley, maize, millet, rice, rye, sorghum, sugarcane and wheat, all from the grass family, and the tubers cassava, potato, sweet potato and yam – provide around three-quarters of global food (Figure 2.5). Yet our planet supports no fewer than 7,000 partly domesticated edible species and an estimated 30,000–75,000 wild species that could also provide us with food.

Figure 2.5 Plants under cultivation

Only 2% is relevant for food and clothing today: **150 species**

Just 0.16% provides about 75% of all food and feed: **12 species**

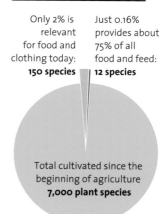

Total cultivated since the beginning of agriculture **7,000 plant species**

There are genetically modified varieties of a number of important human food crops, but few have been commercialised.

Table 2.1 Twelve crops that feed the world, 2012

	Annual production Million tonnes	Yield Tonnes per hectare	GM status	Commercial GM product
Sugarcane	1,832.54	70.24	Yes	No
Maize	872.07	4.92	Yes	Yes
Rice	719.74	4.41	Yes	Yes(?)
Wheat	670.88	3.11	Yes	No
Potato	364.81	19.00	Yes	No
Cassava	262.59	12.88	Yes	No
Barley	132.89	2.68	?	No
Sweet potato	103.15	12.75	Yes	No
Yam	58.75	11.66	Yes	No
Sorghum	57.00	1.49	Yes	No
Millet	29.87	0.94	?	No
Rye	14.56	2.62	?	No

Data source: FAOSTAT

Trade and research

World trade and support for fundamental and applied research are also important influences on agricultural production. Mathematical modelling suggests that increased liberalisation of trade could lower food production costs across the world by as much as 10 per cent, as well as reduce food scarcity. Investment in agricultural research and development (R&D) would also be highly beneficial, particularly as R&D expenditure in many countries has tended to decline or stagnate in recent decades, reducing growth in agricultural production. Many – if not most – experts recommend a global expansion in R&D investment, with more support for national research programmes. This would be of particular benefit to food security where land degradation, water scarcity and climate change are serious obstacles.

New genetics has been applied to some orphan crops – including cowpea and cassava – to help address food security and nutrition, and should be applied to others, but progress in Africa is hindered by lack of public acceptance and an unfavourable policy and regulatory climate.

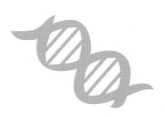

The role of biotechnology

Biotechnology opens up many avenues for crop improvement, both in enhancing plants' responses to their environment and in improving their inbuilt genetic and physiological potential. Yields can be driven up, for example, by increased insect resistance or by modifying a crop's internal processes, as has been illustrated before in this section.

But there is a potential problem here. In North and South America, genetically modified (GM) crops with improved traits such as insect resistance have been extensively cultivated. Other countries, however, have objected to their use because they fear that they would be unable to export their crops to Europe where the cultivation of GM crops has encountered considerable public and government opposition.

Whatever the benefits of the new genetic technologies, then, there has to be a favourable policy and regulatory climate, as well as broad public acceptance, if they are to be realised.

Incentives for farmers

Growers already have considerable knowledge and skills that can help increase crop yields in an environmentally sustainable manner. But they need encouragement to adopt best practices through incentives, especially economic ones. For example, they have at their disposal a variety of methods for improving environmental sustainability, such as increasing the nitrogen efficiency of their crop and livestock production systems or reducing methane emissions. And they could readily sequester more carbon on their farmland by improving soil management. But it has to be worth their while to do what is necessary to achieve this. Farmers need help from the public sector to exploit the most effective combinations of traditional and innovative methods if they are to rise to the challenge.

Food uses up a much smaller proportion of household incomes in developed countries than in those still developing – representing about 10 per cent of take-home pay in the USA and Europe versus 80–100 per cent in some developing countries.

KEY THEMES

- Variety of appropriate technologies.
- Genetic modification: case studies.
- Guide to recombinant DNA technology.
- Drought stress: non-GM solutions.

Farmers need appropriate technologies

Any technology designed to increase productivity or add significant value must be appropriate to a farmer's particular circumstances: the environment, the labour available, the accessibility and affordability of the proposed technology, and so on. Many kinds of technologies can be appropriate:

- *Traditional* technologies are those that fit with local conditions and have been evolved over a long time by communities themselves – such as home gardens or locally developed methods of rainwater harvesting and irrigation.
- *Intermediate* technologies are those traditional ones that have been improved by coupling them with more modern techniques. Examples here include the treadle pump upgraded by modern engineering, and the practice of intercropping.
- *Conventional* technologies are those familiar in industrialised countries where knowledge of modern physics, chemistry and biology has been converted into products for use regionally or globally. Synthetic fertilisers and pesticides coupled with mechanisation are good examples.
- *New-platform* technologies are those that draw on innovations in biotechnology and nanoscience as well as information and communications technology (ICT), all of which have enormous potential in meeting the needs of both industrialised and developing countries. Genetically modified (GM) organisms and drought-tolerant or pest-resistant crop varieties that have been developed using new molecular selection and breeding techniques fall into this category.

Tricky choices

It is not always easy for a farmer to judge which among this extensive array of technologies is appropriate – even when they are accessible and affordable. High cost and the need for labour or concerns regarding environmental damage may make an apparently desirable technology impractical. A crop may well be selectively bred or engineered to resist pests and diseases, but does it also take up nutrients from the soil efficiently enough or reduce the need for water under local conditions? How will it respond to the stresses of global warming? Trade-offs may need to be made.

CASE STUDY Revolutionary new rice through marker-assisted selection

Rice growers in Asia have struggled for generations with extended periods of flooding that submerge their crop, stunting growth and impairing its viability. It is estimated that flooding affects more than 25 per cent of the world's rice-producing land – a proportion that may well rise as global warming increases the likelihood of flooding during the critical seedling stage, keeping the rice plants under water for several weeks on end.

In 2006 a team at the International Rice Research Institute (IRRI) in the Philippines took a big step forward in developing a new strain of submergence-tolerant rice using the relatively novel technology of marker-assisted selection (MAS). This enables the presence and structure of genes responsible for desirable traits to be selected at an early stage of seedling development at the level of their DNA sequences. The researchers at IRRI identified genetic markers associated with the ability to

Abdel Ismail/Dave Mackill/IRRI

remain submerged, yet survive, for more than two weeks. This works through a mechanism that keeps the rice dormant during flooding, then allows it to grow as the water levels drop.

This became the key to a new rice – named Scuba – which is currently being bred using the new MAS technology. New submergence-tolerant varieties are being produced in Laos, Bangladesh and Thailand, and in India where more than 100,000 farmers have adopted one particularly promising variety.

The contribution of biotechnology

Biotechnology has been around for a long time, as long in fact as the centuries-old practices of brewing beer, fermenting wine and making bread. Today, though, the term has a much larger reach. We could define modern biotechnology as any technological intervention that uses biological systems, living organisms or their derivatives to make useful products and processes. At its heart lies our knowledge of the workings of DNA and RNA in determining the genetic basis of characteristics or traits (yield, drought tolerance, pest resistance and so on) in plants and animals. Undoubtedly, one of the best-known applications of these insights is the technique of recombinant DNA – often termed genetic engineering or genetic modification (GM) – in which genes from one organism are directly transferred into another. Box 3.1 describes briefly how it works.

BOX 3.1 A quick guide to recombinant DNA techniques

The basic process of locating and then transferring – recombining – a gene from one organism to another started to become practicable in the early 1980s; a decade later there was a dramatic surge in commercial applications of this revolutionary new technology. Human hormones were produced using bacteria as tiny growing factories, vaccines were engineered in yeasts, and genetically modified crops came on the scene.

Location and extraction

The first step is to locate the section of DNA – the sequence – of interest in the donor organism. This would be a sequence that determines – or codes for – a desirable characteristic or trait such as improved insect resistance or enhanced nutritional value, as with the biofortification of Golden Rice with vitamin A to prevent blindness. This sequence is then snipped out, or cleaved.

Transfer strategies, from bacteria to gene guns

Once extracted, the DNA then has to be relocated within the genome of its new host. One of the first and most successful techniques to be used for plants is a bacterial plasmid carrier or vector – small DNA elements in bacteria. The bacterium *Agrobacterium tumefaciens*, which causes crown gall disease, is commonly used as a vector because it naturally infects plants.

The desired gene sequence is inserted into a small segment of DNA, known as T-DNA (transfer DNA), from the bacterium, which in turn is incorporated into the host plant's DNA, sometimes through a method known as vacuum infiltration, in which plants are subjected to vacuum pressure to increase the contact between the bacterial vector and the plant's tissues.

In an alternative transfer process, the new fragment of DNA is coated onto the surface of gold or tungsten micro-particles which are injected into the host plant's cells with a gene gun, a process known as biolistics. Millions of cells are treated, and those in which the new gene has successfully integrated are selected using genetic markers to identify them. The selected cells are then cultured to grow into the new plant.

The method chosen depends on the target crop, with the *Agrobacterium* plasmid being the most routinely used transfer mechanism.

Advantages over conventional breeding

There are obvious advantages of speed and precision in recombinant DNA methods. And there are also huge potential economic pay-offs in terms of higher yields, greater tolerance to worsening conditions such as drought or increased salinity in the soil, and resistance to pests and pathogens. Fewer crops are lost and the farmer depends less on expensive chemicals such as fungicides and pesticides. Meanwhile the opportunity for no-till cultivation (no ploughing) is among the most significant benefits because it reduces fossil-fuel use as well as soil degradation. Lastly, there are qualitative benefits. Crops can be deliberately engineered to provide better nutrition, delivering higher levels of essential dietary ingredients or bearing valuable micronutrients where before they offered none.

CASE STUDY New Rices for Africa using tissue culture

The rising demand for rice in Africa is not being met by local production: each year 6 million tonnes have to be imported at a cost of more than US$ 1 billion. Biotechnology, in this case advanced tissue culture involving the growth of tissues or cells separately from the organism, is being deployed to meet this shortfall.

A Sierra Leone researcher – Monty Jones – based at the African Rice Centre, has used this technology to develop crosses between the African rice species *Oryza glaberrima* and the Asian species *Oryza sativa*, which typically has a yield five times that of its African counterpart.

The research was not all plain sailing. At first the technique simply did not work well, until collaboration with Chinese scientists provided a new coconut-oil-based culture method that delivered results.

Many new varieties – New Rices for Africa, which grow well in drought-prone upland conditions – have thus been generated. The new varieties also have good resistance to local pests and diseases and require low nutrient input. And they grow vigorously, crowding out weeds.

These new rices give the farmer many advantages, including the typical Asian characteristics of a full growth of grain that is ready to harvest 30–50 days earlier than the more local African crops. As a result, rice imports have been reduced. Uganda, for example, has halved such imports, while also boosting farmers' incomes by US$ 250 per hectare as they switch from maize to these new varieties of rice.

Yields up, imports down, and the farmers' returns on investment are enhanced: a triumph for tissue culture.

Compared to the kinds of innovations opened up by modern biotechnology, conventional breeding, whereby crop varieties with desirable traits are selected and crossed, can be quite slow and imprecise. Conventional breeding also often depends on the appearance of new, beneficial mutations, as was the case with quality protein (high-protein) maize, which only came into being after maize mutants with high levels of desirable amino acids were found quite serendipitously. Biotechnology takes away the waiting, making conventional breeding quicker and therefore cheaper, more targeted and more effective. At the same time, however, the procedure can be costlier and take longer to implement when GM is involved, because of the need to go through regulatory approval processes.

Not just biotech: other appropriate technologies have a role

For all its advantages, biotechnology is but one among a range of useful technologies. It would be wrong to think of it as a high-tech silver bullet for improving crop

production. The usefulness of other methods and approaches is clearly demonstrated by the ways in which farmers have tackled the age-old problem of drought – a threat made even more menacing as a result of global warming. The brief national accounts that follow show the range of these interventions in the face of severe water shortage.

Globally, some 670,000 children die every year because of vitamin A deficiency, and another 350,000 go blind. Southeast Asia is the worst affected region, with 90 million children lacking this essential nutrient.

Bangladesh

Large-scale irrigation systems are often not feasible in some of the least developed countries, where physical geography or low levels of wealth mean that smaller-scale solutions have to be found.

One such country is Bangladesh where, in the early 1980s, local people started to develop a new kind of pump to lift water from wells as an alternative to labour-intensive buckets and expensive oil- or petrol-powered pumps. They came up with a treadle pump: human powered, efficient, easy to use and to maintain, enabling

---

CASE STUDY Two generations of Golden Rice through genetic engineering

Rice is the basic dietary staple in Asia and parts of Sub-Saharan Africa, yet rice, in common with most cereals and other staples, is naturally deficient in essential proteins and other micronutrients. One huge lack is vitamin A, resulting in, among other things, a considerable burden of blindness and death in the human population, especially children. No fewer than 250 million children under five are estimated to be at risk from this deficiency. And more people die from vitamin A deficiency than from HIV/AIDS, tuberculosis and malaria combined.

At the Swiss Federal Institute of Technology, Ingo Potrykus along with Peter Beyer from the University of Freiburg used plant biotechnology to solve the problem. They concentrated on the gene responsible for synthesising beta-carotene, a natural precursor of vitamin A, which is present in both the daffodil and a bacterium. They extracted these genes and transferred them into rice where they began to activate the correct beta-carotene-producing biochemical pathways.

At first, beta-carotene levels in this first-generation Golden Rice (so-called for its distinctive colour) were not particularly high, but further research by scientists at Syngenta, the Swiss agrochemical company, uncovered another gene in maize which drove them far higher. Although it has been a decades-long, complicated and contentious story, this second-generation Golden Rice has already been developed into locally appropriate varieties in the Philippines and India, and these and other countries are expected to adopt it within a few years.

farmers to irrigate their fields either from natural water sources or from man-made wells. The current design enables an individual farmer to irrigate nearly a hectare of land under cultivation without the need for much more expensive pumps and fuel: an excellent example of intermediate technology.

The treadle pumps are also relatively cheap thanks to a combination of public subsidy and community involvement.

Thailand

For 200 years or more, farmers in the valleys of northern Thailand had managed their water supply through an arrangement of stone and timber dams linked to irrigation systems run by local representative bodies. Then in the 1960s and 1970s the Thai government began to construct larger-scale water diversion systems to increase year-round capacity. In doing so, they integrated the new developments with the existing, community-led management systems.

The technology was quite traditional, but the real benefits came from the traditional management structures, which ensured a sufficiently reliable water supply to enable farmers to plant a high-value, third-season crop in the same year.

South Africa

The common practice of tilling (ploughing) the soil before sowing seeds has some drawbacks. It makes soil more vulnerable to erosion and drought, harming its structure and increasing water loss. Farmers in southern Africa are avoiding these problems with another approach – conservation farming – an intermediate technique that protects soils and improves their fertility. It is also labour-saving.

In conservation farming, plant residues from the previous crop are left on the land, helping to minimise soil erosion and providing organic material, and there is no use of the plough. Instead, small hollows – or basins – are carefully dug to avoid turning over the earth, which keeps the soil organisms alive and retains precious moisture and nutrients. Two cupfuls of manure and a bottle top's measure of fertiliser are added. This considerably reduces the need for expensive chemical fertilisers. When it rains, instead of running over heavily tilled land and eroding the soil, the water seeps gently into it. Farmers then plant their new seeds in the basins where they germinate and grow. After harvesting, farmers cover the soil with the stems and leaves of the old crop, leave it fallow for a few months, then sow seed for the next crop in the same basins.

Variants on traditional methods, clever, simple modifications to age-old practices, and updating conventional ideas can all contribute to increased food security.

CGIAR

With the *zai* system it has been possible to increase sorghum and millet yields by 80–170 per cent while also vastly improving the soil's long-term prospects for cultivation.

Despite the need for hoeing to control weeds, less labour is required overall and yields are high. In addition, this system tends to build up carbon in the soil, making the soil structure more stable, and the approach more sustainable than conventional agricultural methods.

Niger

For 50 years, farmers have been looking for ways to use expensive synthetic fertilisers – with their pollutant effects on water sources – more sparingly. The micro-dosing technique developed in Niger is one answer.

"Soda cap fertilisers" involve a soda bottle cap filled with a 6-gram mix of phosphorus and nitrogen fertiliser, which is poured into the hole before a seed is planted. This simple approach, using an everyday household item, has made an astonishing difference. Farmers are using between three and six times less fertiliser than their US and European counterparts, with no loss of efficiency. In fact, they are enjoying a 55–70 per cent increase in millet yield at far lower cost.

Burkina Faso

Even parched regions usually have a little available water. The challenge is to harvest these small amounts cheaply and efficiently. The response in Burkina Faso has involved a traditional technology, developed decades ago, known as the *zai* system. *Zais* or holes, 20–30 centimetres in diameter and 10–15 centimetres deep, are dug in rows across fields during the dry season and allowed to fill with leaves and sand as winds blow across the land. The farmers add manure to attract termites, which dig a complex network of tunnels beneath the *zais* and bring up nutrients from the deeper soils. When it rains, water collects in the holes where sorghum and millet seeds are sown. An arrangement of stone and earth ridges constructed around the fields' contours slows down any run-off. The result is that water capture is enhanced: the manure limits water loss through drainage, while the termites' porous tunnels allow deep infiltration.

With the *zai* system it has been possible to increase sorghum and millet yields by 80–170 per cent and, after five years or so, to upgrade the whole land surface for farming.

Appropriate technologies

The ingenuity of farmers in fighting drought stresses on their crops demonstrates that a high-tech, genetically sophisticated fix is not always necessary. But that is not to say that biotechnology cannot be of help. Improved seed varieties are still a vital basis for boosting yields and resisting pests and drought. The Water Efficient Maize for Africa initiative, for example, has benefited from knowledge of so-called chaperone genes, which help cells to repair damage caused by various stresses, including insufficient water. One such gene found in bacterial DNA and introduced by genetic engineering into maize DNA has shown excellent results in field trials, increasing maize yields by up to 15 per cent in plants subjected to drought, compared to those without the gene.

However, as we have seen, variants on traditional methods, clever simple modifications to age-old practices, and updating of conventional ideas can all play their part. There is a broad array of technologies out there, ancient and modern, from which today's food producers can draw.

The impacts of first-generation genetically modified crops

KEY THEMES

- Higher farm incomes.
- Qualitative advantages for farmers.
- Impact on production volumes.
- Environmental benefits, including reduced CO2 emissions.

The methods and techniques of modern genetic modification (GM) started to become commercially available in the mid-1990s. So what benefits have farmers derived from them? How has the use of GM-enhanced crops paid off in economic and environmental terms? Studies of three major food crops – soybeans, maize and rapeseed – together with cotton, provide some insights.

Impacts on farm income

In general, GM technology has had a significant positive impact on global farm income as a result of enhanced productivity and efficiency. Table 4.1, which tracks changes from 1996 to 2011, shows incomes increasing by US$ 98.2 billion, with the value of GM crops totalling US$ 19.8 billion in 2011 alone. This means that more than 6 per cent was added to the value of the four crops in question.

Looking more closely at cotton, which has shown the biggest yield gains, the new GM insect-resistant variety raised incomes from cotton by an impressive 14 per cent during the period under study. Substantial gains in farm income are also seen globally in the maize sector, where the adoption of GM crops has resulted in both lower costs and higher yields.

Table 4.1 Income benefits from genetically modified crops, 1996–2011
Worldwide

| | Increase in farm income Million US$ | | Farm income benefit in 2011 as % of total value of: | |
	2011	1996–2011	production of crop in GM-adopting countries	global production of crop
GM HT soybeans	3,879.2	32,211.9	3.8	3.2
GM HT maize	1,540.2	4,212.2	1.5	0.7
GM HT cotton	166.9	1,224.1	0.4	0.3
GM HT rapeseed	433.2	3,131.4	1.4	1.2
GM IR maize	7,104.9	25,762.0	6.8	3.3
GM IR cotton	6,559.6	31,263.2	14.7	11.6
Others	83.3	412.0	–	–
Total	19,767.3	98,216.8	6.3	5.9

Source: Brookes and Barfoot, 2013

Notes: HT = herbicide tolerant; IR = insect resistant. Others = virus-resistant papaya and squash and herbicide-tolerant sugar beet. Income calculations are net farm income changes after inclusion of impacts on yield, crop quality and key variable production costs (e.g. payment for seeds and crop protection).

Table 4.2 Income benefits from genetically modified crops, 1996–2011

Selected countries, million US$

	GM HT soybeans	GM HT maize	GM HT cotton	GM HT rapeseed	GM IR maize	GM IR cotton	Total
USA	13,835.9	3,110.5	924.8	241.5	21,497.3	3,769.4	43,379.4
Argentina	12,624.6	510.5	89.0	–	380.7	362.3	13,967.1
Brazil	4,314.5	431.5	82.6	–	1,796.9	19.9	6,645.4
Paraguay	732.4	–	–	–	–	–	732.4
Canada	231.6	66.7	–	2,862.5	820.5	–	3,981.3
South Africa	7.0	3.8	3.0	–	887.3	31.6	932.7
China	–	–	–	–	–	13,067.8	13,067.8
India	–	–	–	–	–	12,579.5	12,579.5
Australia	–	–	58.4	27.5	–	525.4	611.3
Mexico	4.9	–	51.4	–	–	123.9	180.2
Philippines	–	88.2	–	–	176.2	–	264.4
Romania	44.6	–	–	–	–	–	44.6
Uruguay	83.4	–	–	–	11.7	–	95.1
Spain	–	–	–	–	139.1	–	139.1
Other EU	–	–	–	–	16.2	–	16.2
Colombia	–	0.9	14.9	–	29.2	13.7	58.7
Bolivia	327.0	–	–	–	–	–	327.0
Myanmar	–	–	–	–	–	338.7	338.7
Pakistan	–	–	–	-	–	334.2	334.2

Source: Brookes and Barfoot, 2013

Farmers in the developing world have enjoyed a slightly larger share of global income gains from genetically modified crops than those in the developed world.

Notes: HT = herbicide tolerant; IR = insect resistant. Income calculations are net farm income changes after inclusion of impacts on yield, crop quality and key variable production costs (e.g. payment for seeds and crop protection).

While GM varieties cost more owing to the technology fee charged by agro-biotech companies to cover the costs of development and regulatory compliance, they are still being adopted by farmers because they generate greater profit through improved yields.

How are the general income gains reflected in the individual countries that have adopted new genetic crops? Table 4.2 shows how economically important GM soybeans have been in South America and GM cotton in China and India. A range of GM crops in the USA, South Africa, the Philippines, Mexico and Columbia, too, have proven beneficial.

Farmers in developing countries have enjoyed a slightly larger share of global income gains than those of the developed world – with roughly 55 and 45 per cent of the total respectively – largely through the adoption of GM cotton and soybeans. However, the relative cost of switching to the new crops has been substantially lower for farmers in the developing world, representing 17 per cent of their income gains, with the corresponding figure in the developed world being 37 per cent. This disparity may be due to relative weakness in providing or enforcing intellectual property rights, or may be down to differences in relative gains per hectare planted.

Other economic impacts at farm level

The new GM crops appear to have a number of other, less tangible effects on the profitability of farms, which are difficult to quantify. Even so, these seem to be the most important reasons why farmers embrace the new technologies.

Herbicide tolerance

By growing crops that tolerate modern, broad-spectrum herbicides such as glyphosate, farmers have more time for other activities, including off-farm money-generating enterprises. Also, with conventional crops, herbicides need to be applied after weeds and crops are established, and the herbicide often then impairs the crop's growth, so-called knock-back. Novel GM crops are not affected by this because they are tolerant to herbicides.

Herbicide tolerance facilitates no-till systems by reducing the need for mechanical weed control, so there are cost savings on labour and fuel. And minimising soil disturbance improves moisture retention and reduces soil erosion. Improved weed control means, too, that harvesting costs are reduced because crops are relatively weed-free at harvest time.

Soybeans represent a large share of global agriculture, but few make it to the table as beans. Around 85 per cent of the crop is turned into vegetable oil and high-protein meal, and much of this is fed to livestock.

And because GM herbicide-tolerant crops tolerate broader-spectrum herbicides, herbicide use can actually be reduced, with positive implications for soil quality and less damage to follow-on crops from herbicide residues. In addition, lower herbicide levels create healthier conditions for farmers, local people and the broader environment by reducing poisoning from spray drift or inappropriate application methods.

OCPS/pics.tech4learning.com

Insect resistance

Genetic modification takes away much of the worry associated with heavy pest damage – a benefit in itself. But it also reduces insurance premiums for farmers, which in the USA has amounted to savings of around US$ 138 million over just three years. There are also savings in the time and labour spent inspecting crops and applying insecticides, along with a reduced energy use from avoiding aerial spraying.

Crops are of higher quality. Insect-resistant GM maize, for example, seems to show lower levels than conventional plants of mycotoxins – toxic fungal products on maize plants infected by fungi because of damage by corn-boring pests. These plants also have a shorter growing season, allowing farmers in India, for example, to plant a second maize crop in the same season.

As with herbicides, there are health advantages for farmers and farm workers who handle fewer pesticides and for local people from reduced spray drift. And there are also environmental advantages – particularly for beneficial fauna such as pollinating insects.

Putting a monetary value on the less tangible advantages of the new genetic crops is quite difficult. But a number of studies in the USA based on surveys of maize, soybeans and cotton show improvements in value of between US$ 7 and US$ 25 per hectare. This amounted, in 2010, to an estimated total annual benefit of more than US$ 1 billion.

Insect-resistant maize varieties are able to withstand the maize weevil, which attacks crops both pre-and post-harvest. And it doesn't just stick to maize – it also feasts on wheat, rice, sorghum, oats, barley, rye, buckwheat, cassava, peas...

Impacts on production volumes
The improvements in yield made possible by GM technology feed directly into higher crop production totals. Table 4.3 shows the added tonnage worldwide for 1996–2011.

Environmental impacts – the EIQ
Changes in insecticide and herbicide use brought about by GM crops have had a number of positive effects on the environment in its broadest sense, including impacts on the health of both humans and wildlife. One useful measure of these effects is the Environmental Impact Quotient – EIQ – which combines the various environmental and health impacts into one single per-hectare value.

Table 4.3 Contribution of genetically modified crops to yields, 1996–2011
Worldwide, million tonnes

	Additional (GM) production	
	1996–2011 total for period	2011
Soybeans	110.20	12.74
Maize	195.00	34.54
Cotton	15.85	2.48
Rapeseed	6.55	0.44
Sugar beet	0.45	0.13

Source: Brookes and Barfoot, 2013

Note: Sugar beet is for the USA and Canada only, and from 2008.

USDA/PD

Table 4.4 Impact of changes in the use of pesticides owing to genetically modified crops, 1996–2011
Worldwide

	Area of GM crops in 2011 Million hectares	Change in volume of active ingredient used Million kilos	Change in field EIQ Million field EIQ/hectare units	Change in active ingredient used on GM crops %	Change in EIQ associated with pesticide* use on GM crops %
GM HT soybeans	73.2	-12.5	-6,444.2	-0.6	-15.5
GM HT maize	35.1	-193.1	-5,168.0	-10.1	-12.5
GM HT cotton	4.5	-15.5	-420.9	-6.1	-8.9
GM HT rapeseed	7.3	-14.8	-501.5	-17.3	-27.1
GM HT sugar beet	0.46	0.87	-3.3	23.9	-4.1
GM IR maize	37.8	-50.0	-1,884.2	-45.2	-41.7
GM IR cotton	22.2	-188.7	-8,498.0	-24.8	-27.3
Total	180.56	-473.73	-22,920.1	-8.9	-18.3

Source: Brookes and Barfoot, 2013

Like the IQ scale for measuring human intelligence, the EIQ has its limitations, but it does give us a working tool for making comparisons. Worldwide, for example, the use of insecticides and herbicides on the total GM crop area has fallen by 9 per cent since 1996, whereas the environmental impact associated with their use has fallen by practically twice as much (Table 4.4).

In terms of the volumes of pesticides used and the number of hectares treated, the largest environmental benefit revealed by the EIQ is from GM insect-resistant cotton, while in percentage terms it is GM insect-resistant maize that shows the greatest fall in both pesticide use and adverse environmental impact. But particularly impressive is the positive effect of GM soybeans. Here, herbicide use has dropped by less than 1 per cent, but the EIQ indicates a fall in adverse environmental impacts of more than 15 per cent.

The environmental benefits associated with lower use of herbicides and insecticides as measured by the EIQ vary a little between developed and developing countries, with the developed countries enjoying a 55:45 advantage. Most of the developing countries' gains come from insect-resistant GM cotton.

The Environmental Impact Quotient (EIQ) measures the impact of herbicides and pesticides on human and wildlife health. A minus figure indicates improvement.

Notes: HT: herbicide tolerant; IR: insect resistant; *herbicides and insecticides.

Greenhouse gas emissions
New GM crops have already made a considerable contribution towards lowering levels of greenhouse gases, principally carbon dioxide (CO_2). There are two main mechanisms.

Figure 4.1 Growth in genetically modified crops by area and crop type, 1996–2013
Million hectares

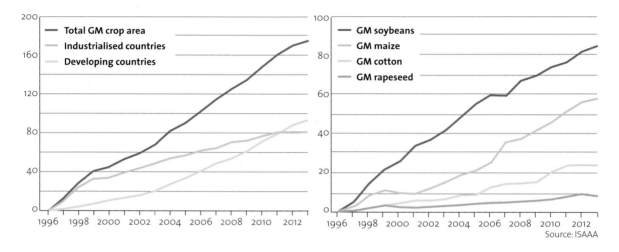

Source: ISAAA

- Less frequent herbicide or insecticide applications means lower fuel use, which in turn drives down CO_2 emissions. In 2010 alone, farmers worldwide reduced their fuel consumption by just over 642 million litres, with the result that 1,715 million kilos less CO_2 found its way into the atmosphere. That is the equivalent to taking 763,000 cars off the road.

- More no-till or low-till farming has a direct impact on the amount of tractor fuel farmers use. In addition, because soil quality is enhanced and erosion reduced, more carbon tends to remain within the soil. This sequestering effect is estimated to have cut atmospheric emissions by 17,634 million tonnes in 2010. Nearly 8 million cars would need to come off the world's roads to reach that figure.

A record 18 million farmers in 27 countries planted 175.2 million hectares of genetically modified crops in 2013, an increase of 3 per cent – or 5 million hectares – on 2012.

Two kinds of contribution

In the 17 years or more since the new GM technologies came on stream, they have improved productivity and profitability for more than 18 million farmers around the world. By 2013, these advantages were seen across more than 175 million hectares of agricultural land (Figure 4.1). Developing countries, with 54 per cent of the global hectarage in 2013, grew more GM crops than industrial countries, with 46 per cent.

These important socio-economic and environmental benefits have come about through a combination of inherent technical advances and by facilitating more cost-effective and environmentally friendly farming practices. Summarising specifically:

Reducing herbicide and pesticide use creates healthier conditions for farmers, their workers and neighbours, as well as the broader environment.

- Direct technological advances in GM insect resistance have improved yields, reduced production risks and decreased pesticide use. This has enabled farmers to enjoy higher returns while, at the same time, being able to practise farming methods that may be less damaging to the environment.
- The herbicide-tolerance traits developed through GM have benefited farmers both by lowering costs and by facilitating changes in farming systems, such as enabling them to use low-cost broad-spectrum herbicides. This in turn has enabled a move away from conventional plough-based production systems to low- or no-till systems.

ROADMAP FOR A CONTINENT
Modern genetics and plant breeding for Africa

Africa can lead the way

The Global Food Security Index, recently created by The Economist Intelligence Unit, identifies and measures the risks to food security in 105 countries, basing its analyses on the affordability, availability and quality of food. It aims not just to describe food insecurities but to provide solutions.

The bottom of the food security table is dominated by Sub-Saharan African countries including Mozambique, Ethiopia, Rwanda and Nigeria, where economies are forecast to grow fastest over the coming years. Africa in general – and Sub-Saharan countries in particular – could be in a position to lead the introduction of the latest agricultural technologies, especially for improving plant breeding, in order to meet their food security needs.

The key crops for solving Africa's food and income security challenges are banana, plantain, cassava, potato and sweet potato, along with other indigenous root vegetables and the staple grain crops of maize, rice and sorghum, of which the first two are being imported in large quantities. These key staples provide an excellent source of cheap calories, but there is an urgent need for new and improved cultivated varieties. How can today's advances in plant genetics help bring this about?

KEY THEMES

- Key role for African plant breeders.
- Current innovations, pros and cons.
- Blueprint for future progress.

Figure 5.1 The Global Food Security Index, 2014

Best environment
Good environment
Moderate environment
Needs improvement
No data

Source: foodsecurityindex.eiu.com

The Global Food Security Index is based on a combination of 27 different indicators covering food affordability, availability, quality and safety, as well as background influencing factors such as literacy and economic opportunities for women.

Genetic variation is the engine that drives advances in crop breeding.

Two main drivers of innovation

Genomics research and its application to plant breeding have reached a stage where two main drivers of innovation have begun to emerge:

- Firstly, there is what could be called the growing democratisation of genomics technology, with the speed and accessibility of gene sequencing accelerating and its cost falling. With sequencing data doubling every five months, the cost per DNA base being sequenced is in free fall.
- Secondly, alongside the cheapness and accessibility of sequence information, dietary and nutritional security is now a global priority, putting agriculture centre stage. The future of farming is pivotal to a sustainable planet based on a viable green economy.

These two factors have combined to change attitudes to plant breeding by opening up the prospect of improving crops in a variety of ways. Now, if exciting new breeding programmes are to flourish, they will need support and insightful leadership.

Next-generation sequencing

Genetic variation is the engine that drives advances in crop breeding. The wider the variation, the greater the ability of a plant species to respond to, and survive in, a changing environment. Those plants that do survive will go on to transmit their favourable genes – and the traits these genes code for – to their offspring. It is this that provides the basis for the selection of plants with desirable characteristics.

A number of high-throughput, low-cost technologies known as next-generation sequencing (NGS) have made possible the completion of reference genome sequences for many important crops, including orphan species such as the pigeon pea, grown by resource-poor farmers in more than 25 tropical and subtropical countries, including in Africa.

In January 2014, the African Orphan Crops Consortium (AOCC), composed of the University of California-Davis, Mars, Inc. and other institutions, announced the 100 African crop species whose genomes will be sequenced. Having the total, detailed genetic sequence of a crop provides a platform for identifying individual genes and discovering genetic markers – short DNA sequences that are invaluable in manipulating genes for beneficial characteristics. There is currently a good deal of interest in one category of marker SNPs – single nucleotide polymorphisms, often called "snips". These vary by only one biochemical unit but can have big consequences for a plant's characteristics.

BOX 5.1 Breeding in brief

Plant breeding is essentially about identifying the best parent plants and crossing them to improve performance. Successful breeders skilfully combine elements of science, art, craft and business acumen.

The methods they deploy, whether traditional, high-tech or both – are determined by a crop's reproductive biology and breeding mechanism. Propagation – the way plants reproduce themselves – is of four kinds:

- *Vegetative* (or clonal) propagation, whereby new individuals develop from specialised structures such as bulbs or tubers on the parent plant. Potato, sweet potato, cassava and yam fall into this category.
- *Inbreeding*, in which crops self-fertilise through pollination, as with wheat, barley, rice, soybeans and cotton. Two-thirds of the world's food crops are inbreeders.
- *Outbreeders*, such as maize and forage grasses, which cross-pollinate with unrelated or distantly related plants.
- *A variable intermediate group* which can partly cross-pollinate, partly self-pollinate. The best-known example is sorghum.

Rapid developments in NGS technology do not just add detail to our understanding of the make-up of a plant's total complement of genetic material. They also open up the promise of new discoveries of genes with important effects on traits and diversity. One example is maize, where genome-wide analysis of 278 maize lines has enabled scientists to quantify the molecular changes that take place during the breeding process. This gives them a sophisticated tool for understanding better the genetic resources within any given plant and for identifying novel variants of genes that could be used in breeding.

Marker-assisted and genomic selection

With the dramatic fall in the cost of DNA-based techniques, methods such as marker-assisted selection (MAS) have taken off; MAS is already widely used in all breeding programmes by the big seed companies. This method of selecting a biochemical marker associated with a gene that codes for desirable plant characteristics has been successfully deployed in submergence-tolerant rice (see Case study on page 32) and in backcrossing programmes carrying transgenes from another species.

However, traditional MAS has limitations because it identifies only a few markers, while many of the crop traits that breeders are trying to put into their plants are complex – controlled by large numbers of regions along the genome, each one with only quite a small effect. Another drawback is that it does not always give a wholly accurate picture of the effect of stretches of DNA linked to genes of interest. A new MAS technique – genomic selection – overcomes these difficulties. Rather than seeking to identify individual markers significantly associated with a trait, genomics uses all marker data as predictors of performance and consequently delivers more accurate predictions.

Plant populations

For many key African crops, however, the bottlenecks that might impede future breeding advances are not so much genomic as population-based. Breeders have a better chance of accessing useful genetic variants if the underlying research focuses on community-based plant populations – populations of plants created from a community of parents and hence likely to contain a range of genetic variants controlling complex systems such as pest resistance, yield, stress tolerance and grain quality. This give a more finely tuned, higher-resolution picture of genetic mechanisms. One such initiative, first developed in maize and called nested association mapping, has already enabled researchers to isolate genes controlling complex plant traits such as pest resistance regulated by a number of genes, not just one. Another experimental design for plant populations – with the compelling acronym MAGIC (Multi-parent Advanced Generation InterCross) – is being deployed in wheat, rice and sorghum.

Theory and practice: closing a gap

Plant breeders are genuinely excited by the dramatic advances made by research on crop genomes: information is pouring out of their laboratories at a dizzying rate, possibly faster than plant breeding practice can keep up.

Plant breeding is resource-intensive and highly dependent on collecting accurate data to support decision making. It also relies heavily on new insights from the even faster-moving fields of human genetics and evolutionary theory. This, allied to the fact that more and more is being discovered about the control of genes regulating complex traits, means that plant breeders' methods are becoming increasingly dependent on accessing new knowledge. Powerful computer simulations now make it possible to evaluate different breeding strategies or to model the way different genes work to help bridge the gap between theory and practice. Nonetheless, any simulation will ultimately need to be tested in a breeding programme.

Many of Africa's major food crops, including cassava and banana, reproduce vegetatively rather than by seed, making them ideally suited to improvement through genetic modification.

Road map for Africa

The new crop science and technology could be of great benefit to African agriculture, but it needs to take a comprehensive strategic perspective that embraces not just technology but the biology of Africa's critically important crop species.

Education, training and skills strongly focused on crop species of relevance are essential. A new generation of African plant breeders needs to be inspired to integrate modern approaches into practical, productive breeding programmes.

Innovative partnerships between funders, breeders, policy makers, urban planners, ecologists, educational institutions and professional communicators are needed to articulate the critical role of plant breeding in agricultural productivity and environmental sustainability.

Plant breeding needs to become more compatible with the goals of African agriculture, to embrace both greater species diversity and farming systems. It is not just a matter of focusing on crops to promote food security. Breeders need also to think about farm incomes and productive employment.

S. Szydlo/CC-BY-SA 3.0

Plant breeders need to focus not just on food security, but on crops that might boost incomes and productivity, such as coffee.

Molecular breeding to improve orphan crops

KEY THEMES

- Need to concentrate on orphan crops.
- Molecular breeding methods.
- Prospects for realising innovations.

Orphan crops: the case for improvement

For centuries, those resources we call orphan crops have provided food, animal feed, fibre, oil and medicinal products. They often manage to thrive in harsh conditions where they have evolved and adapted to the environment, making them ideal for agriculture in these conditions, and playing a major role in feeding the poor in the developing countries of Sub-Saharan Africa and South Asia. But they remain, compared to the most high-yielding crops, neglected and under-researched. They have never received the attention of plant breeders that has been enjoyed by major players such as wheat, maize and rice.

This lack of genetic improvement makes them much more susceptible to pests, weeds and diseases than they could be. So even though a large area in developing countries – some 250 million hectares – is used to cultivate just 27 of the crops defined as orphan, their yields tend to be much lower than those of major crops.

In short, the enormous potential of orphan crops in helping to meet the growing needs of the expanding human population remains unrealised.

Valued for its nutritious fruits and anti-viral properties, the baobab *Adansonia digitata* is the first orphan crop whose genomes are being sequenced by the African Orphan Crops Consortium.

Increasing molecular breeding

This unsatisfactory state of affairs could well be remedied by more investment in modern genetic technologies to bring these orphans in from the cold. Advanced molecular techniques have demonstrated their usefulness for the major crops by giving us unprecedented knowledge of key genes in their DNA sequences. It is now time to deploy these transformational tools more widely, and there are several ways in which this could be done.

Next-generation sequencing for orphan crops

The latest sequencing technologies – next-generation sequencing (NGS) – can produce thousands or millions of sequences concurrently. Genes with desirable properties can be identified far more quickly than in the past, which makes highly accurate reference genome sequences affordable, and promises more effective molecular breeding for trait improvement. So it is now realistic to consider advanced breeding programmes for orphan crops.

Marker-assisted selection

The use of marker-assisted selection (MAS) in improving rice is a major success story. Could this DNA-based technology for increasing our ability to identify genetic variation and develop new combinations of genes be extended to orphan crops?

wholegrainscouncil.org

The speed and affordability of NGS have begun to make this feasible. Researchers have, for example, used NGS with the medicinal plant *Artemisia annua*, which produces the potent anti-malarial compound artemisinin in microscopic structures on the surface of its leaves. They rapidly discovered a large number of genes responsible for artemisinin production, going on to identify thousands of markers associated with the expressed genes. This method of identifying molecular markers has the advantage that they all reside in gene sequences that are switched on – expressed – and therefore actively affecting the function of the genes. Within less than five years, a toolkit was created for marker-assisted breeding of an orphan crop for which, previously, little or no genetic information had been available. More importantly, the researchers began to see incremental improvements in the crop's performance.

Just a kilo of teff grains is needed to cultivate a hectare of the crop, while some 100 kilos of wheat grains are needed for a hectare of wheat.

Likewise, with the perennial plant *Jatropha curcas* – an oil-producing orphan crop that initially excited the interest of researchers as a potential source of biodiesel, and therefore a replacement for petroleum – large-scale production was hampered by lack of detailed knowledge of its genetic make-up. This resulted in very little breeding to improve its characteristics. Again, researchers have, in a similar fashion to their work on *Artemisia annua*, used NGS to build up a fuller picture of the genetic machinery of *Jatropha curcas* and are now working on a molecular breeding programme to identify high-yielding varieties that can be used for biodiesel production.

The use of MAS and NGS has done much to develop plants with potential as medicinal and biofuel crops, and now looks set to have a huge impact on improving the traits of orphan food crops.

Mutation breeding by TILLING

During the second half of the 20th century, breeders of the major crops made use of ionising radiation or chemicals to increase the amount of variation in their stocks by inducing mutations – sudden random changes in the genetic material of the cell. The methods were quite successful, though they did have a few technical drawbacks that limited their usefulness. Over the past decade, however, an updated version of mutation breeding has been developed that extends its applicability, especially to orphan crops. TILLING (Targeting Induced Local Lesions IN Genomes), and a variation called ecoTILLING, have been used in conjunction with NGS for rapid identification of numerous candidate genes associated with specific traits.

Currently, a number of TILLING projects are under way to improve orphan crops such as banana and cassava. Another centres on teff (see Case study), a staple cereal grown on more than 2.5 million hectares, mainly in Ethiopia.

It may well be that new NGS-based screening methods could replace TILLING and ecoTILLING in the hunt for valuable mutations in target genes.

Engineering variation
Genetic modification has already proved its worth in enhancing the yield, quality and environmental impact in terms of pesticide and fuel use of some of the major crops, including soybeans, maize, rice and rapeseed. Indeed, GM foods have been a significant component in global markets for some years.

CASE STUDY Improving teff by TILLING

Teff can grow where many other crops cannot thrive and its light-weight seeds – less than a millimetre in diameter, similar to a poppy seed – make it ideally suited to semi-nomadic life in areas of Ethiopia and Eritrea where it has long flourished.

Teff has a number of desirable characteristics: tolerance to drought and water logging; exceptional nutritional value; and very few post-production problems with pests or diseases. One major weakness, however, is a tendency to stem displacement, or lodging, when the plant falls to the ground under wind and rain, impairing both the quality and quantity of the ensuing harvestable grain.

So far, conventional breeding has failed to find a remedy to the problem. However, a new genetic approach has been to look at several genes that have boosted the yields of wheat and rice while conferring resistance to lodging. These are dwarfing genes that code for reduced height.

Next-generation (high-throughput) sequencing of the teff genome is currently in progress, with promising results. It does appear to carry some of the dwarfing genes, which could be used as targets for TILLING, with the aim of engineering semi-dwarf, higher-yielding varieties of the orphan crop.

CASE STUDY BioCassava Plus

A number of scientists from around the world pooled their expertise in the BioCassava Plus programme, a team effort to reduce malnutrition among the 250 million people in Sub-Saharan Africa who rely on cassava as their staple food.

Over the past five years or so, the team has developed cassava plants with 30 times as much beta-carotene (a source of vitamin A), four times as much iron and four times the protein content of traditional plants. Such enhanced levels would go a long way to meet nutritional needs.

From the laboratory, these crops have gone on to be field-tested and assessed for safety in Nigeria and Kenya – the necessary preparation for getting regulatory approval and, eventually, release for use by farmers.

While not yet fully tested or approved, BioCassava Plus may well influence regulators in Africa. Like their counterparts in Europe, African authorities have been cautious in their acceptance of genetically modified foods, but such high nutritional value may be hard to ignore in the face of Africa's burgeoning population.

However, it has not all been plain sailing: GM foods and crops have incited considerable controversy, especially in Europe, despite widespread scientific confidence in their proven benefits and safety for both human health and the environment. So it is hardly surprising that orphan crops, by definition the relatively neglected contributors to food production, have received little investment for GM development. Nonetheless, the work on GM-improved cassava (see Case study) gives some cause for optimism.

Can the potential be realised?

The experience of, and attitudes to, GM technology in Africa show that there are still some hurdles to the wholesale adoption of molecular plant breeding in order to improve orphan crops.

The cost of complying with regulatory processes, for instance, can deter investors from trying to develop these new crops. But this may change. When analysis was carried out on four GM products in the Philippines – insect-resistant eggplant and rice, and virus-resistant papaya and tomato – the regulatory costs, although significant, were generally lower than the cost of developing the technology. What is more, regulatory costs tend to decline as more experience is gained in these kinds of crops, so should not be an insurmountable barrier.

USGS/PD

On the positive side, molecular plant breeding clearly has huge potential for rapidly improving orphan crops. Next-generation sequencing technologies are making it possible to set up molecular breeding initiatives to target improved crop traits very quickly. Indeed, some of these technologies have reached the stage of "plug-and-play" usability since they are capable of being readily and routinely carried out in laboratories.

The use of new-generation sequencing looks set to have a huge impact on improving orphan food crops such as guava.

One final prospect is that the lowering of cost and the increases in throughput brought about by NGS and associated technologies will enable future molecular breeding work on orphan crops to be carried out in research institutes, academic laboratories and small to medium-sized companies. Its development will not have to depend solely on large multinational organisations.

RESEARCH, DISCUSSION
AND ESSAY TOPICS

- Genetic modification alone is not a solution to the challenge of food security – biotechnology is not a silver bullet.
- Biotechnology is often described as being dominated by multinational companies and not consistent with the interests of poor farmers and the developing world.
- Failure to meet global demand for food would have catastrophic humanitarian and political consequences.
- Despite recent improvements in agricultural production, the benefits are not equally distributed. What factors determine these inequalities?
- If crop yields are to increase in a sustainable manner, much can be achieved using existing knowledge and skills.
- Agriculture is both a victim of climate change and a contributor to it.
- Farmers need technologies appropriate to their particular circumstances – environmental, labour availability and affordability.
- The impacts of genetically modified crops are not simply economic: they reach beyond productivity and profitability.
- Crop plant breeding is a combination of science, art and business.
- This is an exciting time for plant breeders who have new science-based opportunities to improve crops.

FURTHER READING
AND USEFUL WEBSITES

Bennett, D.J. and Jennings, R.C. (2013) *Successful Agricultural Innovation in Emerging Economies: New Genetic Technologies for Global Food Production.* Cambridge University Press, Cambridge. Chapters 1–6.

Brookes, G. and Barfoot, P. (2013) *GM Crops: Global Socio-economic and Environmental Impacts 1996–2011.* PG Economics Ltd, UK.
http://www.pgeconomics.co.uk/pdf/2013globalimpactstudyfinalreport.pdf

Brookes, G. and Barfoot, P. (2014) *Economic Impact of GM Crops: The Global Income and Production Effects 1996–2012.*
https://www.landesbioscience.com/journals/gmcrops/2014GMC0001.pdf

Brookes, G. and Barfoot, P. (2014) *GM Crops: Global Socio-economic and Environmental Impacts 1996–2012.* PG Economics Ltd, UK.
http://www.pgeconomics.co.uk/pdf/2014globalimpactstudyfinalreport.pdf

Donald Danforth Plant Science Center. BioCassava Plus.
http://www.danforthcenter.org/scientists-research/research-institutes/institute-for-international-crop-improvement/crop-improvement-projects/biocassava-plus

Encyclopaedia Brittanica. Recombinant DNA technology.
http://www.britannica.com/EBchecked/topic/493667/recombinant-DNA-technology

European Academies Science Advisory Council (EASAC) (2013). *Planting the Future: Opportunities and Challenges for Using Crop Genetic Improvement Technologies for Sustainable Agriculture.*
http://www.easac.eu/fileadmin/Reports/Planting_the_Future/EASAC_Planting_the_Future_LAY_SUMMARY.pdf
http://www.easac.eu/fileadmin/Reports/Planting_the_Future/EASAC_Planting_the_Future_SHORT_SUMMARY.pdf
http://www.easac.eu/fileadmin/Reports/Planting_the_Future/EASAC_Planting_the_Future_FULL_REPORT.pdf

European Commission (2013) Special Eurobarometer 401.
http://ec.europa.eu/public_opinion/archives/ebs/ebs_401_en.pdf

Food and Agriculture Organization of the United Nations (FAO). FAOSTAT Database.
http://faostat3.fao.org/faostat-gateway/go/to/home/E

Food and Agriculture Organization of the United Nations (FAO). Food Prices Index.
http://www.fao.org/worldfoodsituation/foodpricesindex/en/

Food and Agriculture Organization of the United Nations (FAO) (2013) *Food Outlook: Biannual Report on Food Markets.*
http://www.fao.org/docrep/019/i3473e/i3473e.pdf

Food and Agriculture Organization of the United Nations (FAO). *The State of Food Insecurity in the World 2013.*
http://www.fao.org/publications/sofi/en/

Foresight (2011). *The Future of Food and Farming: Final Project Report.*
https://www.gov.uk/government/publications/future-of-food-and-farming

International Assessment of Agricultural Knowledge, Science and Technology for Development (IAASTD) (2009). *Agriculture at a Crossroads: Global Report.*
http://www.unep.org/dewa/agassessment/reports/IAASTD/EN/Agriculture%20at%20a%20Crossroads_Global%20Report%20(English).pdf

International Food Policy Research Institute (IFPRI) (2014.) *Food Security in a World of Natural Resource Scarcity: The Role of Agricultural Technologies.*
http://www.ifpri.org/sites/default/files/publications/oc76.pdf

International Food Policy Research Institute (IFPRI). Global Hunger Index.
http://www.ifpri.org/book-8018/ourwork/researcharea/global-hunger-index

International Service for the Acquisition of Agri-biotech Applications (ISAAA). Crop Biotech Update.
http://www.isaaa.org/Kc/Cropbiotechupdate/Default.Asp

International Service for the Acquisition of Agri-Biotech Applications (ISAAA). *Global Status of Commercialized Biotech/GM Crops 2013.* ISAAA Brief 46-2013.
http://www.isaaa.org

Mars. African Orphan Crops Consortium (AOCC).
http://www.mars.com/global/african-orphan-crops.aspx

Organisation for Economic Co-operation and Development (OECD) (2014) *Factbook 2014: Economic, Environmental and Social Statistics.*
http://www.oecd-ilibrary.org/economics/oecd-factbook_18147364

Organisation for Economic Co-operation and Development (OECD) and Food and Agriculture Organization of the United Nations (FAO). *The OECD-FAO Agricultural Outlook 2013–2022.*
http://www.oecd.org/site/oecd-faoagriculturaloutlook/

Paarlberg, R. (2010; 2nd ed. 2013) *Food Politics: What Everyone Needs to Know.* Oxford University Press, USA.

Royal Society (2009) *Reaping the Benefits: Science and the Sustainable Intensification of Global Agriculture.*
https://royalsociety.org/~/media/Royal_Society_Content/policy/publications/2009/4294967719.pdf

The Economist Intelligence Unit. Global Food Security Index.
http://foodsecurityindex.eiu.com/

United Nations Department of Economic and Social Affairs Population Division. (2013) *World Population Prospects: The 2012 Revision.*
http://esa.un.org/wpp/

United States Environmental Protection Agency. Climate Impacts on Agriculture and Food Supply.
http://www.epa.gov/climatechange/impacts-adaptation/agriculture.html

SECTION TWO

NEW GENETICS IN THE EMERGING WORLD

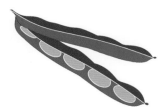

Orphan crops are vital to the economies of developing countries due to their suitability to local agro-ecological and socio-economic conditions.

This section looks in depth at the ways in which the modern revolution in plant science, including our newly discovered capacity to alter crop characteristics through marker-assisted breeding (MAS) and genetic modification (GM), is currently being applied to the challenges of food security in both the developed and developing worlds. The innovations described here result from our increasingly detailed understanding of the information contained within the genomes of plants as well as the pests and pathogens that threaten production. Integration of this information through so-called "-omics" technologies (such as genomics and proteomics), bioinformatics and modelling, coupled with suitable agrochemicals and farming practices, gives us the best chance of meeting global challenges of supply and demand in a sustainable manner.

A recurring theme here is that all available technologies – both conventional and modern genetic ones – should be evaluated and deployed as appropriate. Conventional plant breeding, for example, can be combined with genetically engineered traits such as insect resistance and herbicide tolerance to create crops with better pest and weed control. This has been successfully demonstrated in many of the major staple crops – maize, rice, cotton, soybeans – resulting in the decreased use of agricultural chemicals and improvements in productivity.

Argentina's triumph

There are several encouraging, if not dramatic, instances of economic and environmental benefits from the new agricultural genetics. In Argentina, for example, the introduction of a GM soybean which is resistant to the herbicide glyphosate rapidly transformed the whole agricultural sector – a success only possible because of the existence of the appropriate mechanisms for smooth technology transfer, biosafety regulation and technological assessment.

Africa's potential

The particular problems of Africa are also examined in this section, with a wide-ranging overview of the major challenges facing African smallholder farmers and the positive impacts on productivity that can be achieved by combining native traits, MAS and GM approaches with more conventional methods. For potential benefits to be realised on a wide scale, however, public attitudes towards plant breeding and GM technology – and its safety – also need to be taken into account. The fact that only four African countries have embraced GM crops at the time of writing may reflect the ambivalent, if not hostile, attitudes towards GM crops of many non-governmental organisations and a large section of the people of Europe, one of Africa's principal trading partners. This is reflected in the Declaration of the 9th Annual Meeting of African Science Academies, which took place in November 2013 in Addis Ababa.

What is the potential scope for improving the yields of crop plants by modern genetic methods? To date, the primary goals of plant breeders and farmers have been to maximise the macronutrient and calorific yields of the major grain crops such as wheat, maize and rice. Other important staples and so-called orphan crops – banana, sorghum, cowpea, pigeon pea, plantain, millet, sweet potato and cassava, for example – have been relatively neglected. These make up a group of crops that are vital to the economy of developing countries due to their suitability to the agro-ecology and socio-economic conditions, but which remain largely unimproved. In the future, this imbalance should be addressed. Not only should science play its part in improving macronutrient levels (carbohydrates, proteins and fats), it must also contribute to enhancing the micronutrient content (essential vitamins and minerals) in the interests of human health. Genetic engineering and conventional breeding have already been used to improve the content of essential vitamins and minerals in a number of crops – such as vitamin A in Golden Rice.

Insect resistance

Another key target for genetic improvement is insect resistance. For many people in Africa the black-eyed pea – or cowpea – provides a rich source of protein, starch, vitamins and minerals. Mainly cultivated by women farmers, it is economically and nutritionally the continent's most important legume, thriving on poor soils and with extremes of rainfall. But for all its versatility the cowpea has been a neglected – orphan – crop. Although breeders have managed to produce plants with high poten-tial yields, these have suffered immense losses through insect infestation. Now, though, a GM insect-resistant transgenic cowpea has been developed to overcome the expense, inefficiency and harm to people and the environment from poisoning through insecticide use.

India's issues

The food security problems facing India are also explored in this section. Despite the fact that the Green Revolution in India in the 1960s turned the country into a net

Science should play its part in enhancing the micronutrient content of crops like sorghum, one of Africa's most important staples.

H.F. Schwartz/USDA

China has invested heavily in developing transgenic varieties of crops, including sweet peppers.

food-exporting country, India has failed to benefit from more recent biotechnological developments, including GM food crops, in improving yields and meeting regional needs. Currently there is something of an impasse facing the adoption of GM crops – such as insect-resistant aubergine (brinjal) and Golden Rice – due to widespread anti-GM activism. The tangle of issues that have eclipsed India's efforts to help its poor through technological innovation are analysed in some detail.

Investment in China

A different kind of problem faces China. Here, industrialisation, urbanisation and general economic development have eaten into the land available for farming. Yet the relentless demand for food of an expanding population, and for animal feed as increasing wealth leads to greater meat consumption, continues apace. Since 1978, China has enjoyed considerable success, however, in developing new germplasm and hybrid breeding technologies which, along with high agrochemical use, have substantially increased the productivity of rice, maize and wheat. Over the past 30 years, China has invested no less than US$ 3.5 billion in transgenic research on 52 species of crop plant (and some animals), which will undoubtedly have positive impacts on food security and productivity in the future – provided appropriate regulations are adopted.

MANY CHALLENGES, MANY OPPORTUNITIES
Crop biotechnology and biosafety in Africa

7

Clear-cut benefits of biotechnology

Global food security needs a two-pronged attack: reducing demand for food along with increasing sustainable crop production. Both will be necessary if recent developments in plant science are to be harnessed optimally. Technological innovations will be most effective if rolled out as integrated components of agricultural systems, as the case studies in this chapter illustrate.

Agricultural biotechnology has already brought significant benefits to African farmers, but in only four countries so far – South Africa, Burkina Faso, Sudan and Egypt. Small-scale producers growing commercial genetically modified (GM) crops, in particular, have enjoyed substantial advantages: increased gross margins of 114 per cent; pesticide costs down by 62–96 per cent; and yield improvements of 18–29 per cent compared with conventional crops.

Improved pest control resulting from new plant strains is particularly noteworthy. Some African communities can lose up to 90 per cent of their food crops through diseases caused by bacteria, viruses and fungi, as well as other organisms such as plant-eating nematodes and mites that greatly impair growth and yield.

There are other benefits too from the new crops. They make farmers' lives simpler and more convenient as well as being safer for both human health and the environment. They also have the great advantage of being compatible with conservation-oriented farming practices. The opportunity to use fewer agrochemicals, for example, has a positive impact on the diversity of pollinating and other beneficial insect populations.

Underperforming agriculture

For more than 30 years, African agriculture – on which 60 per cent of the continent's labour force depends – has been underperforming compared to those parts of the developing world that benefited from improvements associated with the Green Revolution. Nonetheless, agriculture is still a major economic driver in Africa, both domestically and, in a number of countries, in terms of foreign currency earnings. There are many reasons for underperformance, including:

KEY THEMES

- Underachievement in agriculture.
- Pan-African initiatives on genetically modified organisms.
- Dramatic repositioning of investment in farming.
- Current biosafety and desirable goals.
- The need for integrated effort.

- poor-quality seeds;
- unpredictable rainfall and lack of irrigation together with climate change;
- degraded soil health and fertility;
- low-technology farm inputs;
- instability of world prices;
- a predominance of small farm holdings (1–2 hectares or even less in Africa);
- lack of farming organisations;
- poor infrastructure, such as lack of roads and bridges;
- neglecting the needs of women farmers, often the chief food producers;
- HIV/AIDS leading to a decrease in the availability of labour;
- an aging farming population;
- migration from rural areas into the cities.

Despite such limiting factors, Africa's demands and patterns of food consumption are predicted to change, with a doubling of the population from 1 billion to 2 billion by 2050, expanding urbanisation, and rising incomes likely to bring about increased overall demand, especially for high-value and processed foods. There has been a measure of agreement across Africa that more scientifically and technically trained people are needed to evaluate and further the cause of biotechnology.

Freedom to Innovate places great emphasis on building cohorts of appropriately trained experts who can advise countries on all aspects of biotechnology.

Common stance on biotechnology

The African Union (AU), through its New Partnership for Africa's Development (NEPAD), has adopted a common position on all issues arising from biotechnology and biosafety. The AU has also put in place the African Model Law on Biosafety to guide member states in drafting their own national legislation, and the African Strategy on Biosafety which provides member states with frameworks for regional and national biosafety initiatives and helps enhance regional capacity to carry out biosafety measures.

These guidelines complement the recommendations in AU-NEPAD's publication _Freedom to Innovate_, which places great emphasis on building cohorts of appropriately trained experts who can advise states on all aspects of biotechnology, including regulation, and food and environmental standards.

Regional priorities

Freedom to Innovate also stresses the need to identify biotech priorities that are geographically relevant to Africa's development. It suggests the following breakdown of activities:

FREEDOM TO INNOVATE

Biotechnology in Africa's Development
Report of the High-Level African Panel on Modern Biotechnology

- Southern Africa should concentrate on health biotechnology;
- North Africa on biopharmaceuticals;
- West Africa on new crop technologies;
- East Africa on animal biotechnology;
- Central Africa on forestry.

Genetic modification in agriculture

In addition to the above recommendations, the Conference of AU Ministers of Agriculture in 2006 came to a common African position, specifically on the use of GM organisms in agriculture. They recommended that member states should:

- enhance training in biosafety and biotechnology;
- establish regional GM testing laboratories;
- develop policies to enhance public-private partnerships in biotechnology;
- be encouraged to build regulatory capacity on issues surrounding biotechnology and biosafety.

Extent of commercialisation

What impacts have these pan-African initiatives had? Clearly some countries have been harnessing agricultural biotech innovations and integrating them into their

Figure 7.1 Numbers of confined field trials in Africa

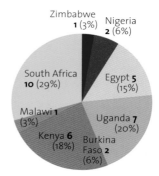

Total number of confined field trials: 34

Source: NEPAD/ABNE

Table 7.1 Confined field trials in Africa

	Crop/trait
Burkina Faso	*Bt* cotton (approved for commercialisation); cowpea (insect resistance, application pending)
Egypt	Maize (insect resistance, approved for commercialisation); cotton (salt tolerance); wheat (drought tolerance); potato (viral resistance); cucumber (viral resistance); melon (viral resistance); tomato (viral resistance)
Kenya	Maize (insect resistance); cotton (insect resistance); cassava (viral resistance); sweet potato (viral resistance)
Malawi	*Bt* cotton (insect resistance)
Nigeria	Cassava (nutrient enhancement); cowpea (*Maruca* insect resistance)
South Africa	Maize (drought tolerance); maize (herbicide tolerance); maize (insect resistance); maize (insect resistance and herbicide tolerance); cassava (starch enhancement); potato (insect resistance); sugarcane (alternative sugar); cotton (insect resistance and herbicide tolerance)
Uganda	Banana (fungal resistance); maize (drought tolerance); *Bt* cotton (insect resistance); cotton (herbicide tolerance); cassava (viral resistance); sweet potato (weevil resistance)

Source: www.nepadbiosafety.net

national agenda. But for all the agronomic, environmental, and nutritional and health benefits of the new technologies, only four countries have commercialised GM crops: South Africa, Burkina Faso (see Case studies), Sudan and Egypt. Figure 7.1 and Table 7.1, however, show that a number of other African countries are also conducting field trials for GM crops, so the signs are optimistic.

Dramatic change in direction

Agriculture across the continent has been repositioned in the development agenda through the Comprehensive Africa Development Program. This is a visionary attempt to make radical changes to the way in which Africa sets about making future agriculture fit for purpose. African leaders, for example, agreed in the 2003 Maputo declaration of the AU to increase public investment in agriculture by a minimum of 10 per cent of their national budgets, and to raise productivity by at least 6 per cent.

Target 2015

The ultimate aims of African leaders in the near future are as desirable as they are ambitious:

- vibrant agricultural trade within and between African countries and regions;
- farmers as active players in the market economy;
- Africa to become a net exporter of agricultural products;
- more equitable distribution of wealth for rural populations;
- environmentally sound production;
- a culture of sustainable management of natural resources;
- Africa to become a major strategic player in agricultural science and technology.

Challenges and constraints

For all this determination to ensure that Africa benefits fully from modern crop biotechnology, not to mention the fact that, globally, it has now been safely applied for nearly two decades, the pace of adoption has been relatively sluggish. The 2003 Maputo declaration of the AU is a very positive sign, and most countries have made significant progress towards the target of raising investment in agriculture by 10 per cent of national budgets, but only eight out of 54 (Burkina Faso, Ethiopia, Ghana, Guinea, Malawi, Mali, Niger and Senegal) have actually met or exceeded it, and only 11 have reached the 6 per cent productivity goal.

Many factors are at play here. Some are essentially political, such as the absence of biosafety regulations in most African countries and a lack of political will to

While the symptoms of cassava mosaic disease are seen on the leaves, the impact on tuber growth is so severe that the virus can cause serious financial losses as well as devastating food shortages.

FAO

CASE STUDY Cotton in Burkina Faso

The cotton crop of Burkina Faso is notoriously prone to pests. Before 2003, farmers were spending more than US$ 40 million annually on pesticides in an effort to fight production losses of 50–70 per cent. They badly needed the benefits promised by the new technologies.

From 2003 onwards, trials began in many locations on cotton crops modified with a suitable protective gene derived from a soil bacterium, *Bacillus thuringiensis,* which produces toxins that kill many insect pests when ingested. The new *Bt* cotton worked well, culminating in 2007 in 20 demonstration tests in fields at a suitable isolation distance from conventional cotton. By 2009, commercialisation of the *Bt* cotton began, with excellent results. Today, 80 per cent of Burkina Faso's cotton production, grown on more than 350,000 hectares, is from the *Bt* variety. Other genetically enhanced crops under evaluation include insect-resistant cowpea and sorghum biofortified with vitamin A.

The planting of *Bt* cotton has paid off handsomely, giving farmers average yield increases of more than 18 per cent compared to conventional varieties, and a rise in per-hectare profits from US$ 39 to around US$ 62. On the national scale, the estimated economic benefit of growing *Bt* cotton is over US$ 100 million, as yield increases reach 30 per cent and insecticide spray use falls by at least 50 per cent.

One further by-product has been an increase in honey production in areas where *Bt* cotton is under cultivation.

embrace new technologies – as well as concerns about safety implications. Others relate to the lack of strong seed industries and weak links between industry and research and development (R&D) bodies. In addition, investment in the new technologies has been uneven. Even when national research centres have the potential to apply the new biotechnologies, greater capacity in molecular biology, biochemistry, genomics, plant breeding and bioinformatics is needed.

The reasons for this are not just a lack of skilled personnel, funding or local infrastructure. Many laboratories are concerned that the regulatory procedures governing biosafety are inadequate for this kind of innovative research.

Status of biosafety measures

Of the 54 states in the AU, only 18 have laws, regulations, guidelines or policies relating specifically to modern biotechnology. The reasons for this shortfall are many and complex. Some relate to the international obligations and national priorities of individual countries. Others turn on the state of their biotech R&D.

Peggy Greb/USDA/ARS/PD

Certainly, it appears that some countries tend to focus their policy making more on the risks of the new genetics than on its potential benefits. Some also tend to evaluate it using socio-economic rather than scientific criteria, imposing risk assessment requirements that are incompatible with normal product development. Regulations are imposed that are simply unaffordable or unenforceable in practice.

The introduction of insect-resistant cotton in Burkina Faso has been bad news for pink bollworm – one of its major pests – but good news for local bee keepers as well as cotton farmers.

There is often a lack of cooperation and coordination between the government departments responsible for biosafety measures, as well as inadequate operational budgets. Inefficiencies and delays in processing applications for permits are also common. Matters are not helped by legal complexities, with biosafety laws that are unreconciled with existing laws.

A recipe for biosafety

A United Nations University Institute of Advanced Sciences report in 2008 – *Internationally Funded Training in Biotechnology and Biosafety: Is it Bridging the Biotech Divide?* – made the following recommendations for a functional, national biosafety system. It should:

- make science-based decisions on developing and using biotech products;
- be clear, transparent and predictable for all stakeholders;
- be flexible in adopting new technologies;
- take into account inputs from the public;
- ensure that biosafety policies and regulations are workable in practice.

CASE STUDY South Africa leads the way

In both research and development and in the cultivation of genetically improved crops, South Africa is the continent's frontrunner. Its list of crops under research is impressive: insect-resistant and herbicide-tolerant cotton; virus-resistant and drought-tolerant maize; fungus- and virus-resistant grapevine; starch-enriched cassava, and sugarcane with higher yields and raised sugar content.

These new crops are being developed by various organisations: seed companies, research institutions, academia and industry. To date, no fewer than 13 genetically modified crops have been approved for commercial release – eight cotton, four maize and one soybean line.

The rise in yield for the new maize compared to conventional plants ranges from 31 per cent to 134 per cent. In addition, those smallholders cultivating genetically modified cotton have seen their yields increase by 11 per cent, which means an extra US$ 35 per hectare.

Table 7.2 Some genetic modification research and development activities under way in Africa

Country	Crop	Trait	Institutions/companies involved
South Africa	Maize	Drought tolerance, herbicide tolerance, insect resistance, insect resistance/herbicide tolerance	Monsanto, Syngenta, Pioneer
	Cassava	Starch enhancement	Agricultural Research Council-Institute for Industrial Crops
	Cotton	Insect resistance/herbicide tolerance, herbicide tolerance	Bayer
	Potato	Insect resistance	Agricultural Research Council-Onderstepoort Veterinary Institute
	Sugarcane	Alternative sugar	South African Sugarcane Research Institute
Kenya, Tanzania, South Africa, Mozambique	Maize	Drought tolerance	African Agriculture Technology Foundation, National Agricultural Research Institutes, CIMMYT (International Wheat and Maize Improvement Centre), Monsanto, Bill and Melinda Gates Foundation, Howard G. Buffet Foundation
Kenya	Maize	Insect resistance	Kenya Agricultural Research Institute (KARI), CIMMYT, Monsanto, University of Ottawa, Syngenta, Rockefeller Foundation
	Cotton	Insect resistance	KARI/Monsanto
	Cassava	Cassava mosaic virus disease resistance	KARI, Danforth Plant Science Center
	Sweet potato	Viral disease resistance	KARI/Monsanto
Uganda	Cotton	Insect resistance/herbicide tolerance	National Agricultural Research Organisation/Monsanto, Agricultural Biotechnology Support Project II, USAID, Cornell University
	Banana	Black sigatoka (fungal disease) resistance	NARO-Uganda, University of Leuven, International Institute of Tropical Agriculture, USAID
	Cassava	Cassava mosaic virus disease resistance, cassava mosaic and brownstreak disease resistance	National Crops Resources Research Institute, CIP (International Potato Centre), Danforth Plant Science Centre
Nigeria, Burkina Faso, Ghana	Cowpea	*Maruca* (insect) resistance	Institute for Agricultural Research, Zaria/INERA (Institut de l'Environnement et de Recherches Agricoles)/SARI (Savanna Agricultural Research Institute)
South Africa, Burkina Faso, Kenya	Sorghum	Nutrient enhancement	Consortium of nine institutions led by Africa Harvest Biotechnology Foundation International and funded by the Bill and Melinda Gates Foundation

Table 7.2 continued

Country	Crop	Trait	Institutions/companies involved
Nigeria	Cassava	Nutrient enhancement	National Root Crops Research Institute, Umudike, Danforth Plant Science Center, International Institute of Tropical Agriculture, USAID
Egypt	Maize	Insect resistance	Monsanto, Pioneer
	Cotton	Salt tolerance	Agricultural Genetic Engineering Research Institute
	Wheat	Drought tolerance, fungal resistance, salt tolerance	Agricultural Genetic Engineering Research Institute
	Potato Banana Cucumber Melon Squash Tomato	Viral resistance	Agricultural Genetic Engineering Research Institute

Source: Bennett and Jennings, 2013

Overview of Africa's current research and development

Despite all the limitations, drawbacks and disappointments surrounding both the development and application of the new biotechnologies and the biosafety structures needed to facilitate them, the outlook definitely remains hopeful.

With the help of development partners and technology developers, African science has built the capacity to make significant progress in creating, developing and producing indigenous transgenic crops. A key event here was the creation of the African Agricultural Technology Foundation (AATF), which has overseen field testing of a number of GM crops across many institutions. Table 7.2 shows the extent of this R&D.

Importance of being integrated

If Africa is to realise its vision of 6 per cent annual growth in agricultural productivity with biotechnologies generating the greatest contribution, a number of issues need to be addressed.

To date, fear and scepticism have made biotechnology a sensitive trade issue across the developed and developing world. There has been a lack of information and familiarity with these innovatory methods and techniques, which has created misunderstandings and influenced public perception. The work of NEPAD is helping to break down these misperceptions, giving member states the information, training, technical support and networks necessary for their policy makers and the general public to make better-informed decisions.

There needs to be greater integration of effort. In those African countries with little or no capacity in biotechnology and biosafety, expertise needs to be pooled, data shared, and regional risk assessment and decision making distributed. Too many countries seem to be taking their own path in developing safe biotechnology, even though no country can ensure biosafety without engaging with neighbouring states. Furthermore, the cost and complexity of steering GM crops through the regulatory processes are prohibitive if approval has to be obtained for each country separately.

Africa has moved towards a critical mass of scientific expertise and can reduce both the costs and the time necessary for biotech development by sharing facilities and equipment. Coordination and cooperation will be key to success.

Africa has moved towards a critical mass of scientific expertise and can reduce both the costs and the time necessary for biotech development by sharing facilities and equipment.

ANATOMY OF SUCCESS
New genetic technologies in Argentina

KEY THEMES

- Importance of innovation.
- Unique experience with crops.
- Economic, environmental and sustainability impacts of genetic modification.
- Keys to success.

Argentina's experience

In using genetically modified (GM) crops to reshape its agriculture, Argentina is a country that has made full use of its potential in both economic and non-economic terms. Crucial to achieving this is that it has benefited from a friendly and effective institutional environment. Applying science and technology in order to speed up agricultural development, improve food security, boost farmers' incomes and generally alleviate poverty goes hand-in-hand with a favourable climate for innovation.

A century of agriculture

As Figure 8.1 shows, the history of agriculture in Argentina from 1900 to 2008 is broadly one of upward trends, as measured by area planted with grains and oilseeds. There are ups and downs, but in a hundred years or so the increase was more than fivefold, from 5 million to 28 million hectares.

Figure 8.1 Evolution of the area planted with grains and oilseeds in Argentina, 1990–2008, and milestones along the way

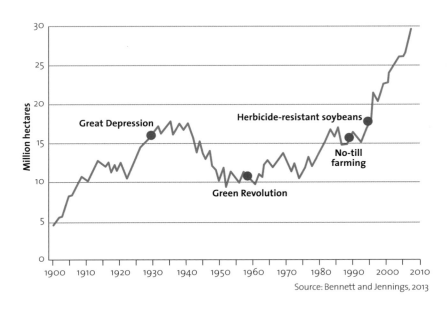

Source: Bennett and Jennings, 2013

73

Strikingly, the peaks and troughs closely reflect technological changes. The first decades, driven mostly by mechanisation, are followed by the Great Depression when planted areas were severely reduced. Yet, by the 1960s, the graph turns upwards following the Green Revolution, when improved dwarf wheat varieties and productive hybrid maize ushered in a new, innovation-based growth cycle that, with some fluctuations, has continued ever since.

Other landmarks include the widespread adoption of no-till farming (no ploughing or harrowing) in 1991, and the introduction of the first GM crop varieties – herbicide-tolerant soybeans – five years later. Together, these created a synergy that surpassed all expectations, outperforming even the USA where both technologies originated.

Genetic modification in Argentina: a unique narrative

The still-evolving story of GM crops in Argentina contains a number of elements that are unique. Analysts have been amazed by the sheer magnitude of the progress in the country's agricultural economy, which cannot be explained just by rising prices in grain and oilseeds. There are synergies at the heart of Argentina's success that can only be accounted for by technological change. How then has all this come about?

The first GM varieties introduced in Argentina were soybeans tolerant of the herbicide glyphosate, which kills a wide range of weeds. The first herbicide-tolerant soybean varieties were commercially available for the 1996/97 crop season, since when a further 20 more GM crop varieties have been approved for planting and consumption as food, feed or fibre. These include herbicide-tolerant and/or insect-resistant maize and cotton, and soybeans resistant to herbicides other than glyphosate.

By the 2010/11 crop season these technologies were being used over approximately 23 million hectares, with the improved soybeans occupying 100 per cent of the total area planted with soybeans, GM maize occupying 86 per cent of the designated maize area, and GM cotton 99 per cent of all cotton. These impressive totals place Argentina third in the world in GM crop area planted, behind only the USA and Brazil, and just in front of India and Canada.

Such progress is almost unprecedented in the history of world agriculture, comparable only to the adoption of hybrid maize in Iowa in the 1930s and certainly

Figure 8.2 Sources of growth in grains and oilseeds in Argentina, 1968–2008

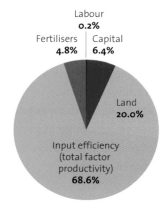

Source: Bennett and Jennings, 2013

much faster than the spread of new technologies in America's corn belt states, or in other countries during the Green Revolution of the 1950s and 1960s.

Speed of adoption apart, another surprising feature of Argentina's deployment of the new GM technologies is that none of these evolved from the country's own research and development (R&D) programme. All of them were developed outside Argentina by multinational seed companies and introduced into the genetic pool of indigenous crops. Yet, despite the fact that no innovations have been locally developed, there is general agreement that both the strength of Argentina's internal breeding programmes and the existence of an efficient seed industry have been critical to the adoption of the new genetic technologies throughout its agriculture.

Economic impact of the new biotechnologies

The new GM technologies, especially herbicide-tolerant soybeans, have had huge economic impacts, and not just because they reduce farmers' production costs. Farming practices have changed as well. By cutting the idle time between the wheat and maize harvest and the sowing of soybeans, short-cycle soybeans can be used as a double crop to take advantage of a newly created window of growing opportunity. Double cropping of two crops each year of wheat or maize and soybeans now takes place in areas where it was previously impossible. The net effect of this has been to enlarge the effective growing area by an estimated 3.5 million hectares.

At the same time, the new technologies made soybeans very financially competitive compared to other crops – maize and sunflower – as well as in comparison with livestock production. This encouraged farmers to intensify their use of the new technologies, which resulted in marked gains in livestock productivity even with less land devoted to cattle and more to soya, much of which is fed to cattle. During 1996–2005, for example, pasture land was cut by more than 5 million hectares with no drop in beef production.

The cumulative gross benefits to Argentina derived from growing GM crops (soybeans, maize and cotton) between 1996 and 2010 amount to an estimated US$ 72.65 billion. Figure 8.3 shows how this was shared out, with farmers enjoying the largest portion of the increased income.

Indirect effects on the economy

Alongside the direct economic benefits of GM crops are other, indirect gains. During the period 1996–2010, 1.8 million jobs were created, a substantial figure

Figure 8.3 How the benefits of genetically modified crops have been shared in Argentina, 1996–2010

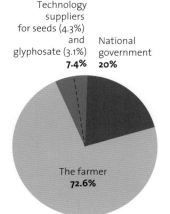

Technology suppliers for seeds (4.3%) and glyphosate (3.1%)
7.4%

National government
20%

The farmer
72.6%

Source: Bennett and Jennings, 2013

given that Argentina's total workforce was no more than 17 million. Moreover, this was during a period when the country's economy as a whole was contracting by about 10 per cent while unemployment rose to more than 21 per cent.

Environmental benefits

Expanding the number of GM varieties under cultivation has led to a dramatic increase in areas under no-till farming. This has had two main environmental consequences:

- no-till helped to reverse the negative impacts on the physical structure of the soils caused by conventional tilling and ploughing practices, which had prevailed up to the beginning of the 1980s;
- greater energy efficiency was achieved through a reduction in fuel consumption and a concomitant fall in CO_2 and other polluting emissions.

The cumulative effects on the Pampas region of water and soil erosion caused by traditional farming methods had severely affected yields – and therefore the economic viability of agriculture. By the end of the 1980s it was becoming clear that, in order to recover this lost productivity, changes were necessary, among them the introduction of no-till farming.

Breakthrough came in the late 1990s when the new strains of herbicide-tolerant soybean came on stream, enabling no-till farming to pick up speed and rapidly establish itself as the predominant strategy. The practice increased coverage from just 300,000 hectares in 1990/91 to 25 million hectares today.

This combination of no-till and herbicide-tolerant crops integrates two technological concepts: new mechanical means of modifying the soil-crop interaction; and the use of a total broad-spectrum herbicide – glyphosate. Although capable of controlling most kinds of weeds, glyphosate has no residual effects, so has less of an impact on the environment.

The effects of this synergy between two technologies are hard to quantify, but there is no doubting the positive pay-offs in terms of soil fertility and land productivity. There is also a contribution to mitigating the greenhouse effect thanks to a reduction in the amount of organic content lost from the soil.

These technologies have even more pronounced effects on the farming industry's contribution to climate change. So great are the reductions in fuel consumption

scsphotogallerytamu.edu

A century of land conversion has taken its toll on the Argentinian Pampas, exposing the soils to erosion from wind and rain. Thanks to advances in biotechnology, things are looking up; however, the extent of monocropping of export crops like soybeans continues to cause concern.

associated with no-till farming that the atmosphere has been spared an estimated 5.19 million tonnes of CO_2 that would have been generated by conventional practices. Annually, Argentinian farmers consume 13.5 million litres of fuel less than under the old agricultural regimes.

Similar improvements have been seen in carbon sequestration – the soil's ability to capture and store carbon from the atmosphere. The new reduced or no-till cultivation of soybean crops alone may be sparing the atmosphere more than 50 million tonnes of unwanted CO_2.

Phosphorus fertiliser can be organic, as is the case with guano, but very little of that is available. So the vast majority has to be mined from finite deposits of phosphate rock – 50 per cent of which are in the Arab regions – and transported over huge distances.

Sustainability and the soybean

The dramatic transformation of Argentina's agriculture brought about by introducing GM crops in the mid-1990s is not without its downside. A predominance of monocultures and low levels of fertiliser use, especially in those regions where ecosystems are relatively fragile, have created significant soil-nutrient losses. The long-term effects of the continual export of nutrients from the soil, particularly phosphorus – essential to all life – are serious and throw a question mark over the issue of sustainable production. Many millions of tonnes of phosphorus are lost over time – an estimated 14 million between 1996 and 2010 – which can only be replaced at huge cost to the farmer and the environment.

Argentina on the world stage

As the world's third-biggest soybean producer, exporting nearly all its output to Europe, China and Southeast Asia, Argentina is an international player of huge importance to consumers. Soybeans are a major component both of a large number of processed foods for humans and of much farm animal feed. By adopting novel technologies, the country has been able to reduce the price of the commodity compared to what could have been achieved using conventional practices. In monetary terms, this means a saving in consumer expenditure of US$ 89 billion for 1996–2010, such is the power of the new genetics.

Conditions for success

The story of GM crops in Argentina highlights a number of conditions that are necessary for a country to benefit from the new technologies. These include:
- early adoption of novel crops made possible by having in place institutions able to deal with technology transfer and diffusion;
- biosafety regulations and the infrastructure available for assessing new technologies;

- an active and efficient seed industry to enable the rapid introduction of new genes into commercial varieties of crops.

Together, these advantages have been more important than a local R&D capability for generating innovation. GM technologies seem to travel well. This is seen not just in Argentina but in many other parts of the world too.

www.soils4teachers.org

Phosphorus deficiency results in stunted growth and a dark reddish-purple hue to the plant's leaves.

What really matters is to have the right tools in place to extract maximum benefit from innovation when it becomes available. Smooth technology transfer at farm level, for example, depends on having in place proper biosafety and intellectual property frameworks. Policy makers, too, need to be alert to ensure that land use, input prices, market regulation and so on are all taken into account to avoid any negative effects of these paradigm-shifting innovations.

THE NECESSITY OF NEW TECHNOLOGIES
China's experience, yesterday and tomorrow

KEY THEMES

- Urgent productivity needs.
- New technologies, especially transgenics.
- Complex biosafety problems.
- Essential future role of biotechnology.

"Food is heaven for the people"

This ancient Chinese saying encapsulates the immense importance of an adequate food supply in ensuring stability and prosperity, sustainable development and peace. Food security has always been a core issue.

To maintain its food supplies, China has to cope with a perennially difficult tension between supply and demand. Its population, currently over 1.3 billion and rising at a rate of more than 5 million per year, puts huge pressure on agriculture. Yet Chinese arable land occupies a relatively small area, just 126 million hectares, which is being cut back all the time by rapid industrialisation, urbanisation and infrastructure development. How can China, which accounts for more than 20 per cent of the global population, feed its people from only around 8 per cent of the world's arable land?

Many problems, many challenges

Over the past 30 years a number of important changes have taken place. China has a long agricultural history: before the 1980s, agriculture involved more than 85 per cent of its workforce; today, in the wake of industrialisation and the wholesale relocation of rural populations to cities, it employs less than half of the population.

Figure 9.1 World arable and cropland by region

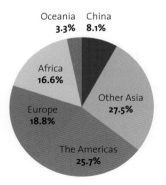

Total world arable and cropland 1.55 billion hectares

Source: FAOSTAT

Over the same period, alongside loss of labour and the progressive shortage of resources such as farmland and water, the use of pesticides and chemical fertilisers has risen sharply. Indeed, overuse has severely degraded many agricultural eco-systems – which are expected to come under yet more stress as a result of global climate change. This means that if China pursues traditional methods and practices, by 2030 it may well suffer a shortfall in food supplies of 120–170 million tonnes per annum: a severe threat to food security. The move to higher meat consumption as the economy continues to develop puts even greater demands on the supply of animal feed. In short, China has an urgent need to enhance crop productivity in an environmentally friendly, cost-effective and resource-efficient manner.

One solution is to use the existing genetic resources – the germplasm – within its crop plants more efficiently. Another is to draw on the new technologies to drive up productivity.

79

New germplasm and breeding technologies

Under the traditional style of farming, rice – one of China's most important staple foods – had poor levels of productivity, yielding less than 2.7 tonnes per hectare. For some decades, China has been making considerable efforts to drive this up by improving the crop.

The first milestone was the development of new semi-dwarf rice bred by creating hybrids of traditional semi-dwarf crops and high-yielding varieties. The newly bred varieties were shorter in height, resisted lodging (flattening down and so being more difficult or impossible to harvest) and produced more grain. They were widely cultivated from the early 1960s when many semi-dwarf crops were developed in different parts of the world – fruits of the Green Revolution. These new rice

CASE STUDY Transgenic cotton shows the way

China is one of the world's leading cotton producers, though it used to lose a significant proportion of the crop – worth tens of millions of dollars each year – to pests, especially cotton bollworm. Heavy pesticide use not only had highly adverse effects on agricultural ecosystems; it also led to the rapid development of resistance in the insect pests, making insecticides ineffective. The whole cotton industry was teetering on the edge.

Then, in 1991, came a research programme to develop transgenic insect-resistant cotton using artificially synthesised *Bacillus thuringiensis* (*Bt*) genes to confer resistance. By 1997 the relevant transgenic cotton technologies gained patents and a biosafety go-ahead for commercial production. The following year, about 5 per cent of China's total cotton-growing area was given over to the new transgenic varieties, which were then rapidly adopted across the major cotton-planting areas.

In 2003, China's locally produced insect-resistant transgenic cotton made up 50 per cent of its crop, rising to 75 per cent by 2011 – a total of 3.9 million hectares. Seven million smallholder farmers benefit from the new cotton, with their incomes markedly boosted and their use of chemical insecticides falling to less than 30 per cent of that in conventional crop fields. The environment is healthier, as are farm workers and their families who suffer fewer cases of spray-induced poisoning.

Another important beneficiary is the whole agricultural biotechnology enterprise. The practical and commercial success of *Bt* cotton has promoted research and development of other transgenic crops such as wheat, papaya and tomato, and vindicated the decision of researchers and governments to follow the transgenic route, when appropriate, for driving up agricultural efficiency.

www.goldenrice.org

In the past, the production of hybrid rice strains was limited by rice's inherent propensity to self-pollinate. This was overcome when scientists developed a method which relies on various types of male sterility, thus preventing self-pollination.

crops exceeded yields of 4 tonnes per hectare and did much to overcome China's food security problems in the 1960s and 1970s.

A second milestone came at the end of the 1970s with improvements to breeding technology which made it possible to produce higher-yielding hybrids by relying on male plant sterility, along with the development of more semi-dwarf hybrid varieties that benefited from hybrid vigour. This is an increase in growth, survival and fertility resulting from crosses between genetically different parent crops.

The ensuing hybrid varieties showed a 20 per cent increase in grain yield compared with conventional semi-dwarf plants, which drove an expansion of the areas set aside for their cultivation from 5 million hectares in 1978 to around 16 million in 1990. This had profound effects on productivity. Although the total cultivated area of all rice varieties declined during 1975–2005, the total rice grain yield increased.

This use of elite genetic resources and new breeding techniques has paid off with crops other than rice – such as maize, wheat and rapeseed. Here, too, semi-dwarf varieties and hybrid vigour have led to huge increases in productivity.

Adopting these new varieties, however, has brought with it some drawbacks. Outputs are certainly high, but so too are inputs in the shape of chemical fertilisers and pesticides. This high-input/high-output system has led over time to degradation of the land, affecting its long-term productivity.

The need is clear for what has come to be called sustainable intensification – which focuses on achieving environmental sustainability through an ecosystem approach – aiming to maximise crop production through the careful management of biodiversity and ecosystem services. One strategy for overcoming limitations and meeting the need for sustainable intensification is to look to biotech solutions.

Figure 9.2 Rice yields in China, 1961–2012

Tonnes per hectare

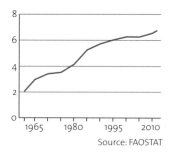

Source: FAOSTAT

Transgenic biotechnology takes off

In the mid-1980s the Chinese government launched the first National High Technology Research and Development (R&D) Programme, which identified R&D in transgenic biotechnology and its application in agriculture and pharmaceuticals as an important aspect of the country's development strategy. National research projects focused specifically on transgenic crops and their commercial application. Since then, China has built up its capacity in the areas of whole genome sequencing, in which it is probably now the world leader; gene mapping and cloning; genetic transformation; transgenic breeding; biosafety assessment and management; and the commercialisation of transgenic products. To date, researchers have explored the potential of more than 52 plant species, including cotton, rice, maize, potato, tomato, wheat, rapeseed, soybeans and poplar tree. More than 100 transgenes have been used to create a large number of transgenic lines of crops with traits such as insect resistance, herbicide tolerance, improved grain quality and drought tolerance.

By March 2011, no fewer than 1,560 biosafety certificates had been issued for various crop species, with many more transgenic lines undergoing biosafety assessment. By the same date, a number of transgenic varieties were in commercial production (Table 9.1). Despite these advances, however, the commercial growing of transgenic crops in China has come under increasingly critical scrutiny. While the government strongly supports Chinese development of genetically modified (GM) varieties, there has been public concern about US control of the country's food supply through its biotech companies, as well as food scares.

Poplars are one of China's most commonly planted species. A fast-growing tree used for veneers, plywood and timber, it is also used for reforesting areas that have suffered from intensive logging.

Vital financial support

China's productive experience with cotton underscores the need for adequate funding for the substantial investment needed to deliver new technologies to the farmer in the field.

Direct funding came from central government through national research programmes sponsored by both the Ministry of Science and Technology and the Ministry of Agriculture. Provincial administrations, too, allocated funds, as did local

CASE STUDY A lesson in biosafety

As long ago as 1992, China cultivated, in Yunnan province, transgenic tobacco that was resistant to two viruses which cause the plant severe damage – tobacco mosaic virus and cucumber mosaic virus. The new varieties could have been extremely important both for farmers and for the export market, but cultivation was stopped by biosafety shortcomings.

At the time of the new tobacco's development, China lacked a well-established national biosafety regulation and assessment system, so was unable to carry out the proper regulatory procedures; it certainly could not export the new products internationally. So some excellent, front-end research and development had to come to a close.

Table 9.1 Genetically modified species commercialised or having biosafety certificates in China

Crop	Species	Year of commercialisation or biosafety certificate	Trait	Status of application
Cotton	*Gossypium hirsutum*	1997	Insect resistance	3.9 million hectares
Petunia	*Petunia hybrida*	1997	Flower colour change	Small-scale
Tomato	*Lycopersicon esculentum*	1998, 2000	Virus resistance, storage endurance	Small-scale
Sweet pepper	*Capsicum annuum*	1998	Virus resistance	Small-scale
Poplar tree	*Populus tremula*	2005	Insect resistance	Small-scale
Papaya	*Carica papaya*	2006	Virus resistance	About 10,000 hectares
Rice	*Oryza sativa*	2009	Insect resistance	Biosafety certification
Maize	*Zea mays*	2009	Phytase for improved feedstuff	Biosafety certification

Source: Bennett and Jennings, 2013

research institutes and universities. Commercial companies and non-governmental organisations also played their part in the overall investment.

Biosafety: a complex problem

In China, as elsewhere, the extensive cultivation of transgenic crops has aroused huge concerns over biosafety – a central topic for debate which simply cannot be avoided if the new technologies are to be developed and applied. Following biosafety assessment, any GM crop must, by law, receive a biosafety certificate or deregulation permit before it can be commercially cultivated.

Earlier experience with transgenic tobacco in China shows how essential it is to deal with biosafety matters properly if biotechnology producers are to succeed in the marketplace (see Case study).

Biosafety in the context of GM and other innovatory technologies is a complicated business which needs consideration at every stage: threats to human and environmental health can exist in the research laboratory as well as in the fields or supermarkets. There are several biosafety concerns:

- potential health risks to humans, livestock and wild species from consuming GM products;
- environmental and ecological risks from extensive cultivation of the new crops in monocultures;
- useful and informative labelling of commercial products and the detection of transgene-derived protein if they are not so labelled;
- ethical and socio-economic concerns;

- public perception/acceptance of these products;
- regulatory procedures for GM products;
- risk assessment systems governing commercial release and cultivation.

One can see many of these considerations in play in the case of gene flow – the flow of genes from cultivated to wild relatives or between crops – a topic which has aroused much debate, even worldwide, both within the scientific community and among the public at large.

China's biosafety response

In 1993 the Ministry of Science and Technology issued an important legal document – *Safety Administration Regulation on Genetic Engineering* – to serve as a

---

BOX 9.1 What's the worry over transgenes?

The central concern turns on the potential ecological impacts of transgenes flowing by cross-pollination from genetically modified (GM) crops to the equivalent non-GM crop or wild species, transporting engineered genes to new hosts where they could have damaging effects. A gene coding for herbicide tolerance, for example, might make its way into the related weed population and create superweeds that frustrate a farmer's attempts to control them. Other objections are that transgenes flowing from GM crops might limit biodiversity or even cause the extinction of local wild plant populations.

In certain cases, crops may interact with related wild plants to form crop-weed complexes – for example between cultivated sugar beet and wild sea beet. These weed populations can act as reservoirs of foreign genes, potentially including genes introduced by genetic engineering. And they can also act as

bridges, allowing gene flow between crops and wild species that are usually unable to interbreed.

Then there is a health worry: that transgenes coding for antibiotic resistance might flow into bacteria, causing new antibiotic resistance problems for humans. We all have anything up to a kilo of bacteria in our intestines, which for the most part already contain antibiotic-resistance genes, due in part to excessive or inappropriate use of antibiotics by people and the medical profession.

The questions raised by transgenes have influenced decision makers considering the commercial application of GM crops as well as the general public and consumers. And that, in turn, has caused difficulty for scientific researchers who have had to think hard about how much data is needed to prove whether or not GM crops are safe for consumption or to be released into the environment.

The development and cultivation of virus-resistant transgenic papaya – in which the plant is "immunised" with a gene from the virus – has largely solved the problem of papaya ringspot virus, which used to cause major setbacks for papaya growers.

framework on all biosafety matters, ranging from research and experimentation to commercialisation, labelling, import and export. Further regulatory documents have followed since then, as has the establishment of a top-level panel of experts forming the National Biosafety Committee.

Today, China has in place a rigorous procedure for taking any GM crop proposal through biosafety assessment and on to commercial exploitation. To receive a biosafety certificate, a novel crop has to go through a five-step process: confined laboratory safety investigation; restricted field tests; enlarged field testing; production-scale tests over more than 2 hectares; and finally safety certificate application. This is essentially the same procedure as for any crop that is approved for market in the developed world.

Future prospects for new technologies

China has come to a decisive conclusion to ensure its future food security. It believes that, in order to feed its swelling population in an environmentally friendly, sustainable manner, it needs to apply new technologies in general and transgenic crop technologies in particular. These are powerful tools that cannot be ignored.

Biotechnology for food production is firmly on the government's agenda, inspired by the huge success of transgenic cotton, which has rescued China's cotton industry, and other GM crops. Many R&D projects are now under way, particularly ones following the transgenic route.

Genetic modification and biotechnology have already significantly improved the efficiency of the country's agriculture: reducing pesticide use, improving herbicide resistance and thereby labour practices, and increasing yields. They have become – and will continue to be – intrinsic to China's food supply and security in the future.

A STRUGGLE FOR RECOGNITION
Food security in India through genetically modified crops

10

India's urgent needs

India's agriculture, like that of its easterly neighbour, is confronting a massive population. The country's 1.21 billion people, increasing at an average rate of more than 10 million a year, are expected to reach 1.69 billion by 2050 – compared with China's 1.4 billion in 2025.

For nearly three-quarters of India's people living in some 820,000 villages, agriculture has been a way of life. But the pressures on output are enormous, as incomes rise along with demand for more and higher-quality food. At the same time, the area of cultivable land is being lost to degradation, and irrigation facilities remain largely inadequate. These restrictions have put India at the bottom of the productivity ladder in the developing world and placed it 63rd (out of 78 countries) on the 2013 Global Hunger Index. Some 76 per cent of India's people are living on less than US$ 2 per day. To ensure its food security, India needs more than 65 million more tonnes of food grain every year.

Agriculture under stress

Indian agriculture has to refocus itself to align production with the growing demands of its booming population. Modernisation and mechanisation are urgently needed, as are many more hectares of useable land, which could be acquired through technological innovation to enhance soil health and improve water supply and irrigation. The water table is dropping very rapidly, and electricity for irrigation pumps will not be free to the majority of farmers forever, as it is now. Productivity also needs to improve. Indian food crop yields have not kept up with those of the USA, China and Egypt, and compare very unfavourably with world averages in general.

In short, after the beneficial effects of the Green Revolution began to be seen in the late 1960s, the country's agriculture seems to have reached a plateau. Its areas fit for farming cannot be appreciably expanded and its water resources, forever subject to the vagaries of nature, are restricted, sometimes to alarmingly low levels.

Even agricultural extension programmes for guiding farmers on their choice of seeds, fertilisers, insecticides, irrigation methods and alternate cropping patterns based on

KEY THEMES

- Agriculture under stress.
- Limits to the Green Revolution.
- Variable success of genetically engineered crops.
- Activism, public opinion and politics.

Figure 10.1 Cereal yields in India relative to other major producers, 1961–2012
Tonnes per hectare

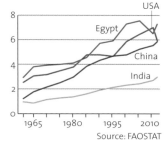

Source: FAOSTAT

Native to India, the mung bean is an orphan crop with a short growing season. It is also heat and drought-resistant and has few insect or disease problems, making it a valuable food source.

soil analyses and other factors have all been largely ineffective. Sometimes this is for purely agricultural reasons, such as the unsuitability of soils. Sometimes the human element intervenes: farmers can be lured into making poor choices by the prospect of better financial returns.

What did the Green Revolution achieve?

India's Green Revolution, launched in the 1960s, was designed to:

- establish scientific and agricultural research bodies for improving technologies and crop varieties, and introducing the new dwarf cereal crops;
- improve fertilisers, pesticides and herbicides;
- address irrigation deficiencies;
- promote effective management.

By and large, this plan worked, showing that barriers to food production could be overcome and that the country could be transformed, through technological innovation, from an import-dependent nation to a net food exporter. Unfortunately, however, the Green Revolution's benefits to India did not last. Although they initially reduced fluctuations in food production, increased incomes, assuaged poverty and brought about more sustainability, over time the pendulum began to swing back. A number of warning signs were simply ignored by those managing India's agriculture, with serious adverse consequences.

The overzealous use of agrochemicals rendered large tracts of farmland uncultivable, while overstretched irrigation facilities meant that no further land could be brought under irrigation. Any benefits from improved crop varieties started to level out, and the farmers' need of cash crops lowered their output of millet, pulses and oilseeds. Alongside all that, financial hardship and electric power shortages eroded the chance of sustaining any hard-won gains.

Strong governmental response

This alarming situation called for powerful and urgent remedial measures. In 2011 the Indian government tabled its Food Security Bill to facilitate heavily subsidised, adequate grain supplies for poor families. This aimed to alleviate the food-supply problems of up to 75 per cent of the rural population and 50 per cent of urban dwellers, at enormous cost to the public purse.

But reducing malnutrition and hunger-related deaths in India needs concerted management and technological effort if it is to be sustainable. Conventional agricultural

CASE STUDY *Bt* cotton proves its worth

India, like China, has enjoyed immense success with *Bt* cotton. In the decade 2002–2012 the *Bt* crop area under cultivation grew phenomenally, from 0.5 million hectares to 10.6 million hectares, while the number of cotton farmers rose from 50,000 to 7 million. Average yield went up by more than 60 per cent and total production soared from 13.6 million bales to 35.5 million.

This transformation allowed India to stop being a cotton importer and instead become the world's second-largest exporter. The new cotton enhanced total farm income by US$ 3.2 billion in 2011 alone, much to the benefit of the country's 7 million resource-poor small farmers.

The biggest gains came from the reduced use of insecticides – more than 38 million kilos less since 2002. Yields went up, as did the physical and psychological health of farm workers and local people.

practices could never deliver the much-needed 65 million additional tonnes of food each year; new technologies are seen as the only option.

Genetically engineered crops: a chequered history

India has around 60 universities, 10 autonomous institutes and 65 companies now involved in the research and development (R&D) of genetically improved crops. They are looking to develop some 80 desired characteristics in around 30 crops, with pest resistance being the most common trait.

India also has a biosafety regulatory system that is more elaborate and rigid than that of most other countries. At first sight, its structure of research, guidelines and standards, checks and balances before field trials and commercial release are approved appears highly rigorous. In practice, however, the top-level governing body – the Genetic Engineering Appraisal/Approval Committee (GEAC) – has often dismayed the scientific community with what the latter regards as irrational decision making. At the same time, the GEAC has attracted the disapproval of anti-GM activists at various stages of development of novel plants. Their criticisms reached a peak with the commercial release of *Bt* cotton in 2002 and *Bt* brinjal (eggplant or aubergine) in 2009.

For all the attempts of the Indian government to create a smooth regulatory path for the new technology, consulting widely with all parties, including the public, there

Bt brinjal was developed to combat losses caused by the brinjal fruit and shoot borer – the larval phase of the moth *Leucinodes orbonalis*.

is still some way to go. Whereas *Bt* cotton has been a success, the introduction of insect-resistant *Bt* brinjal has foundered.

The power of activism

A decade of persistent intense activism has profoundly affected India's development of new crop technologies. Medical and environmental biotech products, on the other hand, escape the attentions of activists who, so far, have concentrated their opposition on GM crops. Even the commercialisation of Golden Rice, which became available to India without any technology costs, has been slowed down by political activism, with scheduled field trials having to be postponed.

CASE STUDY *Bt* brinjal hits a barrier

How different from *Bt* cotton is the story of *Bt* brinjal (aubergine or eggplant) – a valuable food crop which is now under an indefinite moratorium curbing its commercialisation. Both cotton and brinjal were opposed by activists: one crop made it, the other did not.

Bt brinjal contains the same gene from the universally occurring soil bacterium *Bacillus thuringiensis* as cotton and several other crops such as maize and soybeans, which have been safely consumed since 1996. The *Bt* gene controls shoot, fruit and now root-boring pests. Normally, high-quality non-*Bt* brinjal is sprayed with insecticides up to 40 times.

Development of the new brinjal crop started in India in 2002 and gained all the necessary official permissions from the regulatory system. Many institutions and hundreds of experts evaluated the efficacy, field performance and biosafety of the *Bt* brinjal, culminating in the Genetic Engineering Appraisal/Approval Committee (GEAC)

accepting recommendations for commercial release in 2009. But within a matter of months things went drastically wrong.

The Minister of Environment and Forests chose to impose a moratorium on the new crop, not on scientific, safety or environmental grounds but for political reasons. He argued that *Bt* brinjal would have met with public disapproval and expressed a fear that the majority of genetically modified seed would be under the control of one multinational company – Monsanto's Indian subsidiary, Mahyco, the Maharashtra Hybrid Seeds Company – which had simply provided the transgene and had no commercial interest in the ensuing *Bt* plant.

This moratorium has had serious effects on India's research and development of genetically engineered crops as a whole. Public investment has slowed down, and both India and foreign private investors have become hesitant about any future enterprise.

Why have anti-technology activists been so powerful? One reason is that they have the support of the pesticide industry, conventional seed developers and the organic farming lobby – all of which feel threatened by the large-scale adoption of GM crops – together with non-governmental organisations that are antagonistic to many forms of globalisation, including multinational companies and the perceived power of the USA.

Public opinion too has been shaped by such tactics as petitions in India's Supreme Court, and the vandalising of R&D sites and crops in official field trials. Activists have also made use of the media to spread information – some would say misinformation – on issues with a strong emotive pull on the general public. They argued, for example, that the risk of *Bt* brinjal crossing with its wild relatives might jeopardise their use in indigenous medicine.

Notwithstanding a voluminous peer-reviewed literature on the safety and benefits of GM crops, biosafety is a central preoccupation of activists. They argue, for example, that GM crops have adverse consequences for ecology and biodiversity, even though 10 years of experimental field research and commercial cultivation have shown no scientific evidence of environmental harm. They argue too that the new crops threaten indigenous varieties and hybrids. Despite these objections, however, the Indian government has decided to allow companies and institutions to put more than 200 transgenic varieties of rice, wheat, maize, castor and cotton on field trial to check their suitability for commercial production.

Tangled interests

Anti-GM activism has also been fuelled by broad political and industrial antagonisms. In 2002 for example, the Indira Gandhi Agricultural University and Syngenta International – the Swiss multinational company involved in sequencing the rice genome and co-developing Golden Rice – proposed a collaborative research project. Their aim: to identify rice varieties and genes to develop novel hybrids of benefit to farmers. But there was immediate opposition from activists uneasy about the role and influence of multinationals. Negative and unsupported campaigning about farmer suicides due to the growth of *Bt* cotton over the years fuelled the fire. Threatened by violent agitation, Syngenta withdrew from the proposed arrangement.

Similarly, activists and opposition parties in the Indian government strongly opposed a deal made by the Indo-US Knowledge Initiative on Agriculture which aimed, among

Bt cotton is grown on about 90 per cent of India's cotton-growing area, making India the country with the largest GM cotton area in the world.

Earthnoo/CC-BY-SA 3.0

Some of the objections to *Bt* brinjal reflected concern about gene flow to wild relatives of the crop, which are used in Ayurvedic medicine.

other things, to build agricultural cooperation in biotechnology. On another occasion, an Indian state government – Bihar – blocked the development of GM crops for political rather than scientific reasons.

Untangling biosecurity issues from a mix of political, economic, social and ethical considerations would be a decisive step forward in India's deployment of the new genetic technologies. As things stand today, the country runs severe risks, in the opinion of the distinguished Indian expert Professor Chavali Kameswara Rao: "Today any GE [genetically engineered] crop can be released for cultivation in India, provided the developers do not say that it is GE, and in the process can as well save enormous amounts of time and money by bypassing the regulatory regime, benefiting farmers and consumers..."

There have already been several unconfirmed reports of illegal cultivation of pest-resistant and herbicide-tolerant cotton, virus-resistant papaya and *Bt* brinjal. So, clearly, urgent action is needed to balance the interests of a concerned public with that of India's future as a food-secure nation in which biotechnology needs to be given a fair hearing. Public education and informed dialogue are needed to address prejudice and ignorance, as well as vested interests, both political and commercial.

MORE FROM LESS –
A LASTING SOLUTION
Genetic improvement and sustainable intensification

11

Necessity of genetic improvement

Meeting the food needs of a rising global population while adapting to the threats of climate change and reducing our environmental footprint presents the global agricultural community with an unprecedented challenge. Without the genetic improvement of crops by a combination of conventional breeding, marker-assisted selection (MAS) and genetic modification (GM), it is difficult if not impossible to see how this challenge can be met.

There are several components, though, to a sustainable farming future, not just genetically improved seed. More effective land and water use, integrated pest management strategies and fewer harmful chemical inputs are all essential. Sustainability, in other words, is multi-factorial.

Health effects

No technology is sustainable if it is harmful to human or environmental health. There is broad scientific consensus that, after nearly two decades of cultivating GM crops planted over a cumulative total of more than 1.5 billion hectares, there have been no apparent adverse effects on people's health from the new bio-technologies. Nor have they demonstrably damaged the environment.

The USA's National Research Council and the European Union's Joint Research Centre have both concluded that they have enough knowledge to address the safety of GM foods. They state that the processes of genetic engineering and conventional breeding are effectively alike in terms of any unintended consequences to human and environmental health.

That is not to say that every new variety – whether produced by GM or conventional methods – will automatically be benign. Each new GM crop has to be assessed individually through a strict multi-agency process. As it happens, conventional crops are not regulated in this way, and, to date, the only compounds that have been shown to harm human health have originated in foods developed through conventional breeding. One example is the family of naturally occurring toxic compounds found in conventionally bred varieties of celery – psoralens, which

KEY THEMES

- Elements of sustainability.
- Benefits of genetically modified crops.
- More from less in the future.

The three pillars of sustainable agriculture.

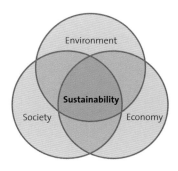

BOX 11.1 What is sustainability?

The idea of sustainability rose to prominence after the concept of sustainable development was explored by the Brundtland Commission in its 1987 report *Our Common Future*. The report defined sustainable development as: "Development that meets the needs of the present without compromising the ability of future generations to meet their own needs."

"Sustainability" has since been applied in many contexts, and is a guiding principle for any human endeavour, including agriculture.

Sustainable agriculture basically means farming founded on sound ecological principles, rooted in the relationships between organisms – plant and animal – and their environment. It implies an integrated system of production practices tailored to environmental conditions that will endure over the long term.

Practices that might cause long-term damage to the soil such as excessive tilling leading to erosion, might be termed unsustainable. So too might the use of synthetic fertilisers that, although appearing to sustain local production over time, could have severe effects away from the farm such as polluting rivers or coastal waters.

In considering sustainability one needs to take a broad view and embrace issues that go beyond agriculture itself. One is energy – essential all along the production line from cultivation through crop processing to storage and transport. Climate change issues, dwindling supplies of fossil energy and rising costs make this of major concern when considering agricultural sustainability.

Then there are socio-economic factors to take into account. Inefficient agricultural methods that deplete finite natural resources to the point where they become unaffordable has huge implications for food security.

International policy is important as well. Sustainable agriculture is very much on the international agenda, especially in the context of the threats posed by climate change.

Urban planning too plays a part. Debates are taking place on which forms of human habitat fit best with the sustainability ambition. High-population towns and cities, or eco-communities that closely link producers and consumers?

Any genetically improved crop must, therefore, be integrated into an ecology-based farming system and judged on its environmental, economic and social merits: the three pillars of sustainable agriculture.

deter insect pests. But they have also been found to cause some farm workers to develop severe skin rashes.

New biotechnology and health

Ever since the American conservationist Rachel Carson, in her 1962 book *Silent Spring*, drew the world's attention to the dangers to humans and the environment of

---

CASE STUDY Californian alfalfa

In California's Central Valley most alfalfa farmers have been using the herbicide diuron to control weeds. This is one of a class of toxic chemicals that can contaminate groundwater as well as persist for a long time in the environment, to the detriment of biodiversity.

Now, though, they have started to plant new herbicide-tolerant varieties that make it possible to use less toxic herbicides, which is expected to improve water quality and enhance biodiversity. The Animal and Plant Health Inspection Service is currently evaluating these varieties with a view to extending their use.

---

unthinking pesticide use, researchers have been looking for ways to reduce reliance on insecticide sprays.

This was the driving scientific motivation behind the first generation of GM crops, such as *Bt* maize and cotton engineered to control caterpillar and beetle pests without the need for insecticides. Although the *Bt* toxins worked well on their target organisms, they caused little or no harm to other, beneficial insects, wildlife and people. Indeed, *Bt* toxins in sprayable form were used long before the new GM crops were developed, and are still extensively deployed today by organic growers and others. So, before granting approval to *Bt* crops, the US Environmental Protection Agency and the Food and Drug Administration had decades of human exposure on which to base their decision.

Human health also benefits from the new generations of herbicide-tolerant crops. Glyphosate herbicides, used appropriately, are the least toxic ever developed – they rapidly break down in the environment and do not persist in groundwater. Novel GM crops including maize and cassava have been engineered to tolerate glyphosate so that growers can use this herbicide to control weeds without harming their crop, farm workers or the wider environment.

Many of the sprays used over the past 100 years are to a greater or lesser extent toxic to humans and animals alike. Bordeaux mixture, for example, a combination of copper sulphate and slaked lime invented in the Bordeaux region of France in the late 19th century and still in use as a fungicide in vineyards, fruit farms and gardens to prevent infestations of mildew and other fungi, is harmful to farm workers as well as to fish, livestock and earthworms due to a build-up of copper in the soil.

Crops engineered to discourage insect or plant pests are part of the broader picture of integrated pest management, which combines a range of techniques to achieve a healthy crop with the least possible disruption to natural agro-ecosystems.

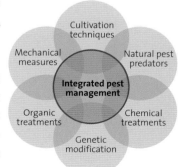

Biodiversity: another goal of sustainability

The planting of *Bt* crops has been shown to support increased biodiversity. An analysis of 42 field experiments in the USA showed that insects, spiders, mites and other pests that are not targeted by the novel crops were more abundant in *Bt* cotton and maize fields than in conventional fields managed by insecticides.

Less developed countries too show biodiversity benefits from *Bt* crops. Chinese and Indian farmers growing GM cotton or rice have dramatically reduced their use of insecticides – thereby helping to sustain non-targeted insects.

Between 1996 and 2011 there was an 18.3 per cent reduction in the environmental impact of herbicides and insecticides worldwide through the use of GM crops (Table 4.4, page 43).

Economic advantages

Applying lower levels of insecticides has obvious advantages for the environment. At the same time, the new crops drive another essential component of sustainability: economic benefits. This is particularly true when the pressures put on plants by pests are high. The US Department of Agriculture's Economic Research Service found that farmers derived significant financial gain from lower pesticide use and less insect damage, which more than made up for the higher cost of genetically engineered

BOX 11.2 Summary of sustainability benefits

Research into the sustainability impacts of genetically modified crops shows the following benefits:

- significantly lower levels of insecticides in the environment;
- improved soil quality and reduced erosion;
- farmers saved from losing their crops and livelihoods;
- health advantages to farmers and families;
- economic gains to local communities;
- enhanced biodiversity of beneficial insects;
- fewer pest outbreaks on neighbouring farms;
- higher profits for farmers;
- yield increases;
- reduced losses to pests and diseases;
- more efficient production on the same area of land.

The key to achieving these, however, does not lie in planting novel crops alone. The real benefits come from combining the new genetics with innovations in farming practices: together they create a synergy for sustainability.

seed. It is estimated that Arizona cotton growers saved more than US$ 200 million between 1996 and 2008 thanks to a 70 per cent reduction in insecticide use.

Maintaining topsoil

One further move towards sustainability is low- or no-till agriculture, which leaves fertile topsoil intact and protects it from wind and rain erosion. New herbicide-tolerant maize and soybeans have helped reduce tilling, resulting in a reduction in fuel consumption and greenhouse gas emissions from tractors.

In Argentina, for example, tillage operations for soybeans have been reduced by 25–50 per cent. Combined with similar levels of reductions in the USA, this means that total cuts in carbon emissions are equivalent to taking nearly 7 million cars off the roads – about a quarter of all the private cars in the UK, for example.

Virus-resistant crops

Although by far the largest area of GM crops is devoted to insect- and herbicide-resistant varieties, others have been commercialised which have shown themselves to be effective tools in the drive towards sustainability. One is the GM papaya developed in response to the destruction of virtually the entire crop on the Hawaiian island of Oahu by papaya ringspot virus – PRSV.

Dennis Gonsalves and his co-researchers engineered papaya to carry a transgene from a mild strain of PRSV that had the effect of "immunising" the plant against further infection. Yields increased by a factor of 20 compared to non-GM trees, production rose rapidly and, quite quickly, 90 per cent of farmers began to plant the new crop. Today, 80–90 per cent of Hawaiian papaya is genetically engineered.

Future prospects

Dozens of useful genetically engineered crop traits are in the pipeline – all of which would aid sustainability.

Crops that use nitrogen more efficiently, for example, would lower the cost of synthetic fertiliser inputs, reduce water pollution and cut the greenhouse gas emissions that result from chemically synthesising fertilisers. There is a transgenic plum variety, HoneySweet, resistant to plum pox – a virus that also infects peach, nectarine, apricot and cherry plants. This technology could prevent major disruptions in production of all of these fruits. Non-browning Arctic® apples are an engineered solution to the real-world problem of apple browning caused by the enzyme

Reductions in tillage operations for soybean cultivation in the USA and Argentina have reduced total CO2 emissions equivalent to taking about a quarter of the UK's private cars of the roads.

polyphenol oxidase, which has real economic costs for each link in the supply chain from tree to consumer.

Other promising applications of the new biotechnology are in staple crops such as rice, which is grown in 114 countries and on six of the seven continents. Given the huge impact on the lives of the poor – and the environment – of even modest changes to a crop's stress tolerance or nutritional content, this research has immense importance. One example here is submergence-tolerant rice produced by both conventional marker-assisted breeding and GM. There are already GM varieties that currently provide an excellent solution to flooding in, say, Bangladesh and India. In the future, though, global warming is likely to bring more extremes of flooding, so a new, "submergence-plus" variety is under development.

Conversely, more research is going on with drought-tolerant varieties to improve on today's GM crops such as maize – Africa's key staple – and other food crops.

More from less?

Without the development of high-yielding crop varieties over the past few decades, up to four times as much land would have been needed for agriculture to produce the same amount of food. Can this progressive increase in agricultural efficiency be sustained? If not, the world's cropland will need to double by 2050 to maintain current per-capita food consumption.

One analysis suggests that, if global average yields could be driven up to the levels currently achieved in North America, there could actually be a considerable sparing of land needed by agriculture.

The transgenic plum Honeysweet contains a gene that makes it highly resistant to plum pox virus.

USDA

The challenge is to raise yields without further damaging the environment. To meet it, an integrated approach will be required that combines ecology-based farming practices with the cultivation of newly developed seed varieties. In many countries, this will mean modifying government policies to build local educational, technical and research capacities along with appropriate food processing and storage facilities, in effect treating plant breeding as a public good.

Rural transport, communications and water infrastructure will need to improve as well, as will the ability to handle the many intellectual property and regulatory issues that these game-changing technologies imply. With all this in place, sustainable agriculture in the future is possible on a global scale.

LITTLE THINGS MEAN A LOT
Enhancing nutrition through biofortification

12

The micronutrient opportunity

Since the 1940s, farming has drawn on many new techniques and practices – some conventional, some cutting-edge – which have helped to achieve higher yields of the major staple crops and, thereby, keep pace with rapid population growth. But not all regions or countries have enjoyed equal success, particularly in Africa.

Until recently, improvements have focused on food production as measured in the carbohydrate content of grain crops such as wheat, maize and rice, and many other staples including cassava and plantain, though the latter two are produced in much smaller quantities (Figure 12.1). Carbohydrate content is a good measure of the nutritional calorific content of food. It is, after all, a critical source of energy needed to sustain life. But it is not the whole story.

Humans – like the plants they consume – need more than carbohydrates. We need protein and fat, the other macronutrients that are needed in large amounts. But we also require micronutrients – the vitamins and minerals that are essential to our diet, albeit in far smaller quantities. Often, staple crops contain few or no micronutrients, with sometimes devastating consequences.

Micronutrient malnutrition

Plants themselves synthesise vitamins and their precursors, whereas minerals such as iron, zinc and iodine are absorbed from the environment in which the plants grow. Of course, plants produce or absorb chemicals to suit their own biological needs, but humans and other animals have evolved to take advantage of a broader chemical diversity. So much so that, without it, a number of health problems can arise.

Throughout history, micronutrient insufficiencies have taken a heavy toll. Too little iodine impairs both physical and mental well-being. Until sea salt containing traces of iodine entered our diet, enlarged thyroid glands, producing a swelling of the neck known as goitre, were commonplace.

Other longstanding problems include the nervous system and cardiac disorder beriberi (deficiency in thiamine and vitamin B1), scurvy (vitamin C), the childhood

KEY THEMES

- Micronutrient deficiency and malnutrition.
- The role of biotechnology in biofortification.
- Arguments in favour.
- Resistance and underfunding.

Figure 12.1 Wheat, cassava and plantain production worldwide, 2002–2012
Million tonnes
Cassava and plantain are produced in much smaller quantities than other staples such as wheat, so are considered orphan crops.

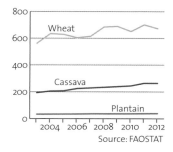

Source: FAOSTAT

Enlarged thyroid glands associated with iodine deficiency were once so common that depictions found their way into medieval manuscripts. The condition is still a feature of a diet poor in micronutrients.

bone deformation condition rickets (vitamin D) and pellagra, which affects both the skin and mental functioning (vitamin B3).

Lack of vitamins and minerals in the diet is not simply of historical interest. Today, the Copenhagen Consensus meetings of top-level economists consistently list micronutrient provision as a high priority in solving mankind's most pressing problems. Rickets is still a scourge in some societies as a result of too little exposure to sunlight, which helps synthesise vitamin D in the body. Insufficient folic acid (vitamin B9) in the diet of pregnant women is another common deficiency that can cause deformities in babies. Ample green vegetables would overcome this, but are often inaccessible among impoverished populations.

The most prevalent micronutrient deficiency of all is that of iron, estimated to affect half the world's entire population. The debilitating physical and mental effects of iron deficiency are often irreversible. Equally worrying is the lack of vitamin A in the diets of people in developing countries. A recent World Health Organization estimate suggests that perhaps 250 million people are vitamin A deficient, predominantly children under five years old, due to lack of fruit, vegetables and animal products in their diet. This is having a massive impact on health. Vitamin A deficiency is the single biggest cause of preventable blindness as well as a widespread cause of many common diseases resulting from impaired immune function.

These nutritional insufficiencies would be overcome if more people enjoyed greater diversity in their diets, from both plant and animal sources. Unfortunately, however, an estimated 2 billion people worldwide, usually the educationally or financially disadvantaged, are simply unable to access the desired level of dietary diversity. Non-staple foods that contain the most micronutrients have the major disadvantage of being the most expensive. Even those living in the countryside often lack the resources to access a wide variety of foods, and remain dependent on staples that contain few or none of the essential micronutrients. So the poor in developing countries are clearly very vulnerable. They are the ones most likely to suffer malnutrition – of both the macronutrient and micronutrient variety.

Alleviating the problem

There are several ways to address the issue of micronutrient insufficiency. One is to fortify foods and other products during manufacturing. Iodine has been added to salt; vitamins A and D to margarine; folic acid to flour; and fluoride to toothpaste – all with some success in both industrialised and developing countries. In the Lao

People's Democratic Republic, for example, the incidence of goitre in children dropped from 40 per cent to 9 per cent in around 10 years after iodine was added to salt. This kind of fortification, though, does depend on foods undergoing industrial processing and being widely distributed by means of an adequate infrastructure: someone has to pay for this.

Another approach is supplementation – the use of tablets or capsules containing the required micronutrients. Supplements, again, have to be paid for, but they can be highly effective. Since the early 1990s, 500 million vitamin A capsules have been given to at-risk populations every year in order to cut child and maternal mortality and vision problems. The annual cost is US$ 0.5–1 billion, largely met by US and Canadian government aid funding.

Despite this initiative, however, the number of preventable deaths remains high. Conventional supplementation and fortification programmes run the risk of missing the most needy, most inaccessible and marginalised people.

A third strategy is to modify the make-up of food crops so that they generate the desired micronutrients while they grow: biofortification.

Back to source: the attraction of biofortification

Plants are sophisticated biochemical factories producing or storing all the compounds and chemicals humans and animals need for life. But the distribution of chemicals synthesised or absorbed within the tissues of crops may not be available in those parts of the plants that humans usually eat.

Take, for example, rice. The part of the rice grain that is eaten – the endosperm – is almost totally carbohydrate, along with small amounts of fats and protein, and it is the thin sheath of tissue surrounding the endosperm that contains most of the micronutrient vitamins and minerals. But before rice can be stored as food, it has to be polished to remove the outer layer, otherwise fats there would turn the rice rancid and bad-tasting. In other words, to keep the rice edible means automatically removing the source of valuable micronutrients – an apparent dilemma that a study carried out with a community of nuns in the Philippines helped to resolve (see Case study).

The Nuns Study led to the establishment of the Harvest Plus programme, which is using largely traditional breeding techniques to increase the levels of nutrition

Pearl millet, which remains an orphan crop even though it has been grown in Africa and India since prehistoric times, is a good candidate for biofortification with iron.

W. Roonguthai/CC-BY-SA 3.0

The wild relatives of bananas and plantains grow plentiful seeds. In today's cultivated crops, however, the seeds have diminished to virtual non-existence, making further improvement feasible only through genetic modification.

already present in low amounts in the edible parts of staple crops. Harvest Plus is breeding biofortified (through increased iron, zinc and vitamin A) sweet potato, bean, pearl millet, cassava, maize, rice and wheat. Growers in Bangladesh, Democratic Republic of the Congo, India, Mozambique, Nigeria, Pakistan, Rwanda, Uganda and Zambia are benefiting – or will soon benefit – from the new varieties.

Role of biotechnology

Conventional breeding for biofortification can have limited results. Plants that produce few, if any, seeds – like plantain, cassava and banana – are reproduced vegetatively, so are ill-suited for selective or cross-breeding. And sometimes none of the desired micronutrient can be conventionally bred into the part of the plant that we eat – as in the case of rice. Another way of building in micronutrients is required.

Much proof-of-concept research on the new biotechnologies achieved to date has yet to be applied in practice in developing countries; nonetheless, new varieties are set to help address these problems of micronutrient deficiency. Rice has been engin-eered to produce folic acid to overcome a lack of it in pregnant women and to combat deformities in children. Zinc is another micronutrient currently receiving attention in rice, involving modifying the action of a key gene. Low iron content has also been studied: the genetic control of iron uptake and storage within plants is a complicated process involving perhaps 12 different genes, but two research groups in Switzerland and Australia have used genetic modification (GM) to raise iron levels in rice endosperm. High-iron bananas have also been developed using this technology.

CASE STUDY Lessons from nuns in the Philippines

Removing the outer layer of rice during polishing takes away the crop's iron content. So researchers decided to try differential polishing which allowed them to retain more of the iron-rich sheath. They gave this rice to one group of nuns and to the others – the control group – they gave low-iron rice in which the whole of the outer layer had been polished off.

The results were striking. Even modest increases in daily iron consumption caused by eating the high-iron rice improved the health status of the nuns compared to the control group. This important finding demonstrated not only that the more outer layer is retained, the better the micronutrient content of rice. It also showed that, if rice has to be polished in order to be stored, then breeders would need to concentrate their attention on the endosperm – the part that is eaten. How can this be fortified with more iron?

Best-known of all are efforts to combat vitamin A deficiency through so-called Golden Rice, in which the plant's endosperm has been engineered with two genes for generating the carotenoid, beta-carotene – the necessary biochemical precursor to vitamin A. The carotenoids are also the pigments that give Golden Rice its distinctive yellow colour.

Golden Rice has shown that it can significantly reduce vitamin A deficiency in societies that eat rice, and is as effective as taking capsules or milk and eggs in providing the vitamin. Just a cooked handful can save lives and sight.

Acceptability of biofortification

For all the potential of Golden Rice – and other promising crops with enhanced micronutrient content based on genetic engineering – the path to acceptability of these innovations has not run smoothly.

Suspicion about GM, anti-globalisation feelings, distrust of the motives of the private sector in supporting these technologies, as well as fear of activist attacks have all, primarily in affluent Europe, slowed things down. Golden Rice, as the first generation of genetically engineered biofortified crops, has perhaps been on the receiving end of more hostility than subsequent GM crops might expect.

The Golden Rice story began nearly 30 years ago, shortly after the dawn of genetic engineering of crops, but is still, in 2014, only at the stage of field trials, and those taking place in the Philippines have been wrecked by activists.

Research with resource-poor growers and consumers tells a different story. Poor farmers would like to grow the new rice crop and believe that it would benefit their families. They welcome the fact that the new rice costs them the same as the old one and are not concerned about the way it was developed. They also care more about its nutritional and health advantages than its unusual colour.

There are powerful economic arguments too in favour of Golden Rice and other GM crops:

- the technology lies in the seed so no factory is needed to access its nutritional value;
- no new road infrastructure is necessary;
- no more money needs to be spent on cultivation than with any other rice;
- no special packaging or processing is required;

The successful introduction in Mozambique of orange-fleshed sweet potato, which is naturally higher in beta-carotene than the white or yellow varieties traditionally grown in Africa, could serve as a model for the acceptance of other biofortified food crops.

USGov/PD

- resource-poor farmers in developing countries are free to sow, harvest, save seed, replant and sell locally without having to pay licence fees.

Taking the Asian countries as a whole, the total impact on wealth is estimated to be huge. Even moderate Golden Rice consumption could add up to US$ 18 billion annually to Asian gross domestic product (GDP). There are massive savings to be made too in health-care expenditure. Each case of iron deficiency averted is estimated to save US$ 45; every vitamin A deficiency US$ 96.

Once biofortified varieties of staple food crops have been widely distributed among subsistence communities, there is no further need to supply food supplements – often at considerable expense and with limited uptake.

Cost-effective but underfunded

Biofortified crops – whether conventionally bred or engineered – offer so many practical and economic advantages that they seem to have enormous potential for the long-term sustainable prevention of micronutrient deficiencies. They also fit well with the 1992 United Nations recommendations for locally available food-based strategies to alleviate these deficiencies, relatively cheaply and with excellent coverage of the population.

The extraordinary advances in mapping plant genomes and using sophisticated molecular techniques contribute to rapid progress in biofortification which could well be applicable across a broad range of plants in the future.

Yet for all this promise, biofortification programmes are dramatically underfunded. Although micronutrient-enhanced crops have the potential to save many millions of dollars in health-care costs, investment lags far behind that of pure health-related research. It is surely time for the balance to be redressed.

THE CROP THAT CAME IN FROM THE COLD
Transforming the cowpea, a staple African orphan crop

13

One of the lost crops of Africa

Cowpea – also known as black-eyed pea or field pea among other names – is one of the most important food crops in the semi-arid areas of Africa. It thrives in the Sahel and the dry Guinea savannahs, stretching in a great continental arc from Senegal in the west to Sudan and Somalia in the east, then reaching south into western Kenya, Tanzania, Zimbabwe and northern South Africa.

In all, millions of hectares are under cultivation, and tens of millions of rural poor depend on it for their subsistence and as a major source of protein. In many parts of Africa the crop is predominantly cultivated by women, both to feed their families and for the income it generates in local markets or from travelling traders. Roadsides in Senegal, for example, are dotted with women offering fresh pods for sale.

The plant is a drought-tolerant legume that can be grown even at high temperatures and where annual rainfall is as low as 300 millimetres per year. Commonly grown for its grain, which like all legumes is rich in protein, the cowpea also has protein-rich leaves that can be eaten raw or cooked. All round it offers an excellent source of nutrition for humans as well as for animals, as cowpea hay is valuable fodder. Like the great majority of legumes, it is also capable of fixing nitrogen from the air in its root nodules, which not only promotes growth, but releases the nitrogen to the soil as the plant dies back, making it available for the next crop.

With an annual production volume of more than 5 million tonnes – 94 per cent of global production – the cowpea is the most important legume crop in Africa. Most is consumed there as well, although it would have potential markets in Europe, Brazil and India were it not for the fact that production is inadequate, quality is not assured and internal demand is so high. Africa, then, could clearly benefit from increased yields through improvements such as better insect resistance.

Hungry insects

Over the past 30 years African breeders have worked hard to develop a higher yielding cowpea, and have in fact bred varieties with the potential to produce as much as 1.5–2 tonnes per hectare. But – even though yields have approximately doubled

KEY THEMES

- Importance of an overlooked crop.
- Transformative technology.
- Factors determining uptake.

Figure 13.1 Global cowpea yields, 1961–2012

Tonnes per hectare

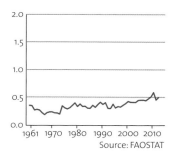

Source: FAOSTAT

Like the great majority of legumes, the cowpea is capable of fixing nitrogen from the air in its roots, where it produces nitrogen compounds that promote plant growth. When the plant dies, the fixed nitrogen is released, fertilising the soil for the next crop.

over recent decades – full potential yields are rarely achieved in the field because of immense losses to insect infestation (Figure 13.1).

The effective use of insecticides can increase grain yields as much as 20-fold. Indeed, unless farmers apply insecticides, in some years there is no pea yield at all; only the leaves are harvestable. But insecticides are not a good solution either. They are often not available, are too expensive for farmers to buy, are of low quality or just unsuitable for the crop, and farmers may not have the equipment or the knowledge to apply them safely.

The chief pests plaguing the growing crop are the *Maruca* pod borer, thrips, a few species of pod-sucking bugs and aphids. Then, after the cowpea is harvested and stored, it is under more attack from seed-feeding beetles belonging to the bruchid family. The cowpea bruchid can destroy a whole crop after just a few months of storage. Then there are non-insect pests such as bacteria and viruses that cause diseases in the plant, along with parasitic weeds that also decrease yields.

Constraints on the crop

In the face of these obvious pressures on the cowpea, why has its advance as a crop been held back? A variety of social, economic and policy constraints have been hindering development of the cowpea.

- Investment in agricultural research has generally been rather low in Africa compared to investment in urban and industrial infrastructure. Agriculture is regarded as relatively unexciting and the cowpea, being a crop of the poor – and of women – has seemed particularly unworthy of development.
- There is little international trade in the cowpea outside Africa, so it does not attract investment like those crops that promise to bring in significant amounts of foreign exchange.
- Although some of the tools of modern biotechnology have been deployed to improve the plant, the testing of genetically modified (GM) crops has been held back by the slow pace of biosafety legislation and an absence of regulatory processes, which are necessary for new varieties of crops to be tested, evaluated and grown in the field.
- International institutions have simply paid too little attention to this relatively minor crop.

However, decades after the need was first recognised, insect-resistant cowpeas – developed by an international public-private partnership managed and coordinated by the African Agricultural Technology Foundation (AATF) – are now expected to be available to farmers within a few years.

How the cowpea has been transformed

Stage one: Some 20 years ago a group of researchers saw a need for a genetically transformed cowpea. Other scientists along with African cowpea breeders agreed. A meeting was held in Dakar in 2001 and the Network for the Genetic Improvement of the Cowpea for Africa was set up, supported by a number of other institutions.

Stage two: The search began for a method to transform the cowpea. The new technology focused on introducing resistance to the *Maruca* pod borer, which can reduce yield by more than 50 per cent, and to the bruchid beetle *Callosobruchus maculatus*, which does severe damage during storage.

Stage three: It was known that sprays of *Bacillus thuringiensis – Bt –* could control *Maruca*, so the researchers used a synthesised version of a gene from this naturally occurring soil bacterium that could be expressed – switched on – in the crop host. The protein encoded by the gene was designed to kill MPB caterpillars and larvae and confer protection to all parts of the growing plant.

Stage four: The gene was incorporated into a carrier – a DNA vector – derived from a bacterium that would be capable of taking sections of DNA into the plant's cells where it was incorporated into the plant genome in the nucleus. Once integrated, these genes were passed on to succeeding generations. Thus transfer and regeneration were achieved, which is termed transformation.

Stage five: Research is now continuing on this transformation in several laboratories. Scientists are currently putting the transformed plants through stringent selection procedures in order to find the most suitable parents for a breeding programme. Field trials are being carried out in Sub-Saharan environments: so far four have yielded promising results.

Making the innovation acceptable

Several issues have to be addressed before the new crop – if and when it becomes commercially possible – is widely accepted.

The cowpea appears to have originated in the Horn of Africa before spreading to the west of the continent. Any potential danger of gene flow from the GM varieties

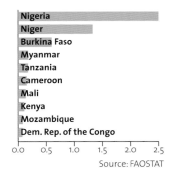

Figure 13.2 Top ten cowpea producers, 2012

Million tonnes

Source: FAOSTAT

to wild cowpea species needs to be built into risk assessment procedures. In addition, the question of movement of *Bt* cowpea across national borders needs attention during any safety assessment prior to its commercialisation. The new crop needs a roadmap to ensure proper insect-resistance management and safe use.

In sum, there has to be a sound regulatory system in place under which *Bt* cowpea can be grown in the field. If harmonised at a regional level this would go a long way to meeting any transboundary problems, and steps are currently being taken to ensure that such a system will be put in place.

Public awareness

There is still ambivalence towards GM crops among the general public in Africa, despite the efforts of some African heads of state to promote the new varieties. Some resistance may be an overhang from Africa's European colonial past, which could still be causing antagonism towards these technologies.

Those GM crops being evaluated in confined field trials are the subject of much dialogue and public debate. Some progress in addressing concerns is being made by the Open Forum for Agricultural Biotechnology in Nigeria, Kenya, Uganda, Egypt and, to a lesser extent, Tanzania. If *Bt* cowpea is shown to be effective in controlling yield losses due to insect infestation and to be successfully grown by smallholder farmers in the next five years or so, like all GM innovations it will need appropriate, responsible and cost-effective regulatory systems, strong political will and continuing provision of varieties of crops that meet the needs of the relevant countries in Africa.

Cowpeas tolerate poor sandy soils and can grow in the shade, making them an important component of traditional intercropping systems.

Importance of seed systems

Widespread adoption of *Bt* cowpea will depend critically on having effective seed-growing and distribution systems in place, and on developing agricultural extension services to provide advice on cultivation.

West Africa has to build a workable system to ensure access to seed, comprehensive quality control and competent stewardship. The improved cowpea has to be affordable for smallholder farmers and reduce poverty while increasing food and income security. Some help may well come from governments and other donor agencies but, ultimately, for true sustainability, the solutions will have to be those that enable the many millions of smallholder farmers to become financially self-reliant by selling at least some of their harvest so that they can reinvest in future crops.

RESEARCH, DISCUSSION
AND ESSAY TOPICS

- Every technology has its downside.
- The future for sustainable agriculture lies in harnessing the best of all available technologies, conventional and modern.
- European attitudes to biotechnology have had a powerful influence on Africa.
- A tangled mix of political, economic, societal and ethical issues has held back genetically engineered crops in India.
- Why has African agriculture performed so poorly over the past 30 years?
- Despite the many benefits of genetically modified crops, only four African countries have commercialised them up to now.
- A biotech-friendly environment is essential for genetic modification to realise its potential.
- Why has Argentina been so successful in exploiting genetically modified crops?
- The Chinese government has invested very heavily in transgenic R&D technology. Explore the reasons for this.
- Biosafety issues cannot be ignored if the new biotechnology is to flourish.
- "If undernutrition were a disease, such as H1N1, and unprocessed food were a drug or a vaccine, both would have the full attention of the entire international community." *Lancet* 374: 1473 (31 October 2009)
- The emerging economies need a second Green Revolution, this time based on modern genetics.
- New genetic technologies are the only options for ensuring adequate nutrition and promoting health, especially in the developing countries.
- Genetically modified crops are more dangerous to the environment and human health than other forms of plant breeding.

FURTHER READING
AND USEFUL WEBSITES

African Agricultural Technology Foundation (AATF).
  http://www.aatf-africa.org/
African Biosafety Network of Expertise (ABNE).
  http://www.nepadbiosafety.net/
Academy of Science for South Africa (2012) *Regulation of Agricultural Technology in Africa.*
  www.assaf.co.za/wp-content/uploads/2012/11/K-9610-ASSAF-GMO-Report-Dev-V8-LR.pdf
African Science Academies (2013) *Declaration of the 9th Annual Meeting of the African Science Academies.*
  www.eas-et.org/AMASA9_Doc/English%20Declaration.pdf
Bennett, D.J. and Jennings, R.C. (2013) *Successful Agricultural Innovation in Emerging Economies: New Genetic Technologies for Global Food Production.* Cambridge University Press, Cambridge. Chapters 7–14.
Cotton Made in Africa.
  http://www.cotton-made-in-africa.com/en/the-initiative/where-we-work/burkina-faso.html
Food and Agriculture Organization of the United Nations. Integrated Pest Management.
  http://www.fao.org/agriculture/crops/thematic-sitemap/theme/pests/ipm/en/
HarvestPlus.
  http://www.harvestplus.org/
International Centre for Genetic Engineering and Biotechnology. Biosafety Web Pages.
  http://www.icgeb.org/~bsafesrv/
International Service for the Acquisition of Agri-Biotech Applications (ISAAA). *Biotech Crops in Africa: The Final Frontier.*
  https://isaaa.org/resources/publications/biotech_crops_in_africa/download/Biotech_Crops_in_Africa-The_Final_Frontier.pdf
US Environmental Protection Agency. Integrated Pest Management (IPM) Principles.
  http://www.epa.gov/opp00001/factsheets/ipm.htm

SECTION THREE

POLICY IMPLICATIONS OF THE NEW CROP TECHNOLOGIES

Converting beneficial science into publicly acceptable farming practices seems an uphill struggle.

This section explores the relationship between advances in plant technology, especially genetically modified (GM) crops, and policy makers faced with converting beneficial science into publicly acceptable farming practices. On the face of it, this seems an uphill struggle. In Europe, politicians of all kinds have had to cope with the scepticism of the public, with GM attracting three times as many opponents as supporters. In 2010 fewer than 25 per cent of Europeans appeared comfortable with GM foods while more than 60 per cent expressed considerable concern.

Yet not all GM research provokes such hostility. The majority of Europeans approve of GM when it is used for medical purposes. Furthermore, so-called cisgenic crops – those that have genes imported only from the same species or from plants that can be crossed using conventional breeding methods – are deemed quite acceptable.

The need to achieve public acceptance of modern plant science is severe. It is estimated that around 700,000 lives may be lost each year through malnutrition and unhygienic food and water – a toll that could be reduced by implementing advanced agricultural methods such as GM. Yet countervailing arguments including

What Europeans think of genetically modified food

In answer to the question: *"Do you agree or disagree with the following?"*

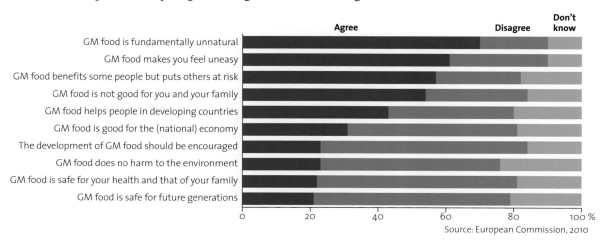

Source: European Commission, 2010

the notion that the activities of agro-multinational companies amount to "genetic colonialism" continue to be aired. How can this policy stalemate be broken?

Policy makers need to learn three key lessons. Firstly, new knowledge does not get translated into benefits by default. It needs the drive, commitment and communication skills of good entrepreneurs to spread the word. Secondly, decision makers need to be clear about what they are addressing: they have to recognise when they are dealing with issues of science rather than policy-related priorities. And thirdly, there has to be universal clarity in distinguishing good regulations and practices from bad. This places the onus on decision makers to understand all the options available and to consider their consequences.

The role of governments is critical. They need to be alerted to any potential controversies at an early stage in order to harness the best scientific advice available to them. They have to ensure that any consultations they undertake reach the broadest possible range of interests and that any analyses they commission rest firmly on transparency and objectivity.

In short, if we are to avoid a dangerous drift away from the real needs of food security and production, there must be a genuine dialogue between advocates, decision makers and critics, in which any uncertainties relating to science or policy are freely and honestly debated.

There must be a genuine dialogue between advocates, decision makers and critics, in which any uncertainties relating to science or policy are freely and honestly debated.

THE SEVENFOLD PATH TO INNOVATION
Enabling factors for new agricultural genetics in African countries

KEY THEMES

- Seven enabling factors.
- Assessing innovation readiness.
- The role of government.
- The needs of smallholder farmers.

Africa's agricultural exports currently total some US$ 55 billion, but the continent suffers from a negative balance in food trade, importing more than it exports.

Creating suitable conditions for innovation

If the crops of new genetics are to succeed in Africa they have to exist in an agricultural landscape capable of embracing innovation. It is not simply a matter of having access to desirable technologies or improved seeds.

An analysis of the potential applications of genetically modified (GM) crops, present and future (Box 14.1), shows how much these innovations could contribute to improving African farming. But for this to happen, certain key enabling factors have to be in play.

Seven enabling factors

To explore these factors in detail two countries have been selected – Ghana and Tanzania – with several considerations in mind: geography, governance, willingness to adopt new technologies, and levels of corruption.

Located in West and East Africa respectively, Ghana and Tanzania are close to nations that have either commercialised the new technology (Burkina Faso) or are near to doing so (Kenya and Uganda). As the following analysis shows, Ghana has made more rapid progress than Tanzania.

Factor one: current modifiable crops

Both Ghana and Tanzania have considerable potential for introducing GM varieties of a wide range of existing crops. In fact, for several crops there is no ready means of improvement without modern genetics. Conventional plant breeding does not work easily with bananas, for example, because they do not produce seeds, while the cowpea has too little natural genetic variation from which to select desirable traits.

Ghana's main crops are yam, cassava and bananas (including plantains), with maize, tomatoes and rice also important to its agricultural output. Given that GM maize and tomatoes are already grown elsewhere in the world and that GM yams, cassava and rice are in development, there is clearly scope for expansion. Sorghum and coconuts too could be added to the list. A rough estimate of Ghana's potential might be the value of its modifiable agricultural produce of US$ 3 billion per year.

BOX 14.1 Potential applications of GM technology

Current
- Tolerance to broad-spectrum herbicide in maize, soybeans, brassica.
- Resistance to chewing insects in maize, cotton, oilseed, brassica.
- Nutritional biofortification in staple cereal crops, sweet potato, banana.

In 5–10 years
- Resistance to fungus and virus pathogens in potato, wheat, rice, banana, cassava, fruits, vegetables.
- Resistance to sucking insects transmitting viruses in rice, fruits, vegetables.

- Improved storage and processing of wheat, potato, fruits, vegetables.

In 10–20 years
- Drought and salinity tolerance, improved nitrogen use efficiency and high temperature tolerance in staple cereal and tuber crops.

In more than 20 years
- Apomixis (reproduction without fertilisation), nitrogen fixation and conversion to a perennial habit in staple cereal and tuber crops.

In Tanzania, bananas are the chief agricultural product, followed by cassava, cowpea, chickpea and pigeon pea, and maize. Cotton is also significant. If one considers GM crops either being cultivated or in development, Tanzania could benefit from modified maize, cotton, cassava, bananas, rice, sweet potatoes, sorghum and potatoes. The total value of the country's potential GM crop is estimated to be US$ 2.2 billion.

Factor two: laws and regulations

A proper legal and regulatory structure must be in place for the commercial release of GM crops. Globally, the framework governing GM is based on two United Nations commitments (Box 14.2).

Ghana has a positive stance on GM crops and has made progress towards an enforceable regulatory framework. Parliament signed its Biosafety Bill in 2011, paving the way for confined field trials of crops such as insect-resistant *Bt* cowpea and GM sweet potato. Steps are also being taken to put in place a framework for the commercial cultivation of GM crops.

The situation in Tanzania is at present uncertain. Despite publicly announcing its support for the new crops, the government has been less than clear on its policies.

There have been press reports and quotes from government ministers that field trials have taken place for GM cotton, tobacco and maize. However, current legislation contains a strict clause that is likely to hamper both confined field testing and adoption of GM crops.

Factor three: trade flows

An important influence on whether a country adopts GM crops is the effect this might have on its international trade potential. If its main agricultural exports are to countries that do not accept GM products, there is little to gain from developing GM varieties of those crops. Conversely, there is much to be gained from developing crops with GM potential that are primarily for domestic consumption or for markets that welcome such products.

If a country's main agricultural exports are to countries that do not accept genetically modified products, there is little to gain from developing engineered varieties of those crops.

In 2010, Ghana exported agricultural products worth nearly US$ 6 billion, representing roughly three-quarters of its total revenue from exports. But only a very small share of these exported products are crops that have GM potential.

Tanzania's exported agricultural goods totalled US$ 1.2 billion, with crops that have GM potential representing a slightly higher proportion than is the case for Ghana. But even so, this was still a fairly small fraction.

This means that there is no obvious trade-related reason against adopting GM crops in either country. Any improved varieties now in development are not, as yet, important for export, especially to the large European market, which is the most reluctant to accept them.

BOX 14.2 The international framework

The Convention on Biological Diversity of 1993 is an international commitment to conserving biological diversity, sustaining the use of biological resources and sharing fairly the benefits arising from genetic resources.

The Cartagena Protocol on Biosafety of 2000 is an international regulatory framework that reconciles the needs of trade and environmental protection in the context of the transboundary movement of genetically modified organisms. Countries that sign and ratify (or accede to) this protocol are bound by its provisions. By 2014, 41 of the 51 Sub-Saharan African countries had done this.

Factor four: research capacity

Agricultural innovations need to be supported by adequately funded and appropriately skilled research. Generally, agricultural research and development (R&D) in Sub-Saharan Africa were profoundly neglected during the last two decades of the last century. But this is changing, with African policy makers recognising that agricultural development is an engine of economic growth.

Between 2001 and 2008 there was a 20 per cent increase in investment in agricultural R&D. Ghana and Tanzania were among the highest spenders in the so-called Big Eight, along with Nigeria, South Africa, Kenya, Uganda, Ethiopia and Sudan. In 2008, these eight countries accounted for 70 per cent of public agricultural R&D expenditure in the region and 64 per cent of all the region's researchers.

Alongside public spending on R&D are contributions from international donors and funding agencies. Here, too, Ghana and Tanzania have been beneficiaries.

The broad picture for Ghana is that it has committed itself to an investment of 1 per cent of GDP in R&D. It has at least six institutes capable of agricultural biotechnology research and around 28 current projects in this area, of which just one involves GM work. Like other countries, Ghana is also beginning to take an interest in studying the genomes of orphan crops.

Overall, Tanzania's agricultural research capacity resembles that of Ghana. It has at least four institutes able to carry out agricultural biotechnology and an estimated 22 projects, one involving GM technology. The general aim, like Ghana's, is to drive up research investment in all sectors to 1 per cent of GDP and to increase researchers' salaries by more than 80 per cent.

In short, both Tanzania and Ghana recognise the significance of agricultural research as an enabling factor in developing and adopting the new technologies.

Factor five: intellectual property protection

Most African nations are some way from filing their own GM crop patents, with South Africa being to date the most advanced. Even so, Ghana and Tanzania are both members of the African Regional Intellectual Property Organisation — an intergovernmental body for hearing patent applications. Each country has only filed a couple of patents so far, but with improved funding for agricultural research in recent years, the number of applications is likely to go up.

One thing threatens Ghana's ability to maintain its current research capacity: an ageing pool of scientists with qualifications that have changed little since the 1990s.

Factor six: transport, power and communications

Good infrastructure is a key enabler of innovation. An efficient transport system, for example – as measured in road density, proportion of paved roads or motor vehicle ownership – is vitally important for seed distribution and access to markets. Sub-Saharan Africa generally has a high proportion of unpaved roads, with negative impacts on access.

Ghana has been active in improving its infrastructure over the past 30 years. Its ports are above average for Sub-Saharan Africa, but access to electricity – an indicator of readiness for technological innovation – is only around half the region's average.

Tanzania's roads are in a slightly worse condition than Ghana's, with road density lower than the regional average. Power consumption lies well below average, with large parts of the population, especially in rural areas, having only limited access to an electricity grid.

Technology-driven communication is most simply measured by mobile phone coverage or internet access. Mobile phone usage has soared across Africa in recent years: there are now more than half a billion mobile phone subscribers. That is comparable with the entire population of the European Union. The penetration of internet use is lower, however, with 13.5 per cent of the whole continent online in 2011, well below the world average of 32.7 per cent.

These trends suggest that there is some potential for information and communication technology (ICT) as a driver of agricultural extension services in rural areas in both countries, with mobile phones currently being a more viable communication channel than the internet. Ghana lies ahead of Tanzania in some areas of infrastructure development, but both countries are aware that more investment is needed if transport, power and communications are to be adequate to sustain agricultural innovation, including modern plant genetics.

Factor seven: macroeconomic and political stability

Macroeconomic stability has a profound impact on a country's competitiveness: no government can provide services efficiently if it is crippled by high debt. The current economic climate, with its effects on commodity prices, capital flows and foreign investment, is taking its toll on Africa's growth. Shrinking, recession-bound, conflict-prone and corruption-weakened economies impair the fight against poverty.

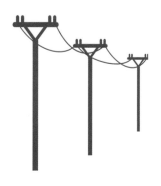

Access to a reliable electricity supply is a prerequisite for technological development.

Table 14.1 Enabling factors for the adoption of genetically modified crops in Tanzania and Ghana

	Innovation readiness	
	Ghana	Tanzania
Current production of modifiable crops	High	High
Laws and regulations	High	Average
Importance of trade flows	Not relevant	Not relevant
Agricultural research capacity	Average	Average
Intellectual property protection	Low	Low
Transport, power and communications	Average	Low
Macroeconomic and political stability	Average	Average
Enabling factors, overall score	*High*	*Average*

Source: Bennett and Jennings, 2013

Both Ghana and Tanzania experienced GDP growth of around 5 per cent during 2003–2008, but both countries score weakly on macroeconomic stability, with poor central government balances and high inflation rates. This does not necessarily mean that their adoption of new technologies will stall: Burkina Faso has managed to succeed with GM cotton despite being in a similar macroeconomic position. But persisting uncertainties surrounding the willingness of banks to lend money to private investors are certainly slowing things down.

Inward investment across Africa is also negatively affected by the continent's high levels of corruption as measured by the Corruption Perceptions Index (CPI). Ghana scores relatively well, coming sixth out of the 45 Sub-Saharan African countries listed, although its economic effectiveness is quite low. Tanzania occupies 19th place, but is still seen as a relatively stable country.

Readiness to adopt new genetic technologies

Both nations can be classified as being of "average readiness" to adopt GM and other technologies. The World Economic Forum's *Global Competitiveness Report* summarised this as follows:

- Ghana has excellent public institutions and governance but has been losing macroeconomic stability. Overall there is good public trust in politicians, a relatively independent judiciary and low levels of corruption for the region as a whole. Some aspects of infrastructure – roads and ports – and financial markets are relatively good. However, education levels lag behind international standards, and the country is not making the most of new technologies such as ICT to enhance productivity. High government deficits and interest rates and double-digit inflation suggest inefficiencies in Ghana's financial system.

- Tanzania's public institutions are also characterised by reasonable levels of trust in politicians, government even-handedness in its dealings with the private sector and good security by regional standards. Financial markets have also become more sophisticated. On the other hand, poor-quality roads, ports and electricity supply weaken its infrastructure. Primary education enrolment is high but secondary and university enrolment rates are among the lowest in the world. Related to this is poor take-up of new technologies such as the internet and mobile telephony. Another serious concern is the health of the workforce, with high levels of diseases such as malaria, tuberculosis and HIV/AIDS.

Support from government

The fact that a country fails to embrace all seven enabling factors does not mean that it will be incapable of adopting new crop production technologies. What is essential though is that it has political commitment and support from its national government.

Burkina Faso, a small, poor country, managed to adopt a GM crop – cotton – and put itself perhaps a decade ahead of other countries in the region. The government created an enabling regulatory framework and prepared its institutions to review and approve new technology in line with the Cartagena Protocol on Biosafety. All the necessary steps were taken to introduce its new *Bt* cotton, with stakeholders being informed right down the line as to what the technology would mean for farming practices, and for both human and environmental health.

Illegal, non-certified seed markets could cripple a country's ability to make the most of opportunities offered by the new genetics.

If governments act on modernising their seed sectors, provide credit and access to markets, enact regulations and coordinate the work of research institutes and government bodies, the way is open. Of course, there are still challenges, especially in establishing proper biosafety systems and preventing a surge in illegal seed markets. But it can be done; how quickly will vary.

Help for smallholders

The needs of subsistence smallholder farmers make up one final, key piece in the GM adoption jigsaw. Small farmers have to get help and advice on matters such as crop types, partnerships with private, public and non-governmental organisations, investment, and financial incentives. External organisations providing this help need to respect local demands and understand the different constraints and priorities that operate in different countries.

Effective communication is key here. Farmers need to know about many aspects of the new technologies and advances in plant breeding in order to manage their farming competently.

Also – and this is vital if innovation readiness is to be achieved – a country must address several questions:

- Does smallholder demand for innovations such as GM crops exist?
- Are smallholders aware of the potential benefits of all aspects of modern plant breeding and of the problems associated with farm-saved seed?
- Are the nation and its people ready, informed and able to fulfill smallholder demand?
- What improvements are necessary for readiness to be achieved?

There are now many informative agricultural apps available to the half a billion registered mobile phone users in Africa.

15 WINNING THE OBSTACLE RACE
Regulatory systems for agricultural biotechnology

KEY THEMES

- The genomic misconception.
- Regulatory obstacles.
- Major reforms needed in the developing world.
- Improving regulation.

The cultivation of *Bt* cotton in six northern provinces of China during 1990–2010 halved the use of pesticides and doubled the numbers of ladybirds, lacewings and spiders.

Andreas Trepte/www.photo-natur.de

The revolution that faltered

What happened to slow progress in the adoption of the new biotechnologies? After decades of research, debate and self-examination, scientists arrived at a consensus: genetic modification (GM) could be used safely and effectively to engineer microorganisms, plants and animals with genes in their cells designed to solve practical problems in medicine, agriculture, food processing, environmental remediation and industrial production. It seemed as if a biological revolution was gathering pace.

But the optimism was short-lived. It fell foul of the forces of scepticism, misunderstanding, technophobia, antagonism, domestic and international politics, overzealous regulators, commercial interests and a determined protest lobby of non-governmental organisations with other agendas.

The genomic misconception

At the heart of opposition to GM, in the words of the Swiss botanist Klaus Ammann, lies the "genomic misconception". Many people believe that GM technologies create new, unique and unprecedented risks to human and animal health, the environment, farming practices and agricultural development. And this view manifests itself in the regulatory structures that governments around the world have adopted.

The genomic misconception stems from an emphasis not on the *product* of GM technology but on the *process* by which it was produced.

When the USA set up the machinery to regulate agricultural biotechnology, it adopted a policy of using existing legal and administrative agencies and an approach focusing on the end product rather than the means of production. In practice, however, things worked out differently.

The US Department of Agriculture, Animal and Plant Health Inspection Service created a new category of "regulated article" for field trials and the commercial release of GM crops. The Environmental Protection Agency also created a new category for genetically engineered insect-resistant crops called plant-incorporated protectants. And the Food and Drug Administration also modified its demands for foods containing ingredients from GM crops. Thus, the USA's regulatory agencies all subject them to extra, intensive oversight.

The European Union (EU) from the outset has had totally new laws and regulatory procedures for predominantly agricultural GM products. These new laws and procedures are focused solely on the process by which such products are produced and emphasise both risks and speculative hazards. They demand close to zero risk before granting approval, and tend to downplay, if not ignore, the benefits of agricultural technology.

At a broader level, the genomic misconception is represented in international law through the Convention on Biological Diversity's clause calling for a binding agreement on trade that deals solely with GM products. Likewise, the Cartagena Protocol on Biosafety singled out agricultural GM products as special cases of risk and liability. Indeed, the Protocol uses the term "benefit" only three times and "risk" 67 times.

Plants engineered to absorb contaminants from the soil might help to convert polluted sites into safe agricultural land, playing a crucial role in environmental remediation.

Predictable and unfavourable consequences

Not surprisingly, these regulatory structures have had adverse effects on agricultural GM. In 2011, the US regulatory agencies approved a nutritionally enhanced soybean and a drought-tolerant maize for commercial release. By 2013, the country had approved 165 applications for commercial release of GM traits in eight different major crops – maize, soybeans, cotton, rapeseed, sugar beet, alfalfa, papaya and squash – and 70.1 million hectares were planted with GM seeds that same year. So on the face of it, the US regulatory structure seems very accepting of GM innovation.

In practice, however, the approval process has become increasingly time-consuming, costly and effort-intensive. The approval of GM products costs ten times as much as for conventionally bred products – multi-millions of dollars – and takes a far longer time, usually five to seven years. The necessary documentation also far exceeds that needed for conventionally bred non-GM products.

Even more discouraging is the fact that some GM products languish in a regulatory limbo for a very long time without getting a decision: GM salmon has been more than 10 years in the regulatory waiting room. Another promising product – rice with proven benefits for children with diarrhoea – was eventually abandoned because of costs, delays and over-heavy regulatory demands.

One final hurdle in the USA is that the GM regulatory structure creates a litigation risk. Many lawsuits have been brought by opposition groups based on a number of statutes governing approval. Whatever the outcome, these lawsuits impose delays, expense and huge uncertainty on GM products. So it seems as if a GM product must not only steer its way through the US regulatory structure; it must also find a path through the judicial system.

In Europe, the complex and intricate regulatory structure has mostly resulted in decision-making paralysis. After years of risk analysis and lengthy debate among EU members, the result is stalemate. While the European Commission has approved approximately 40 agricultural GM products for import as human food or animal feed, it has only approved two novel crops – potato and maize – for commercial cultivation on European farmlands. The system is often described as dysfunctional.

In the absence of sufficient political support in the EU, groups opposed to GM crops have dominated the debate in the media and the public at large. Retailers have shunned them, universities have shied away from research on them, and protesters routinely vandalise field trials and GM crops. With seed and chemical companies abandoning Europe for the USA, the EU has become the only region in the world where the development and use of GM technology is declining.

Salmon modified to reach adult size much faster than wild or conventionally bred fish have been around since 1996, but further research into their impacts is deemed necessary before they can become commercially available.

The scene in developing countries is more promising. For all the risk aversion permeating the Cartagena Protocol on Biosafety, developing nations grew 82.7 million hectares of GM crops in 2013, the second year in which the developing world planted more hectares of biotech crops than industrialised countries. Of the 27 countries that cultivated GM crops that year, 19 were developing and 8 industrialised. More than 16.5 million small, resource-poor farmers, representing over 90 per cent of all GM farmers, used the new technologies to improve their yields, the productivity of their labour force, their safety, income and food security. Brazil is currently approving agricultural GM traits for commercial release more quickly and more cheaply than probably any other country in the world.

Developing countries thus seem to offer a more favourable environment for adopting GM innovation than the developed world. But, even here, there are serious impediments. Many nations are uncertain and confused about GM crops, particularly when the EU's regulatory system threatens their exports to Europe. Zambia, Kenya and Zimbabwe have even gone so far as to ban imports of GM grain that would feed populations facing famine, denying hungry people access to agricultural commodities that hundreds of millions elsewhere are eating routinely as part of their diet.

As explored in Chapter 10, India's experience of *Bt* brinjal – eggplant – is another example of poor people being denied the benefits of GM foods. Although the new brinjal was seven years in testing and approval, the Indian government overturned the decision of the approving agency.

Changes needed

Effective and proportionate regulations are necessary, but several reforms would help to overcome barriers erected by burdensome and inappropriate regulatory procedures. As discussed in Section 2, developing countries would benefit from improved funding for public-sector research. Despite impressive results in laboratories and greenhouses, too few publicly funded GM crops have reached farmers' fields. Public research institutions need funding to cover heavy regulatory compliance costs that can run into millions of dollars for one GM product, which they cannot otherwise afford and which therefore deters them from undertaking such research.

Developing nations need to build capacity in the latest plant-breeding techniques offered by modern biotechnology, but young scientists, perhaps daunted by the complexity both of regulations and of intellectual property law for patenting, appear reluctant to enter GM research, often leaving the field entirely or just using conventional or modern non-GM breeding techniques. In addition, scientists need to have access to lawyers and regulators to help negotiate the legal and regulatory requirements. Plant biologists might show more interest in GM research if there were more skilled personnel able to steer GM products through these complex procedures.

The new GM technologies are critical for food security, safety and nutrition in developing countries. Excessive and unnecessary regulation does not simply have negative impacts on their economies; it costs lives through hunger and malnutrition. The lesson of biofortified Golden Rice, trapped in red tape for more than a decade, needs to be learned: many valuable crop traits have to be engineered through genetic modification. There is no other way.

Figure 15.1 Global yields of major crops, 1961–2030
Tonnes per hectare

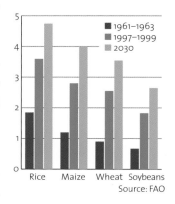

Source: FAO

While it is unlikely that yields will grow as much in the first few decades of the 21st century as they did during the last few decades of the 20th, a similar momentum could be maintained if modern biotechnology is widely applied.

Regulatory structures also need to change

The most direct reforms to the world's regulatory systems would come from a change of attitude on the part of governments. If they were to remove the "genomic misconception" from their thinking and treat plant breeding using GM technologies just like any other breeding methods, focusing on product not process, then safe, efficient, socially beneficial and environmentally benign novel crops would populate farmlands more freely.

Even if this does not happen, countries can still improve their regulatory structures by adopting a risk analysis attitude to GM technology rather than an excessively precautionary attitude, which among opponents of the technology is effectively a zero-risk attitude. But zero risk is unattainable. There is risk in every human activity and it has to be balanced against benefit.

Governments should recognise that the experience of agricultural GM technology has been favourable for nearly two decades. A huge amount of research already demonstrates that there is substantial consensus about the biosafety of GM. Governments can, therefore, lessen their heavy data requirements and streamline the decision-making process for new crops and varieties that use genetic traits already approved in other crops and varieties. They can harmonise their regulations with those of other governments and accept the decisions made by competent regulatory agencies in fellow states.

Above all, perhaps, governments could follow the example of Sweden, the UK and the USA, where scientists have recently called on the regulatory system to reflect science-based decisions and to lessen its burden on agricultural GM crops.

In the words of one expert observer: "We need science to come back to farming." The scientific consensus is that the new GM technology is safe, efficacious, beneficial and socially wise. Developing nations and their regulatory systems should adopt this attitude if they are not to be trapped in underdevelopment.

Sustainable and intensive

In making this shift in attitude, developing countries also have to bear in mind the undeniable constraints on agriculture of limited available land and a need to meet environmental obligations. In other words, the future of farming lies not in extensification – opening up new areas for production – but sustainable intensification, getting more from the same, or even less land.

This 14th century portrayal of cotton by John Mandeville – depicting sheep in the place of cotton bolls – charmingly foreshadows the sometimes fanciful fears of modern-day opponents of genetic modification.

John Mandeville/PD

In 2008, the World Bank estimated that as much as 50 per cent of the world's increased crop yields during the 1980s and 1990s came from the genetic improvements made to new varieties. Agricultural GM technology and other advanced methods such as farmed animal cloning, synthetic biology and nanotechnology could bring about the levels of intensive sustainable farming required to maintain this momentum.

In summary, then, in the face of the challenges of the 21st century, present regulatory systems that are hostile to agricultural GM technology must change. Developing nations must set their own independent course for intensive, sustainable agricultural development irrespective of the attitudes and actions of any developed nations regarding science and innovation.

As the Chinese proverb states: "A person who has food has many problems. A person who has no food has only one problem."

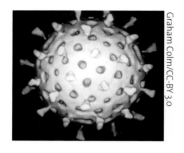

Rotavirus (which causes severe diarrhoea) kills more than half a million people every year. Rice modified to deliver an antibody might have been a solution to the problem...

16

TOWARDS A BIO-ECONOMY
Biotechnology research in the European Union

Biotechnology is a key component of the new bio-economy, which seeks to enable sustainable and environmentally friendly industrial development.

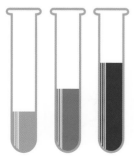

A bio-based economy

Over the past decade the concept of a bio-based economy has emerged. The term refers to an economy that links its industrial development with sustainability, and in an environmentally friendly, socially responsible manner.

The concept was introduced into the European Union (EU) in 2005 as the European Knowledge-Based Bio-Economy (KBBE), and with it came the determination to invest significantly in Europe's knowledge base in order to realise the potential of its most innovative technologies.

The EU's bio-economy sectors have an estimated annual turnover of € 2 trillion, accounting for more than 22 million jobs. Biotechnology is one of the key sectors, with a wide range of tools for using bioresources more efficiently, improving agricultural yields, saving energy and creating industrial processes that are friendly to the environment. The KBBE received support of just under € 2 billion for the period 2007–2013 to cover food and agriculture alongside biotechnology. The fact that these are grouped together underlines their interdependence.

The biotechnology part of KBBE includes:
- novel sources of biomass;
- marine and freshwater biotechnology;
- industrial biotechnology and biorefineries;
- environmental biotechnology for the clean-up of contaminated environments and the development of environmentally friendly industrial processes;
- new trends in biotechnologies (including bioinformatics, systems biology, synthetic biology and nanobiotechnologies).

Controversy, safety and risk assessment

As with all new technologies, the potential risks and benefits of biotechnology in general – and genetically modified organisms (GMOs) in particular – have to be identified and quantified. Safety has to be ensured before products containing GMOs (or where GMOs are used in a production process) can find their way to the consumer or the environment.

In Europe, GM research, development, release and commercialisation are still matters of some debate, so the challenge has been to produce legislation that reflects a broad range of public viewpoints. Such legislation has been in place since the early 1990s, having evolved and been updated over time. In general, the rules and procedures it defines comply with those of international bodies such as the World Trade Organization, the Cartagena Protocol on Biosafety and the Convention on Biological Diversity.

Currently, the main legislation covering agriculture and food safety deals with the deliberate release of GMOs into the environment, GM food and feed, GM micro-organisms and the coexistence of GMOs and non-GMOs.

In investigating the biosafety of GMOs, three steps need to be followed: risk assessment, risk management and continuous monitoring.

Potential risks must be weighed against benefits for any progress to be made with feeding the world.

Risk assessment and management

The overarching body responsible for scrutinising the risk of GM food and feed in Europe is the European Food Safety Authority (EFSA), which draws on highly qualified scientific experts from a number of European countries to conduct its assessments. The EFSA is committed to ensuring that panel members are truly independent.

Figure 16.1 outlines the different stages involved in assessing risk and managing it once a decision to authorise a given GMO has been taken. The assessment stage involves a good deal of formal and informal communication between the EFSA, the applicant and EU Member State authorities. This may be about specific concerns or calls for additional evidence, or it may simply be to clear up un-certainties or misunderstandings.

The United Nations Convention on Biological Diversity is one of several international bodies that help to define the rules and procedures of genetic research.

Once a GMO has been authorised following a favourable opinion from the EFSA, the European Commission submits a draft decision to Member States for their vote. To date, in almost all cases, no qualified majority for or against authorisation of a GMO has been obtained. There has been stalemate. The same has sometimes happened when draft decisions have been forwarded to the governing Council of Ministers. There, too, no majority has been reached over marketing GMOs.

Something comparable also happens when decisions have to be made on the cultivation of a GMO in the EU. Some Member States, unhappy about a novel

Figure 16.1 The authorisation process for genetically modified organisms in Europe

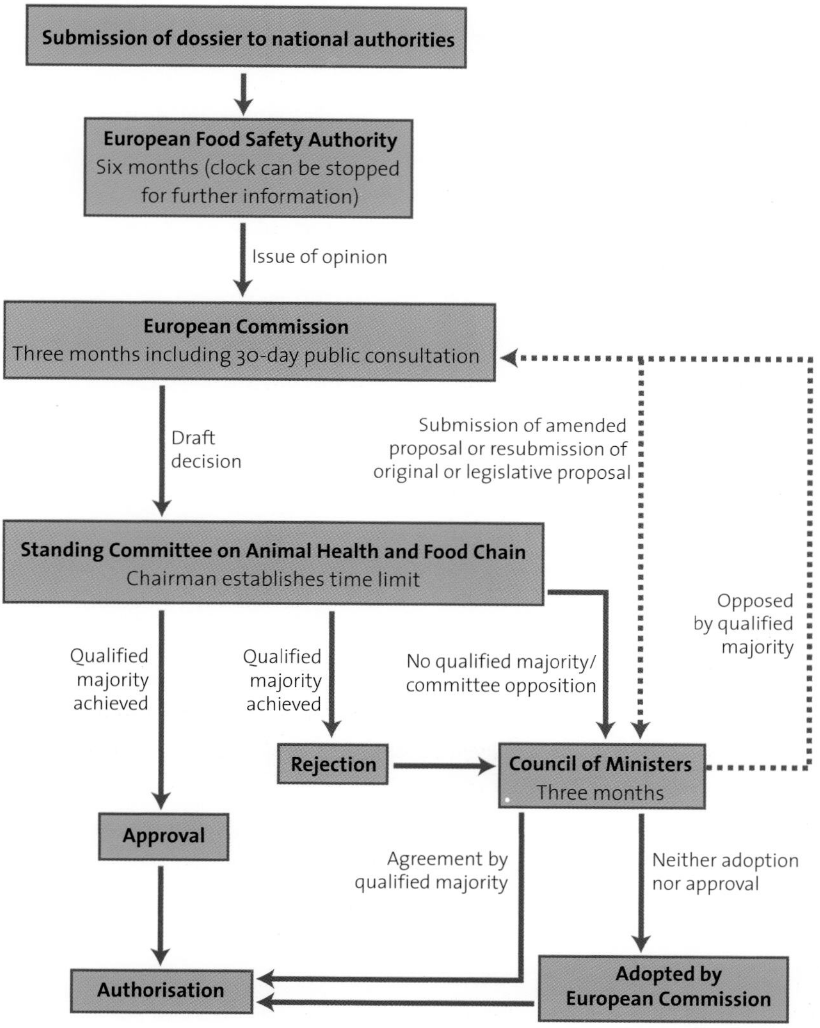

Source: Bennett and Jennings, 2013

organism being grown in their territory, invoke a safeguard clause in the legislation. For example, six states are currently using safeguard clauses to ban the cultivation of a genetically engineered variety of maize – MON810 – although other European countries, along with many more around the world, do grow this insect-resistant crop.

Monitoring

There is a legal requirement to monitor the potential effects of all GMOs grown or consumed within the EU. This takes place at every stage, from initial field trials to commercialisation.

Monitoring can be both general and specific:

- general surveillance is conducted to verify or refute the results of the initial risk assessment where no special monitoring requirements were requested;
- case-specific monitoring can include such actions as surveying the development of the resistance of insects to a pesticide produced by a GMO.

Both these are important tools for decision and policy makers who may need to adjust their positions according to results. If used constructively, they help close the gap between initial risk assessment and practical experience and, thereby, avoid forfeiting the benefits of new products or technologies unnecessarily.

Three decades of research on safety

The EU has undertaken research to evaluate the risks and benefits of GMOs to human, animal and environmental health. These studies were carried out on the basis of the precautionary principle, which can be summarised as "better safe than sorry". This means that, if a technology or novel crop has a suspected risk of causing harm then, in the absence of scientific evidence that it is harmful, the burden of proof that it is not falls on those supporting or endorsing it.

The EU is not alone in following this principle: other international organisations such as the Organisation for Economic Co-operation and Development (OECD) do too, not just in the interests of consumer safety but to harmonise their approach to risk assessment and to ease international trade in agricultural or industrial products.

In 2001, the European Commission published its first overview, *EC-Sponsored Research on Safety of Genetically Modified Organisms*, covering 15 years and 81 projects in more than 400 laboratories. Among the topics were horizontal gene transfer, GM plants in the environment, plant-microbe interactions, GM fish and food safety. A second volume followed in 2010, presenting the results of a further 50 projects involving 400 European research groups. In 2013, a thorough, systematic review of the scientific research conducted on GM crops in the past decade was completed.

Using a technique that turns plants into "vaccine factories", a co-funded EU/Russian research project has developed an exceptionally fast and effective way of creating vaccines to combat some of the most devastating infections affecting farm livestock, including foot and mouth disease.

What does this research tell us about the safety of GM products? The main conclusion to be drawn from the efforts of more than 130 investigations, covering a period of more than 25 years, and involving more than 500 independent research groups, is that modern biotechnology is inherently no more risky than conventional plant-breeding technologies. The research on biosafety came up with a large volume of scientific evidence for these results: data that fail to demonstrate any specific hazard linked to GM technology.

One other conclusion was that today's biotechnology research and applications are far more diverse than they were 25 years ago. This means, among other things, that biotechnology has strengthened its position at the core of Europe's knowledge-based bio-economy by being able to contribute even more towards meeting the challenges of sustainable food safety and security.

European biotechnology on the world stage

The EU has been keen to promote international cooperation in plant biotechnology, both between Member States and with countries outside the EU. A major tool for this is the Partnering Initiative, which foresees increasingly systematic cooperation in research and development programmes that tackle common challenges. To date, Europe has established Partnering Initiatives with India on biomass and biowastes, and with China on fibre crops and genetic crop improvement.

In addition, the European Commission is actively cooperating with industrialised countries including Australia, Canada, New Zealand and the USA on plant biotechnology, along with the so-called BRIC countries: Brazil, Russia, India and China.

The EU has been keen to promote international cooperation in plant biotechnology, both between Member States and with countries outside the EU.

Significant funding has been made available for cooperation with emerging countries in specific areas of research, such as plant vaccines in Russia and sweet sorghum and *Jatropha* (physic nut) in the tropics.

Horizon 2020

The EU's Horizon 2020 initiative will use a budget of € 80 billion during 2014–2020 to drive research and innovation across its Member States, embracing science, industrial innovation, and the major concerns shared by all Europeans such as climate change, food safety and security, an ageing population and so on. With biotechnology explicitly identified as the engine of the bio-economy, the use of new genetic methods and techniques will figure prominently in this wide-ranging, cross-cutting initiative to develop industry and agriculture across Europe.

IN THE EYE OF THE STORM
Genetically modified crops in Europe, past and future

17

A long-running scare story

Europe has seen its share of food crises in recent times. Some are fairly short-lived, such as the scandal over wines contaminated with antifreeze and vegetables containing unacceptably high levels of pesticide residues. Others last longer, as was the case with so-called "mad cow" disease – bovine spongiform encephalopathy (BSE) – caused by feeding meal made from processed animal parts to cattle.

But none has had the persistence or longevity of the controversy over genetically modified (GM) crops and food. Still this rumbles on after decades. It seems as intractable a problem today as it did in the 1990s when it first surfaced. Why is this?

There are several obvious explanations. One is that, from the outset, the climate for "Frankenfoods", as they were called by the UK newspaper *Daily Mail,* was unfavourable. Earlier food scares in the 1980s and 1990s had sensitised public opinion, with people ready to hold their politicians to account on any issue concerning food safety. Secondly, the bureaucratic machinery of the European Union (EU) had not yet become sufficiently developed to create an adequate level of pan-European integration on these issues. And, thirdly, these were exactly the sorts of media stories that helped activist organisations gain publicity and political influence.

These three factors, however, were not enough in themselves to generate the GM food controversy which, by the end of the 1990s, had resulted in a polarised debate. Scientific considerations had become secondary to wider public attitudes and opinions.

Severe marketing failure

Matters were not helped by the behaviour of industrial interests seeking to commercialise the new technology. Companies in general, and the most active one in particular, Monsanto, did not pay enough attention to the context in which they were trying to market their novel products. They failed to appreciate public opinion and sentiment on food-related issues in Europe, and promoted the benefits of the new technology in ways that clearly did not resonate with their intended consumers.

KEY THEMES

- Anatomy of a controversy.
- Complex decision.
- Future prospects for breaking deadlock.

By not emphasising the real benefits to consumers, industrial players had no reservoir of goodwill and enthusiasm on which to draw when later faced with opposition. They had lost half the battle before it had even begun. In other parts of the world, especially the USA, the technology encountered far fewer acceptance problems.

Even so, a failure in marketing alone does not really explain why the controversy took hold and clung on in Europe; nor does the fact that early disagreements between scientists took some time to resolve themselves into today's broad consensus that we should embrace and not reject GM crops and foods.

The heart of the controversy

The dominant reason for GM food becoming so controversial was that it was identified early on by a number of far-sighted, active and ingenious non-governmental organisations (NGOs), notably Greenpeace and Friends of the Earth, later joined by promoters of organic farming, as being a "lightning rod" for a much wider set of concerns that they wanted to advance and popularise.

This was a late-20th century manifestation of ideas initiated by Rachel Carson in her 1960s book *Silent Spring*, an environmental "wake-up call" in which Carson accused the pesticide industry of spreading misinformation and criticised public authorities for accepting industry's viewpoint without question. Three decades later, growing environmental problems came together with the belief that capitalism – especially multinational big business – was responsible for these problems and indeed perpetuating them.

Companies in general failed to appreciate public opinion and sentiment on food-related issues and promoted the benefits of the new technology in ways that did not resonate with their intended consumers.

Those opposed to GM held a world view of global business and its ability to influence governments, at least in the USA and Europe, that set the scene for a great fight between perceived forces of good and evil. They also drew on a worry that our food supply was becoming dominated by too few private multinational companies rather than public-sector organisations. And the manner in which company marketing departments rushed to commercialise their products did nothing to argue the case for GM foods.

As a result, fairly arcane scientific debates and marketing failures transmuted into a discussion about the true meaning of sustainable development. The emphasis shifted to an examination of whether the current global model of political economy was really appropriate for both developed and developing countries. Environmental and social collapse was predicted.

Europe's regulatory response

Against this hostile backdrop, Europe's current legislative framework and policy approach on GM are criticised by most environmental NGOs for being weak, and by business for being unnecessarily strict: both sides seem equally unhappy. At the same time, compared to other parts of the world, the EU's regulatory regime is considered to be highly rigorous and a firm guarantor of consumer safety and environmental protection.

Even so, the stand-off between the two sides persists, as does the controversy surrounding GM products. Some NGOs continue to oppose each new modified crop being considered for regulatory approval, argue that heavy lobbying by business and distorted scientific arguments are having an unfair influence, and mount legal challenges in the courts. Industry associations, for their part, continue to point out that the number of GM crops authorised for cultivation is lower in the EU than in most other parts of the world, and that the whole process is too slow and a disincentive to commercial investment.

Three levels of decision making

What, then, is this much-disliked process of approval and authorisation? It involves scientific consideration by the European Food Safety Authority (EFSA) followed by

Figure 17.1 Layers of influence and the role of science in decision making

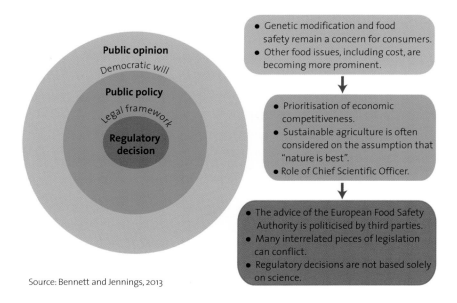

Source: Bennett and Jennings, 2013

Each level of decision making – regulatory, policy, and public opinion – has a set of characteristics that define the way decisions are made, the desired outcome, and the attitudes of those who participate in the process.

Figure 17.2 Characteristics of different decision-making levels

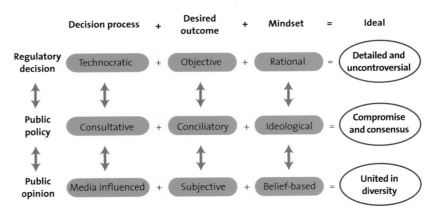

Source: Bennett and Jennings, 2013

expert discussions between national governments and the European Commission (EC), and ends in approval supported by the European Parliament. And it is nothing if not complex.

There are three levels of decision making. The most detailed is a specific regulatory decision on the approval or otherwise of a candidate GM crop. This is taken within the context of previously agreed legislation. The final level of influence is that of public opinion, often transmitted by means of the media as well as through the expression of political preferences at elections. The interrelationship of these different levels of influence on decisions in relation to GM crops is shown in Figure 17.1.

That is the broad picture. But, as Figure 17.2 shows, each of these three levels has its own set of characteristics that define the way decisions are supposed to be taken, the desired outcome and the mindset of participants.

In the case of public opinion, a good deal of subjectivity shapes the attitudes and beliefs of individual participants. Given the diverse histories, cultures and socio-economic situations of Europe's different countries, there is little uniformity in public opinion across the EU. Its own unofficial motto sums it up well: "United in diversity".

A very different picture emerges when one looks at regulatory decisions. These are shaped by a highly technocratic process known as comitology, which implies that all decisions are made rationally and objectively. Many thousands of decisions are taken by the EU each year that never receive any publicity at all. Why then are those on GM crops and food so out of keeping with the norm?

The reason seems to be that there are many voices being heard during regulatory decision making and there is a lot of consultation with third-party stakeholders. The ambition is to reach the ideal of a detailed but uncontroversial outcome. Good compromises and consensus are the aim throughout, so amid this clamour of voices from all different angles – including highly divergent national positions regarding GM crops – it is no surprise that EC officials find it challenging to pin down the European interest.

By not emphasising the real benefits of novel crops when they were first introduced, the industrial players had no reservoir of goodwill and enthusiasm on which to draw when later faced with opposition.

The European Parliament, an institution that should be the sole forum for the direct representation of democratic opinion within the EU, also has a multiplicity of voices through a mix of ideologies of the Left and Right, Greens and others.

Crumbling boundaries

In the case of decisions over GM crops and food, the boundaries between the different levels of decision making – never wholly solid – have almost entirely crumbled. Hostile NGOs have been highly effective in using the issue to exemplify a wider problem. They cast GM as the thin end of the wedge in order to raise public concerns about any development in the technology that meets with their disapproval. They tend to portray such innovations as the creations of business corporations with no public interest in mind.

Combining this with the polarised views of Member States and the EC's commitment to comitology, there is a fear that any decision concerning GM products might be interpreted as an illegitimate imposition by an unelected bureaucracy. Near deadlock has ensued over GM approval decisions for crops to be farmed in Europe. Even the consideration of scientific evidence for a GM crop or food has been politicised in these ways – not the way in which the process was intended to operate.

What future for GM?

Where does this deadlock in decision making leave the EU in future attempts to further GM technology? Certainly, more and more stakeholders are voicing the opinion that the EU's stance has a negative effect on local investment in the technology, with knock-on effects on employment, economic and export potential. Nor does it help in meeting the global challenges of food security and climate change that affect other regions of the world more than Europe.

More importantly perhaps, other regions – notably South America – see things differently. They do not perceive the health and environmental risks of GM to be as dramatic as does the EU and have gone on to exploit the technology through trade in GM food and feed. Indeed, trade in GM has grown to such an extent that it is becoming more and more difficult for Europe to source non-GM varieties and technically more difficult to guarantee that GM and non-GM are wholly separated. In fact, many millions of tonnes of GM maize and soybeans are imported each year into the EU for animal feed, making it difficult to eat steak or eggs from cattle or chickens that have not been fed on one or other of them. In other words, Europe's zero tolerance of GM may end up bringing food security problems even to the EU.

The EC is aware of this and has managed to introduce low levels of GM produce in imported non-GM animal feed. And it is even moving towards doing something similar with food, without provoking much public discussion. Though whether this will really work when it comes to food for direct human consumption is still an open question.

Another development from the EC is a new approach to decision making that might sever the link between those countries totally opposed to the cultivation and use of GM products and those in favour. The idea is that scientifically based risk assessment and consequent approval for cultivation of a GM crop would remain an EU-level task. But the actual decision to cultivate that crop would be taken at national level, thereby giving individual countries freedom to reject it for their own particular reasons.

Even though there is little genetically modified agriculture in the EU, European beef is likely to have been raised on imported biotech feeds.

PDphoto.org

This "re-nationalisation" idea looks attractive, but it does set a precedent for invoking non-scientific reasons for withholding marketing approval for otherwise safe products of any kind. It also effectively presents an inherent barrier to trade in food and feed between EU Member States and to companies whose commercial trade is international, because it is uneconomic and uncompetitive for them to tailor their products to nationally differing markets. This runs counter to the whole spirit of both the European single market and the provisions of the World Trade Organization. So, a creative proposal remains just that: it has not been approved. Pro and anti-GM factions have once more created deadlock.

Getting public endorsement

Considering the three levels of decision making that characterise the EU in relation to GM (and other matters), it is clear that public opinion is critical to the whole process. There seems little hope of reaching solutions at the policy and regulatory levels without having popular support.

Some parts of the EU are seeing signs of change, with other issues becoming more prominent and offsetting GM as the main preoccupation. Opinion polls indicate a slight shift in favour of GM in some countries, including the UK where the government stance has long been favourable even while some media coverage has remained highly charged. But in those countries where governments are opposed to GM there is little sign that opinion is shifting, and this situation looks likely to continue for some time unless a major crisis arises.

However, the price of food may yet have an effect on public opinion. In the UK and elsewhere in Europe, the cost of food has fallen to 10–12 per cent of weekly income, compared with some 80–100 per cent in poverty-stricken developing countries in Africa and elsewhere – that is to say food is, by comparison, very cheap in Europe. But this could change, and if fluctuations in prices were to lower the cost of GM-containing food relative to non-GM food, it would be reasonable to expect a change in attitudes and consumption patterns.

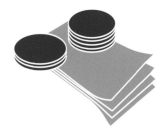

The proportion of household income that Europeans spend on food has fallen from around 30 per cent in the 1960s to 10–12 per cent today.

18

CHAMPIONING THE NEW TECHNOLOGIES
The role of the USA in research and trade

KEY THEMES

- Extensive public support for genetic modification.
- The role of the private sector.
- Cooperation for trade.
- International influence.

Longstanding international engagement

The US government, largely through the US Department of Agriculture (USDA), has a 150-year history of supporting research in the food and agriculture sector, most recently in genetic modification (GM). It also makes strenuous, wide-ranging efforts to promote trade in GM products through bilateral, multilateral and regional networks. Central to both is the active promotion of transparent, predictable and science-based regulatory systems that foster innovation and help the adoption of – and trade in – GM crops.

The latest GM technology is just one tool among many that the USA is targeting in order to tackle global hunger and poverty, but it regards the new genetics as particularly important if farmers are to produce more on less land and with fewer inputs. These technologies also matter hugely in the economy of the USA itself, being essential to its own agriculture and a powerful generator of exports.

Supporting international research

The USDA supports modern plant improvement and biotechnology research through several major initiatives.

- The Animal and Plant Health Inspection Service is concerned with plant and animal health as well as providing information related to food safety, including GM crops. It is also the agency ensuring the safety of GM crop varieties and products imported into the USA. With offices around the world, the Animal and Plant Health Inspection Service links up with the US Foreign Agriculture Service to provide training for scientists abroad and in the USA, with special emphasis on food safety and the import of agricultural goods including biotech products.
- The Foreign Agriculture Service administers and awards fellowships for training scientists and students under a variety of programmes, including biotechnology, biosafety and regulatory issues.
- The Agricultural Research Service conducts and hosts research in several facilities outside the USA. These long-term projects also provide training in fundamental and applied science, including biotechnology.
- The National Institute of Food and Agriculture administers funds provided

Genetic modification technology is just one tool that the USA is targeting to tackle global hunger and poverty.

by several other agencies in the USA for research and training in programmes designed as country-led initiatives.

Many of the USDA's programmes are best described as translational: they convert fundamental research into practical, targeted applications with a direct benefit for health or well-being. They include basic research and training in molecular genomics, the use of advanced breeding tools in plant improvement, genetic engineering of plants, and greenhouse and field evaluation of crops. They also provide training in natural resources and water management, agricultural statistics, economics and rural development.

The National Science Foundation: another research player

The US National Science Foundation (NSF) is another valuable contributor in a number of ways:

- Encouraging and facilitating collaboration between scientists in US universities and research institutions, and between scientists in developing economies and US public-sector researchers. The areas supported by the NSF include plant genomics, genetics and genome evolution, cell biology, biochemistry and other disciplines. The projects funded may involve plant biotechnology and genetic engineering.
- Administering programmes funded by non-NSF sources. One is the BREAD (Basic Research to Enable Agricultural Development) initiative, funded by the Bill and Melinda Gates Foundation, which is designed to support innovative basic research into the key constraints on smallholder agriculture in the developing world. This fundamental work feeds into agricultural improvements through advanced and molecular breeding.
- Another programme is PEER (Partnerships for Enhanced Engagement in Research) funded by the US Agency for International Development (USAID), which has a long history of supporting the development of agriculture-based economies. Its projects have been an important mechanism for training students and other scientists from less developed countries in US institutions in areas such as advanced breeding and GM technologies, and food safety.

University inputs and USAID

The US Agency for International Development also funds research and training programmes in biotechnology at leading universities in the USA, which, in turn, further similar work at universities and research institutes in the developing world.

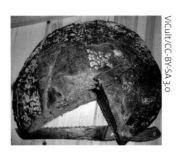

The BREAD initiative (Basic Research to Enable Agricultural Development), funded by the Bill and Melinda Gates Foundation, is designed to support innovative basic research into the key constraints on smallholder agriculture in the developing world.

Along with science and technology, these projects also embrace product biosafety and regulation.

Feed the Future is USAID's most recent initiative, working with ministries in developing countries to achieve food security and build agricultural economies. The approach to improving productivity and marketing is sometimes conventional, sometimes innovative through biotechnology and information technology.

Another recent USAID programme is its Grand Challenges for Development, which enlists scientists and technologists from a variety of disciplines in the USA to find new solutions to both old and new problems in developing countries.

Private-sector involvement

Alongside the work of the US government is support for research from foundations, such as Gates, Ford, Rockefeller and Templeton, private-sector companies and individual donors. These have supported agricultural research, training and capacity building in developing countries, covering advanced plant breeding, biotechnology and other innovative methods for enhancing food production.

Some of the projects funded by the Bill and Melinda Gates Foundation are in collaboration with private companies or foundations. Sometimes this means direct funding, sometimes donations of intellectual property, technical knowledge or services. An example is Golden Rice, which began as a collaboration between Swiss scientists and the Syngenta company. The new rice required more than 40 different patents to reach its goal of high levels of provitamin A. These were donated by different sources, as were funds for related laboratory, greenhouse and field research.

The African Orphan Crops Consortium established a public-private partnership in 2014 to help improve the livelihoods of Africa's smallholder farmers and their families.

Another variant is public-private partnerships in agricultural biotechnology, with private firms supporting public-sector researchers, sometimes in developing countries. Over the past 20 years, many such bilateral or multilateral projects have been funded though, so far, none has resulted in biosafety approval and the commercial release of an agricultural product developed through biotechnology. Lack of biosafety regulations in developing countries, or the unfamiliarity, complexity and/or cost of regulating such products, may be to blame for this.

The African Orphan Crops Consortium (AOCC) established a public-private partnership in 2014 to help improve the livelihoods of Africa's smallholder farmers and their families, reduce hunger and boost Africa's food supply. Its goal is to use the latest scientific equipment and techniques to genetically sequence, assemble and annotate the genomes of 100 staple African food crops to guide the development of more robust produce with higher nutritional content. The consortium includes the African Union's New Partnership for Africa's Development (AU-NEPAD); Mars, Inc.; the World Agroforestry Centre (ICRAF); BGI; Life Technologies Corporation; World Wildlife Fund; University of California, Davis (UC Davis); iPlant Collaborative; and Biosciences eastern and central Africa–International Livestock Research Institute (BecA–ILRI Hub).

Promoting regulatory systems and trade

The food price crisis of 2007–2008, driven by a number of export bans, led to higher prices on the global market and food shortages in many parts of the world, resulting in protests and sometimes violence. Agriculture suddenly came back on the global agenda of priority issues facing governments, highlighting the role that trade plays in either undermining or promoting food security.

The continuing high price of food puts the USA in a quandary. On the one hand, its farmers enjoyed an export boom of US$ 137.4 billion in 2011 – some 20 billion higher than the previous year. But high prices have had a negative effect on global food security, pushing even more people into poverty and hunger. Since nearly half of US agricultural exports consist of – or contain – biotech commodities, the USA has an interest in ensuring that countries around the world have sound regulatory systems for promoting free and fair trade in agricultural products.

The USA is helping to set up an African/European research partnership to explore the scientific and technical issues of biotechnology, including water management.

So, the US government works with developing countries to establish approval mechanisms for both importing and producing GM crops. Partnerships have been formed between USAID and a host of international and regional organisations to strengthen environmental and food safety policies. Building local capacity, including trained staff, to develop science-based regulations covering GM crops is a particular aim.

Cooperation for trade

Alongside these regulatory activities, the USA has been forming bilateral, trilateral and multilateral networks for promoting trade in – and cultivation of – GM crops.

Again, USAID is actively supporting regional organisations in Africa and Asia as they move towards biotechnology policies, engaging in policy dialogues that promote harmonisation of regulations and information sharing.

Figure 18.1 Average size of agricultural holdings

Selected regions, hectares

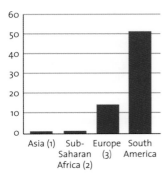

1 Excluding Japan and the Republic of Korea
2 Excluding South Africa
3 Including Russia

Source: FAO

Dialogues have also taken place with the European Commission since 1990, with an EU-US Task Force on Biotechnology Research. Here, however, the focus is not so much on trade as on the scientific and technical issues arising from biotechnology. Senior representatives from the European Commission, the African Union Commission and science ministries from both continents have agreed to set up a research partnership to tackle key issues. Focus areas are set to include the sustainable enhancement of the agricultural and food chain in Africa; the role of small and family farms in food and nutrition security; and water management for sustainable agriculture and food security.

The USA also has links with China through technical and biotech working groups, and discussions on agriculture, commerce and trade. And it has less formal links with countries such as Australia, Brazil and New Zealand that have common interests in a sound regulatory system.

Multilateral organisations

The USA actively participates in multilateral bodies involved in GM technology, regulations and policies, such as the Cartagena Protocol on Biosafety and the Convention on Biological Diversity. It also plays a very active role in meetings of the Codex Alimentarius Commission and its committees. This was established by the Food and Agriculture Organization and World Health Organization in 1963 to develop harmonised international food standards, guidelines and codes of practice to protect consumers' health and ensure fairness in the food trade.

The Codex Alimentarius Commission has taken up the question of GM standards over the past decade or so, establishing two biotech task forces that have:
- successfully established principles and guidelines for assessing the risk of GM crops including nutritionally enhanced plants;
- created guidelines for risk assessment where unapproved GM products are present at low levels.

The Codex Alimentarius Commission has not always been productive, however. Its committee on labelling foods derived from modern biotechnology laboured for nearly 20 years without coming to clear-cut conclusions.

Settling differences?

There are clearly differences between regions and countries in their approaches to GM products. The European Union (EU), for example, stands out as having a moratorium on approving them. The USA has been a front runner, along with Canada and Argentina, in the establishment of the World Trade Organization's Dispute Settlement Body that called for the EU to comply with WTO obligations.

The Settlement Body noted that the EU's moratorium and its Member State bans were inconsistent with the EU's own safety assessments. But the dispute rolls on, with the USA continuing to urge the EU to remove barriers to GM products from its approval system.

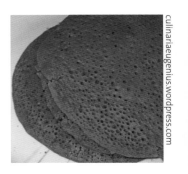

A sense of urgency

The position of the USA on GM crops and food is unequivocal. It regards them as an integral part of its own agricultural system, with a vital role to play in increasing global crop productivity. It has the research experience, infrastructure, capital and capacity to support emerging economies in adopting and implementing the new technologies. It also has the capacity to provide and encourage training in science-based methods for evaluating the safety of biotech products.

Meeting global food needs and building worldwide food security are, it believes, a matter of urgency. Any barriers to trade that reduce access to food should be broken down as soon as possible. The world needs safe and affordable food, with GM crops playing their part in supplying it.

Teff, an African orphan crop rich in calcium, grows from sea level to 3,000 metres. It is made into flour for *injera* bread or eaten as porridge, and is used to make beer and other alcoholic drinks.

RESEARCH, DISCUSSION
AND ESSAY TOPICS

- Global action is needed to avert future food security crises.
- It is essential to create a climate of confidence in scientific and technical progress.
- The agro-multinational companies are practising "genetic colonialism".
- The adoption of genetically modified crops is not just about technology or seeds but also about an appropriate agricultural environment.
- The short history of modern biotechnology reveals a head-on collision between scientific optimism and the reality of hostile societal forces.
- The new crop technologies are being held back by misconceived regulatory systems.
- Sustainability is central to the successful adoption of new farming technologies.
- "Sustainability" is an over-worked term that can mean almost anything one chooses.
- European legislation on the research, development and commercialisation of genetically modified products is simply a mess.
- The controversy over genetic modification in Europe is not, at heart, due to scientific disagreement.
- The USA has a lot to offer emerging economies in the development and implementation of new crop technologies.

FURTHER READING
AND USEFUL WEBSITES

African Regional Intellectual Property Organization.
   http://www.insouth.org/index.php?option=com_sobi2&sobi2Task=sobi2De
   tails&sobi2Id=143&Itemid=68

Africa Renewal (2013) *Africa's Mobile Youth Drive Change.*
   http://www.un.org/africarenewal/magazine/may-
   2013/africa%E2%80%99s-mobile-youth-drive-change

Bennett, D.J. and Jennings, R.C. (2013) *Successful Agricultural Innovation in
   Emerging Economies: New Genetic Technologies for Global Food Production.*
   Cambridge University Press, Cambridge. Chapters 15–19 and 25.

Community Research and Development Information Service (CORDIS). About
   Knowledge-Based Bio-Economy (KBBE).
   http://cordis.europa.eu/fp7/kbbe/about-kbbe_en.html

Convention on Biological Diversity (2000) *The Cartagena Protocol on Biosafety.*
   http://bch.cbd.int/protocol/

EuropaBio (2013) *Pocketguide to GM Crops and Policies.*
   http://www.europabio.org/positions/pocket-guide-gm-crops-and-policies

EuropaBio (2014) *Undue Delays in EU Authorisation of Safe GM Crops.*
   http://www.europabio.org/sites/default/files/position/europabio_undue_d
   elays_update_june_2014_0.pdf

EuropaBio (various dates) Frequently Asked Questions.
   http://www.europabio.org/faq%20

EuropaBio (various dates) Factsheets: Agricultural.
   http://www.europabio.org/filter/agricultural/type/fact%20%20

EuropaBio (various dates) Reports: Agricultural.
   http://www.europabio.org/filter/agricultural/type/report

European Commission (2010) *A Decade of EU-Funded GMO Research
   2001–2010.*
   ftp://ftp.cordis.europa.eu/pub/fp7/kbbe/docs/a-decade-of-eu-funded-gmo-
   research_en.pdf

European Commission. Horizon 2020.
   http://ec.europa.eu/programmes/horizon2020/en

Mars. African Orphan Crops Consortium (AOCC).
   http://www.mars.com/global/african-orphan-crops.aspx

Paarlberg, R. (2010; 2nd ed. 2013) *Food Politics: What Everyone Needs to Know.* Oxford University Press, USA.

Transparency International (2013) *2013 Corruptions Perceptions Index.* http://cpi.transparency.org/cpi2013/

United Nations (1992) *Convention on Biological Diversity.* https://www.cbd.int/doc/legal/cbd-en.pdf

World Economic Forum (2013) *Global Competitiveness Report 2013–2014.* http://www3.weforum.org/docs/WEF_GlobalCompetitivenessReport_2013-14.pdf

SECTION FOUR

SOCIAL, LEGAL, ETHICAL AND POLITICAL ISSUES

Surveys on attitudes to genetically modified crops reveal a rollercoaster ride.

In this section we look at the many different players involved in shaping attitudes and behaviour in relation to new plant science and technology. Although science has proved to be, arguably, the most powerful of all human enterprises shaping our health, welfare, standards of living, lifestyles and the environment, public acceptance of innovation is often a complicated and hard-won process.

Over the past 20 years or more, Europe-wide surveys on genetically modified (GM) crops and their possible future reveal a rollercoaster ride in attitudes. They have swung from early enthusiasm to today's ambivalence. Why so? Certainly, the image of GM foods as unnatural has persisted, as has the belief that they confer few if any benefits. Thus, the outlook for the first generation of modified commodity crops in Europe seems bleak, although in other parts of the world GM crops have been the most rapid and successful technology ever introduced.

However, if the next generation of innovations manages to limit pesticide residues on food crops and confer benefits on the environment by reducing chemical and energy use and by maintaining biodiversity, then the signs are that the public will find them more acceptable. But this will not happen by itself. The public needs to be a participant in the introduction of GM technologies and an enlightened contributor to debates if acceptability and consent are to be achieved.

The biotechnology industry needs to be alert to the hopes, fears and expectations of society. Initially, the industrial view was that the general public would fall in line once people truly understood the science behind the new wave of technological innovations. But this was simplistic. The debate became political, with people expressing deeply held views on freedom, human rights and fairness in combating world hunger.

Central to such discussion has been the media. Journalists and broadcasters have had a crucial role in conveying the radical new ideas emerging from biotechnology laboratories to the public at large, which from the outset has meant wrestling with some difficult concepts and possible misunderstandings. How much does the general public know about the fundamentals of science? About DNA, genes, proteins or biodiversity? What do such everyday terms as "natural" really mean? What are the perceived hazards of GM crops that campaigners talk about? And so on.

And what of the environmental lobbies that have been so active over the past 15–20 years? Non-governmental organisations such as Greenpeace and Friends of the Earth do not simply evaluate GM technology from an environmental or health perspective. They look more widely at the social constitution of new technologies, at issues of control, governance and globalisation and the power of multinational organisations, the distribution of benefits and risks, and at who takes – or should take – responsibility for any problems or hazards that may arise.

Journalists and broadcasters have had a crucial role in conveying the radical new ideas emerging from biotechnology laboratories.

Philosophical perspectives are also relevant in this complex debate. When the pro- or anti- factions consider the health or economic implications of GM technology, they seem to do so from totally different standpoints, considering different evidence and listening to different voices. How can these two worlds be reconciled in the interests of closer engagement and of overcoming universal problems?

A ROLLERCOASTER RIDE
Do genetically modified crops have a future in Europe?

KEY THEMES

- First- versus second-generation genetically modified crops.
- Three fundamental concerns.
- Segmenting the attitudes of consumers.

Potato blight was held largely responsible for the Irish famine of the mid-19th century, when a million people died and the population fell by around 25 per cent.

USDA-ARS/PD

What worries Europeans?

When, in 2010, the European Food Safety Authority commissioned a Eurobarometer survey throughout the European Union (EU) on food-related risks, it emerged that Europeans were most worried about pesticides in their fruit and vegetables, and that their concerns were increasing. They also said that genetically modified organisms (GMOs) were a source of concern, though less so than pesticides.

The impact of ecofriendly varieties

The findings about opinions on pesticide use are thought-provoking in the light of two recent, significant developments in biotechnology.

One is a field trial of new GM wheat that began in the UK in 2013 at the Rothamsted Institute in Hertfordshire. A synthetic gene has been added to this wheat, causing it to give off an insect signalling chemical – a pheromone called farnesene – that deters cereal aphid pests. If the trial is a successful proof-of-concept, then the ensuing GM wheat will need less chemical insecticide spraying, will leave fewer chemical residues and will better support biodiversity.

The second development is a field trial of the Fortuna potato initiated by BASF, one of the world's leading chemical companies. Current potato production in Europe can involve a lot of chemical spraying against the fungus that causes potato blight – as many as 12–15 applications per crop. The Fortuna variety, however, contains two extra genes taken from a wild potato from the mountains of Mexico that is blight-resistant. Again, here is a potential crop with consumer and environmental benefits.

However, a cloud hangs over the future of this GM potato: public resistance has led BASF to end its biotech research in Europe. It makes no business sense for the company to continue developing the potato in the EU, and the research has been relocated to the USA.

Here then is the issue. These ecologically friendly crops that reduce the use of chemical pesticides would seem to herald the long-awaited second-generation GM crops, conferring obvious consumer and sustainability benefits rather than mainly rewarding biotech companies and farmers, as has been the case with first-generation GM crops. But how will such crops be viewed by the European public, with its anxieties over chemicals in food?

Towards the second generation

The Eurobarometer on biotechnology and the life sciences explored attitudes to a second-generation GM apple. Growers typically need to spray their crops frequently with pesticides and fungicides to combat diseases such as canker, scab and mildew. However, the virtually inedible crab apple, which can cross-breed naturally with commercial varieties, contains genes that provide resistance to such pests.

The quickest method of introducing these genes into edible crop varieties is genetic engineering using the process of cisgenics, when genes are introduced from the same or a conventionally crossable species.

The Eurobarometer team wanted to find out whether these cisgenic crops would be more or less acceptable to the public than transgenic varieties, where the genes are introduced from what is frequently a totally different plant species or a bacterium. Respondents were asked whether modifications within a species were more acceptable than those that cross the species barrier. And they were also asked what they thought of GM food in general.

In principle, there should be no difference between attitudes to cisgenics, transgenics and GM in general, as the basic molecular process is similar. In practice, however, as

Responses to questions that used the umbrella term "GM food" got quite different results from questions about cisgenic and transgenic apples, even though respondents had been told that the process for producing cisgenic and transgenic apples and GM food is effectively the same.

Table 19.1 Public perception: safety, environmental impacts and the naturalness of genetically modified foods, 2010

EU 27, excluding "don't know"

Responses (%)	GM food	Transgenic apples	Cisgenic apples
Safe/not risky	27	37	53
Not harmful to the environment	30	55	63
Unnatural	76	78	57
Support	27	33	55

Source: European Commission, 2010

Table 19.1 shows, there were contrasting perceptions of the safety, environmental impacts and naturalness of GM food as a whole, and between cisgenic apples and transgenic apples.

While both GM food and transgenic apples were seen to be "unnatural" by three out of four respondents, transgenic apples were perceived as safer and less likely to harm the environment than GM food in general. This may be because respondents were told beforehand that transgenics have the benefit of limiting pesticide use. Even so, only one in three Europeans was found to support transgenic apples, remaining concerned perhaps about the unnaturalness of between-species manipulation. They do not like the idea of foreign genes.

More than one in two Europeans, however, supported the cisgenic crop, regarding it as safer, environmentally less harmful and not so unnatural. They compared the process to conventional hybridisation, with no worries about crossing a life-form barrier. In other words, there is cause for optimism over second-generation crops engineered using cisgenics. On the whole, however, the picture has been less rosy.

Public opinion, then and now

Figure 19.1 plots responses to Eurobarometer surveys from 1991 to 2010. Respondents were asked how optimistic they were about the potential for biotechnology and genetic engineering to improve people's lives, and whether developments in GM food should be encouraged and supported.

Their answers show a rollercoaster pattern. When biotechnology was at the laboratory stage in the early 1990s, a good proportion of Europeans were enthusiastic about its exuberant claims for feeding the world's hungry. But as the number of

Figure 19.1 Public views on biotechnology and genetically modified foods, 1991–2010

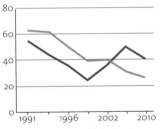

— **Optimism about biotechnology** (zero represents equal proportions of optimists and pessimists)
— **Support for GM foods** (percentage of respondents holding positive views)
Source: European Commission, 2010

applications for the novel technology began to grow, some, such as genetic testing for inherited diseases and disabilities and GM-based medicines gained support, while others – GM crops and food, and animal cloning – did not.

Optimism picked up again with sequencing and analysis of the human genome published in 2001, along with developments in gene therapy, pharmacogenetics, embryonic stem cells and some industrial biotechnologies. Then, between 2005 and 2010, there was another decline.

Support for GM food followed the same trend as optimism about biotechnology until 1999, with both showing a decline. But thereafter, GM lost more ground, driven by several events. Dolly, the sheep, raised fears about where science was going next. The 1996 "mad cow" crisis – bovine spongiform encephalopathy (BSE) – though it

---

BOX 19.2 Genetic modification – a bad start

Fear and distrust have hung over the whole biotechnology enterprise in Europe for a long time. In the late 1980s, even when the technology was still confined to the laboratory, close observers saw public perception becoming negative. According to Mark Cantley, then working in the European Commission: "Public and political opinion was learning to see gene technology, genetic engineering, biotechnology and so on as a single, vague and disquieting phenomenon."

Clearly, education and information were needed to overcome public fears and build trust through scientific, financial, political and environmental accountability. But the warnings went unheeded.

Most scientists, industry and politicians kept their heads in the sand, enthusing over what they perceived as the undoubted health, agricultural and environmental benefits of the new technology. Initially, as the first consumer products came on the market, their confidence was justified.

First to arrive (1987) was vegetarian cheese that had a biotech enzyme in place of traditional animal rennet. Next came the genetically modified tomato, Calgene's Flavr Savr in the USA (1994), subsequently marketed in the UK (1996) through Zeneca's genetically modified tomato purée, which offered 20 per cent more weight than a can of ordinary purée of the same price.

At first, the new products fared well in the marketplace and there was little public debate or consumer resistance, leading industry, shops and government to assume that genetically modified foods had met with consumer acceptance. But this relative optimism over biotechnology and support for genetically engineered food was to erode a great deal over the coming decades.

USDA/PD

The importation of GM soybeans into Europe in 1996 gave rise to media headlines predicting "Frankenfoods".

had nothing to do with genetic modification, pointed up the limitations of scientific expertise. And the importation of GM soya into Europe in 1996 started up a bitter debate: hostility from consumer, environmental and non-governmental organisations, media headlines predicting "Frankenfoods", supermarket boycotts and, eventually, a Europe-wide moratorium on the planting of GM crops.

What really concerns the public?

There is not – and probably never can be – one single cause of Europe's declining support for GM food and crops. The continent has a diversity of social concerns and political opinions, with a wide range of groupings and movements getting involved in the debates, from anti-globalisation lobbies and supporters of natural foods to environmentalists and consumer rights activists.

At the same time, there have been some fairly consistent national attitudes in Europe. From 1996 to 2010, the UK remained the most supportive of GM food while Denmark, Norway, Sweden and Austria consistently showed relatively low levels of support. At the same time, support almost halved in most countries, and in some, such as France, fell even more.

While national events may play a role in these results, the basic causes appear to be common across Europe, namely:

- public perceptions of GM;
- obvious benefits to the biotechnology companies and farmers but an apparent absence of benefits to the consumer;
- food and culture.

Public perceptions of genetic modification

When people read or think about biotechnological innovations their hopes, fears and expectations come into play: their imagination is stirred. They move beyond the reality of any given new technology or product to look at it in the context of past experience or to judge its potential for positive or negative impacts.

Focus group discussions in 11 European countries have tried to capture some of this complexity. From their findings, the public does not seem to be anti-science, but it does have considerable ambivalence about biotechnology, enthusiastically supporting applications designed to cure disease (so called red biotechnology), but worried about GM foods (green biotechnology). They voice this with expressions such as tampering, meddling and interfering with nature. "Nature" here carries two

155

Table 19.2 Public perception: dystopian imaginings

Statement	% of people who realised these statements were false			
	1996	1999	2002	2005
Ordinary tomatoes don't have genes but genetically modified ones do	35	35	36	41
By eating a genetically modified fruit, a person's genes could also become modified	48	42	49	54
Genetically modified animals are always bigger than ordinary ones	36	34	38	45

Source: European Commission, 2006

connotations: a complex biological system that we might disrupt, and a spiritual force. It is this spiritual image that carries the most weight in shaping moral objections, such as those expressed by the UK's Prince Charles.

Eurobarometer surveys spanning a decade of shifting awareness, as shown in Table 19.2, reveal that while the proportion of people rejecting misperceptions about food biotechnologies rose over the period, striking dystopian notions continued to persist among many.

Dystopia, a term coined by John Stuart Mill, the Scottish philosopher and political economist, is an imaginary place in which the condition of life is extremely bad. These misconceptions and concerns run deep. Survey respondents may not have been aware of holding these views before they were posed as questions, but, when asked, they tried to make sense of them and came up with answers shaped by a general unease about the technology, anxieties over food and a kind of magical thinking about adulteration, infection and monstrous outcomes – all of which combined to make them believe the worst.

The human imagination has always populated uncharted territory with monsters of one kind or another – a kind of default response to the unknown. True dragons have yet to come to light.

Who benefits from genetically modified food?

The focus groups also revealed concerns about the absence of perceived benefits from biotechnology, including GM foods. And they raised the possibility of non-GM alternatives to achieve similar ends: why the need to modify food when there is plenty of good, wholesome food in the shops already? Why take risks when tried and tested alternatives already exist for achieving the same claimed benefits? The 2002 Eurobarometer looked at this in more detail. Figure 19.2 shows the results.

Four groups of people emerged. Those who thought GM was beneficial and without risk were labelled "relaxed"; beneficial and risky, "trade-off"; not beneficial and risky,

Figure 19.2 Public perception: risks and benefits of GM food, 2002

Statement		"GM food poses risks for future generations"	
		Agree	Disagree
"GM food will bring benefits to many people"	Agree	**Trade-off: useful and risky** 18% of total sample, of whom 52% encourage GM	**Relaxed: useful and not risky** 14% of total sample, of whom 81% encourage GM
	Disagree	**Sceptical: not useful and risky** 62% of total sample, of whom 17% encourage GM	**Uninterested: not useful and not risky** 6% of total sample, of whom 27% encourage GM

Source: Bennett and Jennings, 2013

"sceptical"; and not beneficial and not risky, "uninterested". A sizeable majority – 62 per cent – fell into the sceptical category, with few of them (17 per cent) thinking that GM should be encouraged. By contrast, 81 per cent of the relaxed group supported GM, but they represent a mere 14 per cent of the European population.

Food, genetic modification and culture

Genetically modified foods date back only a few decades; producing, preparing and consuming food are as old as human society itself.

Over millennia, food has evolved beyond being simply a biological necessity to become a central feature of our culture. With food we not only take in calories, we also absorb beliefs and collective representations of ourselves – we are what we eat.

In the last 50 years, the Western world has moved from food shortages to surpluses, and with this have come anxieties. We are now torn between the appeal of cheap, convenient and palatable – often processed – food and the threats posed by factory farming, pesticides, pollutants and additives that replace natural ingredients. That may be why natural and organic produce has become so popular: it cuts down the perceived distance from farm to fork created by modern processed foods. Naturalness has become a common theme in food advertising – although in fact the amount of organic food sold in the UK and Europe is at most 3 per cent of all food sales and, with the exception of 2013, appears to be in decline.

Agreed EU-wide controls on food labelling were first introduced in 1979. Further controls and a plethora of amendments have since been added, resulting in a complex array of labelling requirements – including ingredients, nutrition, allergens, shelf life, provenance...

157

With modern food production methods, the notion that we are what we eat has been replaced by "we don't know exactly what we eat so we don't know what or who we are". This has led people to try to re-identify with today's food through such strategies as demanding better food labelling, legal protection against chemicals and biotechnology, the adoption of alternative diets – vegetarian, organic, low calorie, low carbohydrate and so on. We look for food that we can trust.

Food biotechnologies appear to clash with these cultural norms and preferences. An extreme example is the cloning of animals for food products. Even though beef and milk from cloned cattle are routinely consumed in the USA, only 18 per cent of Europeans have been found to be willing to support the idea of animal cloning. The bringing together of food – an aspect of culture – with sensitivities about animals and genetic modification, has made the whole idea of cloning unpalatable.

The three explanations discussed above for Europe's resistance to GM food are probably not exhaustive. And their relative importance may differ from country to country.

Segmenting consumer attitudes

A survey of attitudes towards naturalness and the benefits of transgenic and cisgenic apples reveals five different classes of consumer, as shown in Figure 19.3, along with the proportion of Europeans that fall into each category.

Those in category one – giving strong support to both cisgenic and transgenic apples in terms of safety, naturalness and environmental impact – represent just 14 per cent of Europeans, less than those who strongly oppose both techniques (20 per cent). Virtually half of all Europeans are either moderately in favour (26 per cent) or moderately opposed (23 per cent). Most intriguing is the fourth category – strongly negative towards transgenic apples and very enthusiastic about cisgenic varieties. This echoes other survey findings showing support for cisgenic technologies while rejecting genetic transfer between organisms that would not naturally cross breed.

Taking a broader view, the percentage of people attracted by cisgenics is around 30 per cent in 20 of 32 European countries examined, including Denmark, Finland, Germany, Greece, Hungary, Ireland, Sweden and the UK. The question is: will this support increase as people become more familiar with the novel technology?

The introduction of disease resistance genes from crab apples into table varieties takes some 50 years through conventional breeding techniques. Cisgenesis speeds up the process.

Figure 19.3 Public perception: segmenting European consumer attitudes, 2010

Group	1		2		3		4		5	
Expected proportion of Europeans in group	14%		27%		23%		16% Opposition to transgenic; support for cisgenic		20%	
Dominant attitude	Strong support for both		Moderate support for both		Moderate opposition to both				Strong opposition to both	
Item	Trans.	Cis.	Trans.	Cis.	Trans.	Cis.	Trans.	Cis.	Trans.	Cis.
Is promising/useful										
Is safe/not risky and should be encouraged										
Is bad for the environment and makes one uneasy										
Is unnatural										

■ Strongly disagree   ■ Tend to disagree   ■ Tend to agree   ■ Strongly agree

Source: Bennett and Jennings, 2013

Any future for genetically modified crops in Europe?

For the first generation of commodity crops, the outlook seems bleak. It is hard to imagine what might reverse the long downwards trend of public acceptance. For the second generation, however, there are grounds for optimism.

If cisgenic crops achieve the predicted benefits of reducing pesticide residues on fruit and vegetables – the leading food risk concern among Europeans – while supporting biodiversity through reduced chemical spraying, then the public may warm to them.

But public support should not be taken for granted. There has to be transparency about the actual procedures involved in engineering cisgenic crops and recognition that this may raise concerns about unnaturalness. Any benefits should be independently verified, and not overstated.

Lastly, the lessons of the past should not be ignored. The developers of the first generation of GM crops naively, and wrongly, assumed that any public resistance was irrational and would evaporate once GM products were on the market. That did not happen. Trust and consent have to be earned through engaging with the public, treating people as participants, not pawns.

GETTING BACK ON TRACK
Industry's responses to challenges and societal expectations

A host of challenges

The biotechnology industry has faced a range of political, regulatory and public acceptance challenges in recent times. Most of these have come from Europe, which contrasts strongly with countries in North and South America, in particular, which have had high adoption of genetically modified (GM) crops in the past 10–15 years. With GM cotton, the same is true for Australia, Burkina Faso, China and India.

On a global scale, biotechnology is the most rapidly increasing crop technology in the history of agriculture and an integral part of modern farming, with more than half of all GM crops being grown in developing countries since 2012. What has happened in Europe to keep it out of step with – and lagging behind – its global agricultural competitors?

Food is an emotive area

Food advertisers like to stress traditional imagery: the family farm, happy children eating a wholesome breakfast, fresh ingredients ripening in the sun and so on. The general public sees little of the everyday reality of harvesting, producing or processing its food because this would detract from the wholesome, happy vision.

Today's public therefore knows little about modern farming and food production methods, especially people living in richer nations, where the majority are concentrated in urban areas. The whole idea of using modern technology to improve food is alien, and we tend to fear the unknown. Generally, the more we know, the more open we are to innovation.

Cultural traditions also influence attitudes. The population of northern Europe tends to favour agricultural innovation more than those living around the Mediterranean. Take, for instance, the contrast between France and the Netherlands. France is a vast, agriculturally rich expanse producing many desirable foods that are usually marketed as natural or traditionally produced. The Netherlands, on the other hand, is small and densely populated, with a history of being open to new techniques in high-technology greenhouses, hydroponics crops in nutrient solutions, computer-controlled animal feeding systems, animal breeding and so on.

KEY THEMES

- Interest groups opposing genetic modification.
- Poor decision making.
- Misinformation.
- Strategies to overcome hostility.
- Nine lessons learned by industry.

A 2012 UK survey by LEAF (Linking Environment And Farming) found that fewer than half of those surveyed correctly identified butter as coming from cows.

www.drjoanna.com.au

Unsurprisingly, there is widespread aversion to biotechnology in France, while in the Netherlands there is far more support – a direct function of their differing cultural backgrounds and geographic realities.

The scientific ignorance of politicians

Politicians and policy makers can also hinder the acceptance and adoption of biotechnology through their limited understanding of the basic science that underlies it. Few have a scientific background, which means that managing the rules governing the technology or speaking publicly about it is very challenging.

Linked closely to this shortcoming in politicians is the political climate in which biotechnology entered the public arena. People at large lost faith in the ability of the authorities to be honest about scientific issues and protect their health in the wake of "mad cow" disease – bovine spongiform encephalopathy (BSE) – which was first confirmed in 1986. Initially, politicians and scientists alike assured the public that feeding meal made from processed animal parts to herbivorous animals was perfectly safe. But they were proven wrong not just by BSE infection in cattle, but by the emergence of a human variant of the disease a few years later – in 1994. These crucial events shaping public perception of science and politicians in Europe were rapidly followed by the introduction of GM crops.

Genetic modification played absolutely no part in the appearance of "mad cow" disease, but the two became linked in the minds of the public, fuelling fears that modern food production methods could not be trusted.

Some politicians have also played politics with GM to gain advantage. During terrible droughts and famines in Africa, for example, the Zambian president said that his countryfolk would rather starve than eat GM "poison", and rejected food aid from the USA containing GM maize – which had also been claimed to make men sterile. Many European ministers, past and present, still openly attack the safety of the new technology despite thousands of safety assessments and almost two decades of use with no demonstrable adverse health or environmental effects or incidents.

Interest groups

A number of interest groups openly – and not so openly – have reason to manipulate attitudes to biotechnology.

- Food manufacturers and retailers have a variety of attitudes. In most of the Americas there is widespread acceptance and use of GM foods while in Europe there is considerable reluctance. Public resistance and fear of being targeted by campaign groups are probably to blame.
- The main international traders of commodity products may not be opposed to GM products *per se*, but they have a problem. They have to separate out

GM and non-GM supply chains, which complicates their operations and makes them much more costly. In addition, supply and liability problems can occur because a given GM variety may be approved in one jurisdiction but not in another.

- Many organic farming movements oppose GM for both ideological and economic reasons. On the ideological side, it is thought of as unnatural and therefore hostile to organic principles. Economically, the argument is that GM methods are incompatible with organic practices due to possible cross-fertilisation of crops in bordering fields. Ironically, it might well be that since GM production allows for reduced pesticide use, making output cheaper and less polluting than its organic counterparts, it could even be less environmentally damaging. Traditional Bordeaux mixture, for example, composed of copper sulphate and lime, is frequently used in organic farming as a fungicide even though its run-off into streams and rivers is toxic to wildlife.

- Some international development groups are opposed to GM production methods because they fear that they could disempower farmers and so impede development. Others, including leading charities such as the Bill and Melinda Gates Foundation and Oxfam, lend their support to the new technologies.

- Adding to the general uncertainty, countries with large-scale food production compete with other regions cultivating GM products – which is why there has been a race in the Americas to reduce approval time for new crops.

There is ample evidence from international experts and local farmers that modern biotechnology aids development and drives more predictable and sustainable food production.

Unsatisfactory decision making

A major challenge facing the biotech industry is the current state of decision-making systems, which tend to be politicised, dysfunctional or plain non-existent.

In some countries there are simply no legal or technical processes in place for assessing and approving the new technologies, or for allowing field trials. They may have been set up in the past but now lack the financial resources or trained personnel to maintain them. Other countries may have the legal or technical processes but these are just dysfunctional – for example, most Directorates-General of the European Commission do support GM, and it is in the European Council representing the Member States and European Parliament that discord and delay occur.

Most problematic, however, are countries or regions where decision making has been politicised – and the EU is no exception. Here, the approach to approving products is, in theory, science-based. In reality it is not, for three reasons:

- First, the decision-making process sets independent scientific judgements on safety made by the European Food Safety Authority (EFSA) against the political views of national politicians who vote on that safety assessment before approving GM products. The result is a constant calling into question of the scientists' assessments about safety by some politicians, thereby undermining public trust in the science.
- Second, the EU system makes a distinction between approving products for import and those for cultivation. Products for import are regularly approved because they are grown in major commodity-growing countries that export to the EU. However, they are not approved for cultivation. So, Europeans are importing GM produce for both human and animal consumption, but are not allowed to benefit from growing it on European soil.
- Third, the EU has a threshold level above which products with GM content must be labelled. However, Europeans indirectly consume, through animal feed, more than 30 million tonnes of GM protein every year in the form of unlabelled meat, eggs, milk and other animal products whether they recognise it or not. That is the equivalent of 60 kilos of GM product per year for every one of the 733 million European consumers, of which 505 million are in the EU.

The role of misinformation

Some – but not all – of the interest groups opposed to GM have been highly successful in injecting biased information into the public domain. Wild claims and scare stories about GM crops have been promoted over the years since their introduction. But none of these has come true. According to a report by the European Commission in 2010 on *A Decade of EU-Funded GMO Research*, studies of more than 2 trillion GM food meals eaten show no negative effects on health or the environment. Biotech crops have an excellent record.

The claims by anti-GM groups that Europeans are opposed to GM food and crops are often based on incorrect interpretations of opinion polls. The polls themselves can be misleading too. They might, for example, ask people to state how worried they are about GM or to say whether they agree or disagree with statements such as "GM food is unnatural". These kinds of questions effectively prompt answers in a pre-determined direction.

A more open-ended approach can elicit a different response. One of the questions in a 2010 Eurobarometer survey, instead of asking "How worried are you by...", simply

Despite reluctance to accept genetically modified foods, the average European consumes 60 kilos of meat, eggs, milk and other products from animals raised on genetically modified fodder every year.

David Benbennick/PD

asked people to say what things come to mind when thinking about possible problems or risks associated with food. In this case, only 8 per cent of Europeans spontaneously identified worries about GM.

Members of the mainstream media, too, admit that they may have made mistakes in their coverage of GM issues. Early on they were quick to publicise claims by anti-GM groups, casting them in the role of David versus the Goliath of big business dominating our food chain – thereby acting as consumer champions. But now, those same journalists – many of whom lack scientific training – have wondered whether they were too ready to take sides in what was, and still is, an attractive media controversy.

Argentina and the USA are working to simplify and shorten the regulatory process for new genetically modified food crops.

Some governments have also injected questionable information into the public arena. The Ministry of Health of one European government joined with Greenpeace and organised a press conference to present new research claiming possible health damage from GM food. When the research was later shown to be deeply scientifically flawed, the ministry had to publicly retract it.

The cost of regulatory compliance

It takes a great deal of time and money to develop GM crops, from initial discovery to final authorisation and planting. A new biotech trait can take over three years to obtain regulatory approval and cost as much as € 140 million to introduce.

There is also pressure between different regulatory systems. In 2011, Argentina announced that it intended to reduce the time required for product approval, followed in 2012 by the USA saying that it was going to introduce efficiencies to halve the time needed.

The challenge posed by the cost and complexity of the EU's regulatory system for GM crops should, given lack of evidence of harm to people or the environment, lead to a system based on that evidence.

How has industry dealt with these challenges? To combat the factors impeding the progress of new biotechnologies in Europe, a range of strategies has been deployed.

Proactive communications

The biotech industry initially thought that the European public's hostility to GM in the mid-1990s stemmed from a misunderstanding of the science behind the new products and technology. This was wrong. Public opinion was shaped by a more complex combination of lack of scientific knowledge, lack of trust in science and policy makers, and a romantic if misconceived view of food production. In other words, the public's attitude was moulded not so much by science as by feelings and emotions.

The core of the debate was fear of science and its manipulation of nature. Industry should have been focusing on this subjective element rather than trying to communicate how safe, and how like existing products, the new GM products were. No amount of scientific information could dispel the worry created by words such as "Frankenfoods" used by GM's opponents. The fact that scientists seemed to be arguing among themselves did not help matters either, driving up levels of public confusion and anxiety.

After a poor start, industry rallied by embarking on a proactive, locally focused communications effort. Unfortunately, by then, the European approval system meant that no new products were available on which to have a meaningful discussion with the public. Meanwhile, mistrust remained about those products on which governments had imposed a moratorium. The only products that could be discussed were being grown elsewhere and could only be imported into Europe to feed animals, not humans.

Given that Europeans have access to plentiful, inexpensive food, it is not surprising that they remain largely unaware of the benefits that biotechnology can offer.

Small wonder then that industry failed to gain the trust of Europeans who anyway had plenty of cheap food and could not see the need for GM alternatives. More recently, though, the debate has shifted. From trying unsuccessfully to communicate about the science of GM to a public with neither the time nor the interest to delve deeply into the technicalities, industry has moved the focus towards issues such as global responsibilities and freedom of choice. The dialogue today is less about getting safety approval for marketing new products and more about where, when, why and by whom such products are being used and the availability of choice between non-GM and GM foods.

In other words, discussions about GM now centre on the original reason for developing the new products and processes: to produce more and better food, and with fewer inputs, in order to meet the demands of the growing global population. Freedom, human rights and feeding the world fairly, especially people living in food and economic poverty in the developing world, are emotive topics that the public can understand and engage with. This has also resulted in a more balanced exchange of views within the media and among politicians.

Better public affairs effort

In the 1980s, industrial GM organisations had a broad-brush, generalist approach to public affairs revolving around how they managed their relationships with various stakeholders to explain company policies, provide information and debate issues affecting their operations.

This did not work well. Industry began to realise that, with GM, it had to be far more focused in its communications efforts because each region has its own rules for governing the approval and marketing of GM products. Whereas North America, for example, makes assessments based on the product rather than on whether GM is used in the production process, Europe has a process-based approach. A country-by-country strategy is therefore essential.

Because GM commodities are traded globally, the different regulatory systems around the world should not impede the free movement of goods – as laid down by World Trade Organization rules. The industry's public affairs policies have to take this into account alongside its scientific discussions at the heart of the various approval systems around the world.

Summing up: lessons from experience

The biotechnology community has learned nine important lessons from its experience in facing the many challenges to GM over the years.

1 Risk assessment measures devised by politicians without a proper scientific basis do not contribute to improved safety or increased public trust.

2 The influence of anti-GM interests on the EU's decisions means that the rate of uptake of biotechnology is determined by regulatory systems rather than by the needs of farmers or the public, or even scientific progress.

3 Initially, the biotechnology community was ill-prepared for aggressive media campaigns and failed to counter them effectively. Misleading claims should be corrected immediately, as false myths are very difficult to dispel. The only way is through discussion about existing products, consistent safety and clear-cut benefits.

4 The public is not helped by discussions based on science: they need to focus on real, tangible products and benefits.

5 Many Europeans are reconsidering their previously negative position on GM crops and food. They are beginning to see them as an answer to hunger and malnutrition, helping the developing world raise production and counter rural poverty. Europeans are also realising that scaremongering claims are

Figure 20.1 Awareness of genetically modified food
EU 27, 2010

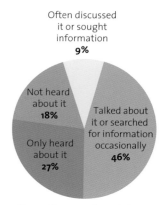

Source: European Commission, 2010

European attitudes to genetically modified food may change as people learn more about it.

overstated and that the rest of the world is adopting GM at a rapid rate, leaving the EU on the economic and development sidelines. In addition, they believe that GM crops could help solve environmental problems.

6 European consumers rely heavily on foreign produce to meet their food needs. But the countries from which the EU imports are becoming less and less sensitive to the non-GM preferences of some Europeans.

7 Most of the countries in the EU that oppose GM have a culture in which science and innovation are relatively undervalued.

8 Worldwide, farmers want to be able to cultivate GM crops because they benefit economically from them. When allowed to, they choose GM and stick with the technology.

9 Europe's foot-dragging over GM crops has slowed uptake of the technology in developing countries that follow or are influenced by the EU's example, especially in Africa.

WHEN BIOTECHNOLOGY HITS THE HEADLINES
A challenge for scientists and the media

21

Surprising rejection of genetic modification

Journalists across the media – electronic and print – were somewhat taken by surprise when the European public rejected genetic modification (GM). The Calgene Flavr Savr tomato, followed by Zeneca's GM tomato paste, had been greeted by mild enthusiasm when they came on the market in the mid-1990s; they were certainly not seen as a threat. Indeed, with the help of obliging chefs making up a pasta sauce, journalists used the arrival of the tomato paste to fill space on a slow news day: a bit of fun. The advent of a new GM cheese using non-animal rennet and suitable for vegetarians also caused no special stir with the public or the media for several years.

In fact, GM technology at the time was far from being a problem for the public. On the contrary, people were aware of the huge medical benefits of advances such as GM insulin for treating diabetes. They were also becoming aware of the basics of the technology: that living entities could be changed or improved by rearranging their fundamental biological components.

The tone of the media's treatment of the new science continued to be quite light hearted. As advances in GM research emerged from specialist journals and conferences, they were reported in "gee-whizz" fashion. Could a jellyfish gene, for example, be inserted into a cereal and be programmed to switch on if the crop became stressed by sudden infestation, glowing in the dark to help farmers direct (and limit) their pesticide sprays? Could ultra-nutritious superfoods be devised? Or fruit carrying life-saving vaccines for the developing world? And so on.

Journalists' limited knowledge

Alongside this slightly jokey approach to reporting GM, the media also encountered a comprehension problem. Many of even the most experienced and skillful writers and broadcasters had trouble understanding the language and concepts of the new technologies.

Journalists were also aware of the fact that the general public, too, would have difficulties with this new vocabulary. Every time they wrote or broadcast a story, the

KEY THEMES

- The nature of science in the media.
- Lessons from the past.
- Need for impartiality and scepticism.
- Value of being proactive with the media.

The Flavr Savr tomato was the first commercially grown genetically modified food to be granted a license for human consumption. Submitted to the US Food and Drug Administration in 1992, it went on sale just two years later.

media needed to give a simple explanation in the hope that this would provide adequate background.

One journalist, the distinguished science editor of the UK's *The Guardian* newspaper, Tim Radford, doubts whether the media had the ability to give sufficient background information, not because they explained badly or because readers failed to understand, rather because of the nature of the media and of the science itself: "People read newspapers very selectively and lose interest very quickly, especially if the stories they read contain almost meaningless acronyms and unfamiliar words such as 'mitochondrion', or 'genotype' ... molecular biology is quite difficult to understand even at the simplest level: most of us are not accustomed to thinking of ourselves as composites of 100 trillion cells of 200 to 300 distinct types, organised by 3.8 billion years of natural selection."

To make matters worse, the biological sciences were rapidly adding thousands of new words and meanings to its lexicon, placing an ever heavier burden on the journalist both to understand what scientists were actually saying and to report on it accurately.

Enter Dolly, the sheep

The cloning of Dolly, the sheep, in 1996 by Ian Wilmut and colleagues at the Roslin Institute in Scotland was a key episode in the public's perception of modern science. Dolly was the first mammal to be cloned from an adult body cell using the delicate process of nuclear transfer. Scientifically, it was a significant advance. Ethically, it rang alarm bells in the minds of the public.

Many of even the most experienced and skillful journalists had trouble understanding the language and concepts of the new technologies.

The cloned animal was regarded by many as science fiction come true, conjuring up visions of Mary Shelley's *Frankenstein* or HG Wells's *The Island of Dr Moreau* and evoking the stereotype of the mad scientist interfering with nature. Then, in the same year, came another reason to distrust agricultural science. The UK government announced that a human variant of the brain disease affecting cows – bovine spongiform encephalopathy (BSE) – might have been transmitted to an unknown number of people.

Scientists, however, had previously stated that this could not happen. More public unease ensued, planting seeds of disquiet for what was to follow later when Britain and other European countries started to reject the notion of GM food as well as research into GM crops.

A wonderful media opportunity

The alarm, outrage and protest over GM surprised not just scientists and journalists, but even the campaign groups that organised anti-GM events. Suddenly, prime-time television news bulletins were giving airtime to opponents of the new genetics, and newspaper editors were hunting for stories to feed the public's interest in bio-technology and its products.

The media exploited this new opportunity in different ways. Some journalists tried to explain the science behind the technology in some detail; others played on public alarm with such headlines as "Scientists warn of GM crops link to meningitis". It was at this time that the UK's *Daily Mail* coined its resonant "Frankenfood" label.

The reaction of scientists also varied. Some vigorously defended the innovative technology, others remained silent. One could argue that the latter group missed an opportunity to put messages across to the public in easy-to-understand, plain language that would help correct any misconceptions.

Dolly, the sheep, proved that a cell taken from a specific part of the body – in this case a mammary gland – could recreate a whole individual. Her eventual fate was taxidermy.

Lessons from the past

What can journalists, or scientists who need to work with the media, learn from these episodes? Clearly, the GM debate as well as research into the molecular biology of plants are here to stay. So, too, are those who are hostile to the technology. Some see biotech advances as needless or valueless. Others find genetic mani-pulation inherently dangerous. Then there are those who regard science not as serving the needs of the hungry and deprived but the interests of multinational companies and global capitalism.

The duty of the journalist is to report all the science accurately and fairly. At the same time, the media in general has a duty to reflect the preoccupations and anxieties of society at large, listening to them and trying to make sense of how these worries arise.

And the media has another preoccupation. It has to sell newspapers and persuade people to watch TV or listen to the radio in a highly competitive industry that is also now trying to come to terms with the internet revolution. That is their job, and it is a different job from that of the scientist. In any future coverage of the GM issue, however, the media should bear in mind several questions about science reporting.

How much does the general public know about science? People are very good at assessing the immediate importance of scientific information when it is properly presented to them. But they cannot be expected to remember technical material from one day to the next: they have many other pressing interests and concerns.

Several decades ago a journalist could not use an acronym like "DNA" without explaining it in general terms. Today, DNA is part of most people's linguistic repertoire even if they cannot define it with any precision. Molecular science is moving quickly, but it takes time to use new terms comfortably, and public understanding struggles to keep up.

Is public suspicion about GM likely to endure? Not necessarily. Today, techniques such as organ transplants and *in vitro* fertilisation – test tube babies – are a familiar part of the medical landscape. But when they were first reported in the media they provoked anxieties, even outrage in some people. Their suspicions ebbed away as the new therapies began to deliver valued treatments.

What do people mean by "natural"? Natural is a tricky word. Modern staple crops – wheat, maize, rice and so on – are very different from their natural wild ancestors, which were first domesticated 10,000 years ago. The Green Revolution has seen dramatic changes brought about both by new crop strains and by improved management through the use of pesticides and fertilisers, irrigation control, careful planting schedules and so on. None of this is natural in the strict sense of being untouched by humankind. And nor are the engineered plants of today that draw on advances in molecular biology.

A survey carried out in the UK in 1989 discovered that one in three people did not know whether the Earth went round the Sun or *vice versa*, and two in three did not know how long it took.

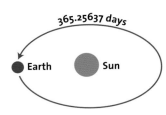

365.25637 days

Earth   Sun

Will GM crops really feed the world? The idea that GM crops provide the answer to the world's food supply problems needs to be looked at closely.

Only about 11 per cent of the planet's land surface is suitable for farming, with a significant fraction already degraded through overgrazing, mismanagement, erosion and excessive irrigation. What is more, projected increases in global population will cut even deeper into the total growing area, while the finite nature of oil supplies will drive more and more farmers to seek commercial gain through planting biofuel crops rather than food, although this is changing as biofuels are developed using crop wastes. When the effects of global warming – sea-level rise and changing rainfall and temperature patterns – are added to the mix, the capacity of the new genetics to come to the rescue, while significant, looks limited.

Certainly, GM crops could help alleviate conditions in some places. New strains are being developed that survive sustained drought and recover with the rains, or flourish in saline soil, or deliver higher levels of nutrition. But GM technology on its own cannot resolve all the difficulties ahead: it is no silver bullet. These problems demand political, social and economic willpower, and cooperation at an international level.

What do campaigners mean by the "hazards" of GM crops? Basically, they appear to mean that synthetically designed strains of crop – as opposed to those painstakingly produced over time by traditional breeding – could deliver unintended consequences. These could be of several kinds. There could be a hazard inherent in the very technique of splicing an alien gene into a food crop. Undesirable effects might result from introducing a trait that natural selection would have eliminated. GM traits could cross species barriers, entering the environment and putting local species at risk. An apparently benign alien gene might turn out to be a health hazard for consumers or other species. A malicious (or even simply unwitting) scientist could devise a dangerous organism. The list goes on.

Only 11 per cent of the world's land area is cultivable. The rest is too shallow (22 per cent), too wet (10 per cent), too dry (28 per cent), has chemical limitations (23 per cent) or is permafrost (6 per cent).

Source: FAO

The media needs to be aware of all these questions and try to see GM in its true perspective. Most modern cereal crops survive only because they are tended, fertilised, weeded, sprayed, harvested and then sown again in cultivated land: in the wild, they would not survive at all. And GM crops would perish just as swiftly as crops bred by traditional methods. In addition, GM crops are most likely to have been modified to reduce pesticide or fertiliser use, and therefore might even benefit their local ecosystem.

Genetically modified crops have been harvested for nearly two decades, during which there has been no demonstrable harm to a single human being eating them. Where then is the evidence that they are dangerous to human health?

The real hazard to biodiversity is not biotechnology, but population growth, intensive farming, climate change, pollution and the destruction of habitat. Compared with these, any additional consequences from GM are likely to be small.

Need for scepticism

The media must remain sceptical but impartial. We cannot know what the future will bring. Just as nuclear technology and medical science have the potential to be misused, so too might advances in GM. In fact, almost anything humans use can be a force for good or ill: a hammer can both build things and kill. It is humans who choose how a technology is deployed.

The fact that acknowledged experts or confident politicians say that something is safe should not be enough to satisfy journalists or prevent them from asking awkward questions. That is their job: to challenge authority in the public interest.

Research on media coverage

A number of academic studies have investigated how the media has dealt with the GM debate. One important finding is that the topic very quickly ceased to be handled solely by science journalists because it had become a social, political and environmental issue, so was picked up by journalists working in these or broader fields. Had it remained with specialist reporters familiar with the language and concepts of biotechnology, it might not have become as contentious as it did for their colleagues with a less scientific background.

At the same time, it is perfectly proper for the media to ask penetrating questions about the purpose, direction, financing and business implications of GM. A science specialist is not always the best person to explore the industrial, economic and human welfare implications – positive and negative – of a technology.

A telling contrast in media know-how

There is no doubt that the public's response to GM was disastrous for the application of the new technology in Europe as compared with the rest of the world.

BOX 21.1 Science and people

Scientists need to come out of the laboratory and engage with the public.

- Everyone pays for science via taxes. So it rests on popular support.
- It follows that there is an obligation on scientists and it is in their interest to explain their science.
- Unfortunately there is no corresponding obligation upon anyone to listen, so scientists should regard themselves as obliged to make themselves heard and see this as an opportunity, not just a duty.
- If they are going to talk to people, they had better use the language of the people.
- This means using a language that is understood and gets attention.
- They must also listen to, understand and respond to people's concerns.

Would it have been better if its advocates had taken a different approach to the media? The introduction of embryonic stem-cell therapy as a possible treatment for serious diseases suggests that it certainly would. Scientists working in this potentially contentious field set about getting the public and the media on their side from the outset. They enlisted the help of charities and patient groups, provoked a national debate, confronted criticism from the world's religions and others worried about moral or ethical questions, and helped politicians to see the strength of their arguments and to make appropriate changes to legislation.

The real hazard to biological diversity is not biotechnology but the burgeoning human population, intensive farming, climate change, pollution and the destruction of habitat.

Most of all though, they had made sure – even before embarking on the research – that the public knew exactly what they were doing and why they were doing it, emphasising clear-cut medical benefits. They trusted the public's judgement.

These scientists were prepared to explain the complexities of their work and its ambitions in straightforward, vivid and easily understood language. The media, for its part, responded eagerly because here were genuinely good stories to tell a receptive public. Many journalists also felt that they were able to make a contribution to public acceptance of the new science.

Contrast this with the early days of GM technology, when scientists and industry seemed to feel that it was enough simply to have a good idea. It did not have to be sold to the public through clear and convincing explanations of benefits and the airing of possible hazards; they did not need to make any special efforts with the media to ensure that journalists sympathised with their efforts. Good science, they felt, was sufficient in itself.

In short, they did too little to persuade others, with the help of the media, that their ideas had genuine value. The ongoing debates and controversies show how misguided that attitude was. It was an experience that, later on, stem cell researchers learned from, as did those working in nanotechnology and other cutting-edge fields.

22

A TALE OF TWO PARADIGMS
The environmental movement's viewpoint

KEY THEMES

- Environmentalists' objections.
- Two conflicting agricultural models.
- Social constitution.

The year 1996 ushered in a battle over the rights and wrongs of genetic modification that has yet to play out.

Sailing into dispute

The year 1996 was a significant one in the history of opposition to genetic modification (GM). It was then that a small fleet of inflatable boats from Greenpeace set out to prevent the first ships carrying Monsanto's GM soybeans from the USA – bound for Europe – from docking in Rotterdam harbour. At the same time, the first banners calling for a halt to GM foods were unfurled at the head offices of major food manufacturers and supermarket chains.

It was as if a starting pistol had been fired. From that point on, many environmental and other non-governmental organisations (NGOs) continued their campaign against Monsanto's soybeans and other GM crops. This had an influence on organic farmers, food producers and retailers, all concerned about possible economic losses ensuing from having GM constituents in their products.

Now, there are signs that the concerns of the food producers are lessening, and that Europe's major consumer organisations have almost given up campaigning against GM. They appear satisfied that EU regulations governing market approval and labelling ensure the safety of GM foods entering European markets.

Many environmentalists, however, remain firm. So what are they really worried about? Why continue to target GM soybeans nearly two decades on?

Petition from Toxicsoy.org

In February 2012, a petition signed by 26,000 people from across Europe was sent by the campaign group Toxicsoy.org to major food retailers in the EU, calling for them to turn their back on GM produce. Their argument was that: "Europe imports 34 million tonnes of GM soya every year, mainly to feed factory-farmed animals, [so] this system can never be called responsible and does not deserve a green label."

This is a typical tactic of environmental NGOs: they draw attention to the organisations in the agri-food chain that use GM soybean ingredients and are close to the consumer. They see Monsanto's soybeans as a key component of factory farming that ends in cheap meat products.

They also object more directly to growing GM soybeans. Monsanto's Roundup-Ready soya has been engineered to be resistant to Monsanto's own herbicide Roundup, which is based on glyphosate and which, according to Toxicsoy.org, has had serious health impacts on humans and wildlife. In order to control weeds, the pesticide is repeatedly sprayed by plane over large areas, without affecting the soybean plants but severely damaging, they claim, humans, water sources and other crops.

The emperor has no clothes

Another attack on Monsanto in particular and genetically modified organisms (GMOs) in general comes from a global coalition of 21 NGOs from North and South America, Europe, Africa and the Asia-Pacific region. They issued a Global Citizens Report with the title *The GMO Emperor Has No Clothes* – a reference to the fable by Hans Christian Andersen in which no one dares tell an authority figure the truth. For the NGOs, the emperor is Monsanto: "Its promises to increase crop yields and feed the hungry have proven to be false; its genetic engineering to control weeds and pests has created superweeds and superpests. Yet the Emperor struts around hoping the illusion will last and the courtiers, not wanting to be seen as stupid, will keep applauding and pretending they see the magnificent robes of the GMO Emperor."

The long report then goes on to examine in detail a series of "false promises":
- *GM crops lower levels of chemical insecticides and pesticides.* The report suggests otherwise: several case studies from the USA, Argentina, Brazil and India are cited which show increases in the use of chemicals and the emergence of herbicide-resistant weeds that demand even more toxic chemicals to control them.
- *Genetically engineered crops can be bred for drought tolerance and other traits conferring resilience to climatic conditions.* When the US Department of Agriculture carried out an environmental risk assessment of Monsanto's drought-tolerant GM maize, it suggested that comparable varieties produced through conventional breeding are readily available. The NGOs contend that the many hundreds of patents taken out on GM are nothing but bio-piracy because traits such as drought tolerance were not invented by genetic engineering: they already exist in nature.
- *GM foods are safe.* The report cites independent studies showing that GM foods can damage health. It also notes that the biotechnology industry has repeatedly attacked scientists carrying out independent research on GMOs and offers evidence that "bad science" has been used to suppress environmental and safety assessments of GM crops.

Opponents of genetically modified crops claim they do not reduce pesticide use, that patents taken out on some crops are effectively bio-piracy, and that the resulting foods can damage human health.

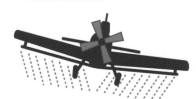

Environmentalists argue that efforts to promote bioscience in the media and political arenas have failed to win public support.

- *GM, conventional and organic crops can co-exist peacefully.* According to many NGOs, this is another falsehood promoted by the biotechnology industry. The report argues that cross-pollination is unavoidable and cites several cases of GM plants contaminating fields.

Importance of patents

The Global Citizens Report argues that the patenting of GM seeds lies at the heart of the agri-industry's interest in GMOs. The GM firms have, by lobbying governments, buying up seed companies and withdrawing conventional seeds from the market, marketed their crops to 15 million farmers. Patents, mergers and licensing agreements give them monopolies on seeds such that nearly half of all sales worldwide are controlled by just three multinational companies: Monsanto, Dupont and Syngenta.

The NGOs argue that the world is losing, along with biodiversity, its seed and food freedom, along with food democracy and food sovereignty. This takes the debate into different territory. The NGOs are assessing the offerings of biotechnology not just from a health or environmental perspective. They are also judging them from a socio-economic standpoint.

The Golden Triangle

Environmentalists see themselves in combat with what has been called a Golden Triangle of interlocking players: government, industry and science. These three factions in many European and other countries around the world express frustration at NGO campaigns that accuse them of irresponsible behaviour, especially in light of the need to confront global challenges such as hunger and climate change.

To counter these accusations, the Golden Triangle has, alongside its expenditure, public and private, on developing GM and other genomics-based plant breeding tools, spent large sums of money on social science research, consumer surveys and public communication.

The environmentalists, meanwhile, argue that after 15 years of efforts to promote the new technologies in the media and political arenas, the Golden Triangle has failed to win the public debate.

A tale of two paradigms

If one looks more closely at this clash between opposing parties, what emerges is a battle between two agricultural philosophies.

The NGOs criticise genetic engineering and the agro-industrial system that supports it on the grounds that they promote what is known as the Life Sciences paradigm – the dominant model of the past 20 years or so. This promises to make agriculture more sustainable through greater efficiencies – by engineering genetically precise changes to plants to protect them from external threats and increase their productivity. Under this paradigm, the research and development agenda favours new knowledge that can be kept in private, commercial hands.

The NGO philosophy is shaped by the very different Agro-Ecology paradigm. This promises to maintain eco-efficiency by keeping growing cycles as short and as closed as possible in order to use biologically diverse resources more effectively, as is the case for example with organic farming.

Herb Pilcher/USDA ARS/PD

According to the Agro-Ecology model, sustainability problems stem from the fact that farmers' knowledge of natural resources and how to use them has been displaced by laboratory knowledge and the demands of distant commodity chains. State-run research has tended to shut out agro-ecology. The incremental improvements made locally by farmers have generally been undervalued by officialdom; the state has valued instead laboratory-based biotechnology research.

Some claim that improvements made by local farmers have generally been undervalued in favour of laboratory-based biotechnology research.

Thus, the Golden Triangle has shifted state research agendas towards specialist laboratory-based knowledge. The environmentalists argue that this has largely dismantled disinterested science and training for the public good, along with extension services designed to take research and new knowledge on agricultural practices out to the farmer. In their place are public-private partnerships based on the belief that scientific research can best drive successful innovation if it is aimed at market opportunities.

There is no doubt that the Life Sciences paradigm has been dominating its Agro-Ecology opposition. Is there any sign of this changing?

A key report: towards a change of direction?
In 2008, a study commissioned by the UN and World Bank was published through the International Assessment of Agricultural Science and Technology for Development (IAASTD), an intergovernmental body involving more than 400 scientists and 30 governments. The IAASTD findings were that the global agricultural system needed to change radically in order to avoid future environmental and social problems. Although recent advances had increased food production,

the benefits were spread unevenly around the world, with more than 800 million people still not getting enough food.

For NGOs this publication was a call to arms. Greenpeace, for example, saw its core message as "the urgent need to move away from destructive and chemical-dependent industrial agriculture and to adopt environmental modern farming methods that champion biodiversity and benefit local communities". At the same time, Greenpeace acknowledged that, although the report was well balanced and scientific, it would take a good deal of work in the coming years to persuade the relevant decision makers of its value.

The prediction was accurate. Although as many as 60 governments signed up to the findings, some major grain producers and heavy users of genetic engineering – Australia, Canada and the USA – rejected the IAASTD report. The biotechnology industry had already pulled out of the consultation process before it was published.

Today, the impact of the report on public and private agricultural research and innovation is still in doubt. Its recommendations do not appear, for example, to have been taken up in the EU's Common Agricultural Policy. The NGOs contend that, given the extensive interests of the Golden Triangle in developed and emerging economies, they are likely to continue to try to shape agricultural research and development (R&D) according to the Life Sciences paradigm – turning farming into a biomass production line for food, feed, fibre and fuel.

The IAASTD suggested that the global agricultural system needs to change radically to avoid future environmental and social problems.

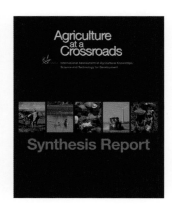

Suspicions about philanthropy
Environmentalists also distrust various philanthropic initiatives such as the Alliance for a New Green Revolution in Africa. Operating across Africa, this programme, which is dedicated to establishing food security, has received millions of dollars from donors including the Bill and Melinda Gates Foundation and billionaire investor Warren Buffet. The NGOs claim that this apparent altruism is opening up huge new markets for the agri-industry by persuading farmers to depend on its seeds and chemicals. They contend that this will, in effect, lay the foundations for the large-scale influx of GMOs into Africa, especially since the Gates Foundation has already stated its belief that GMOs will form part of the solution to the continent's hunger problem.

The issue of social constitution
The clash of paradigms, representing the NGOs on one hand and government, science and industry on the other, clearly encapsulates the position of the

environmentalists towards GM and other innovative technologies. But this is not the whole story.

For the NGOs, the real issue at stake is not the rightness or wrongness of the arguments but what they call the social constitution of the new technology. By this they mean that the political and economic interests of those who own and control the technology will largely determine how it is used.

It would, according to Greenpeace, be disastrous for a new technology to be in the hands of those who care little about environmental or human health, or the social consequences of its use. They advocate thorough public scrutiny, as a matter of democratic right, of any new technology before financial or political commitments make it impossible to go into reverse. If public debate and stakeholder scrutiny are to mean anything, it is argued, they should at least ask the following questions concerning social constitution:

- Who is in control?
- Where can I get information that I trust?
- On what terms is the technology being introduced?
- What risks apply, with what certainty, and for whom?
- Where do the benefits fall?
- Do the risks and benefits fall to the same people?
- Who takes responsibility for resulting problems?

Only by addressing such questions about agricultural research and innovation openly, transparently and democratically can the public controversy over GM in both developed and developing countries be resolved. If the Golden Triangle continues to monopolise agricultural research and innovation, the NGOs will continue, through the media, consumer networks, supermarket chains and food manufacturers, to criticise official risk assessments of genetic engineering technologies and to point out the agro-ecological alternatives.

To overcome antipathy to genetically modified food, scientists, industry and governments must be clear and transparent about:

- **who is in control;**
- **where to find trustworthy information;**
- **the terms under which the technology is being introduced;**
- **what the risks are and for whom;**
- **who stands to benefit;**
- **who takes responsibility for any emerging problems.**

DIFFERENT WORLDS OR COMMON GROUND?
Understanding the social and ethical issues

KEY THEMES

- Two key areas of difference.
- Intellectual property rights.
- The difficulty of reaching common ground.
- Attempts to relocate the debate.

From battleground to common ground

The ferocious debate surrounding genetic modification (GM) has become polarised to the point of deadlock. Both sides, for and against the technology, argue their case with equal conviction and authority. Both make totally contradictory claims about the dangers or benefits of adopting GM. The two factions seem to live in different worlds. Finding a middle way through the debate is extremely difficult.

Bones of contention

There are several areas of difference. One is environmental: the development of superweeds, the levels of pesticides that need to be used with GM crops, whether GM agriculture reduces carbon emissions, and so on. Another argument concerns yield: do GM crops really deliver the promised improvements?

But undoubtedly the two issues that really matter to a world facing global food shortages and hunger through economic deprivation are:
- What are the socio-economic implications of GM crops and food?
- Do GM foods affect human health?

Both sides in the debate are concerned about the welfare of the poor, but they disagree over the capacity of GM to help matters. Advocates see the technology overcoming problems of food production in emerging economies, while opponents regard it as an exploitative tool in the hands of multinational companies.

Whatever their other views, opponents and advocates of genetically modified food are concerned about the welfare of the poor and food deficient.

Pros and cons

The socio-economic argument over GM concerns wealth creation and distribution. Its advocates argue that the technology will contribute to the productivity and livelihoods of farmers worldwide, especially poor smallholder growers in emerging economies. Opponents take a different stance. They believe that GM will not benefit those who need it most but rich multinationals, with knowledge and wealth being in the hands of a few.

The health debate runs like this. The pro-GM lobby argues that there is no evidence of harm to human health from GM foods. People have been eating them for many years with no adverse reactions. The anti-GM campaigners say quite the opposite and point to cases such as tobacco smoking or asbestos use, where similar claims were made but turned out to be wrong.

Where do scientists fit into this polarised picture, alongside the multinationals and the non-governmental organisations (NGOs) with their black and white positions? In general, the scientific community supports the development of these technologies – a power for good that will bring benefits to humankind, alleviating hunger and helping to bring about global equity. At the same time, however, scientists believe that the fruits of their research should be not in private hands but

BOX 23.1 Birth of an industry

Today's biotech industry can be said to have started with the Californian company Genentech. In 1978 it brought the first commercial application of genetic modification to the market – a bacterium modified using recombinant DNA techniques to produce human insulin, the hormone needed to control diabetes.

But there was a problem. There was no protection for the intellectual property in the modified bacterium: the USA had a longstanding policy of not issuing patents for products of nature, including forms of life. In other words, Genentech's research and investment were not secure. Anyone could make use of – and money from – their efforts.

That changed in 1980, however, when the US Supreme Court narrowly found in favour of an appeal from a biochemist at General Electric – Ananda Chakrabarty – against a similar ruling from the US Patent Office on a bacterium engineered (not using GM techniques) to disperse oil slicks. Chakrabarty's organism was not considered a product of nature but a man-made living organism and so could be patented.

The way then was open for Genentech to patent their organism, and for industry to pour investment into research on novel organisms, without fear of plagiarism by competitors. In the following 20 years, biotechnology companies grew in size and number as they assembled the expertise, techniques and materials needed to put genetically modified organisms on the market.

Concurrently, scientists in universities and academic research institutes were also intensifying their efforts to create genetically modified organisms that would confer benefits to society, including crops engineered for improving health and nutrition in the developing world. Ingo Potrykus and Peter Beyer, in conjunction with the company Syngenta, with their Golden Rice to curb vitamin A deficiency, were among the most successful. Unlike some of the companies, though, their motivation was not for profit but altruism, as the new rice was and remains intended to be made available for use by small-scale farmers with a royalty-free licence.

Genetic modification, unlike hybridisation, produces seed that breeds true. So the producers of genetically modified seeds license their use by farmers subject to an agreement that any resultant seed will not be held back and used for the next year's crop.

with the public at large. They ask whether we, the taxpayers, should support plant breeding as a public good. So they share both the multinationals' interest in furthering GM technology and the NGOs' interest in global equity.

Multinationals and ownership

The early history of the biotechnology industry shows that, for a commercial company to invest and expand its activities, it has to make a profit by owning and protecting its products through intellectual property rights. In the case of GM seeds, ownership remains with the corporations that market them throughout the entire lifetime of those seeds and their descendants, and for the lifetime of the patent, which is some 20 years. Corporations do not sell the seeds outright but license them for a fee to farmers who then buy new seed each season. Of course farmers do not *have* to use GM seed – but many do because of benefits such as higher yield or pest resistance.

This system greatly concerns the opponents of GM. They contend that intellectual property rights in seeds undermine food security: they want farmers, or at least their nations, to own GM seeds without the need for perpetual licence fees. National food security depends, they say, on national ownership of the means of production. But we live in a capitalist society and companies have to make a profit to invest in research and for people to invest in them. The alternative would be for the taxpayer to pay for the research and make it freely available to society.

One solution might be to create public licences such as exist for free computer software, but it is hard to see the biotechnology industry agreeing to a measure that eats into its profits. For this reason, environmentalists such as Friends of the Earth cannot envisage GM crops (not, it should be said, biotechnology as a whole) ever contributing to global food security or sustainable farming.

Impacts on human health

The anti-GM movement's current position on the health risks of GM foods is well summarised in *GMO Myths and Truths,* an evidence-based examination of the claims made for the safety and efficacy of GM crops.

This cites several cases showing evidence of health risk, including that of biochemist and nutritionist Arpad Pusztai, which caused a worldwide furore both in the media and in academic circles. In 1998, Dr Pusztai, a distinguished plant scientist and a world expert on a group of proteins found in plants called lectins, publicly announced some startling research results. These, apparently, demonstrated that rats fed genetically modified potatoes containing a lectin gene from the snowdrop plant suffered damaged immune systems and stunted growth of vital internal organs. GM food, it seemed, was potentially harmful to health.

This was a bombshell that reverberated beyond newspaper headlines and into the high-level political domain. Four days after Dr Pusztai's announcement, he was suspended from his job at the Rowett Research Institute in Aberdeen. But other scientists joined the controversy by springing to his defence. The distinguished medical journal *The Lancet* even published the research.

For commercial companies to invest in biotechnology, they need to make a profit by owning and protecting their products through intellectual property rights.

But Pusztai's career was over and, when the UK national academy of science, The Royal Society, carried out its own investigation, it concluded that the research was severely flawed and that the case for possible toxicity of GM potatoes had not been proven. What is clear from this episode, though, is the ferocity of the debate surrounding GM technology. In this case, conspiracy theories abounded. The anti-GM lobby, meanwhile, remained convinced that Pusztai's research revealed a valid representation of the dangers.

The anti-GM lobby also continues to worry a good deal about food crops genetically engineered to produce the *Bt* toxin from *Bacillus thuringiensis*. The toxin acts as an insecticide in crops such as Monsanto's *Bt* maize, rendering them resistant to pests. The obvious concern is that humans, in eating the toxin-containing maize, might damage their health. One Canadian study in an agricultural township in Quebec, for example, appeared to show that traces of *Bt* toxin from the maize were found in the blood of 93 per cent of women and in the umbilical cord and foetal blood of 80 per cent of them. Could the developing embryo be at risk from this?

Supporters of GM argue that the *Bt* protein breaks down in humans during digestion and there is no receptor for it in humans or animals so the fears are unfounded. Coincidentally, *Bt* bacteria are one of the few insecticides approved by organic farmers, and it is used as a commercial product by organic growers who spray it on vegetable and greenhouse crops. But still the arguments roll on, with one piece of research being put up only to be shot down by another.

Why is the debate so complicated?

It seems, on the face of it, as if the conflict between pros and antis should be resolved simply by applying objective scientific methods to examine their claims and counterclaims. If one side believes, as a result of a scientific experiment, that a particular GM product is harmful to health, then it should, in an ideal world, be possible to test that finding with another experiment to replicate – or disprove – the claim.

However, with GM as with other contentious sciences and technologies, we do not live in an ideal scientific world. Here, a clutch of non-scientific interests are in play, which leads to different preferences about which claims are accepted. Indeed, in this debate, each side is keen to point out the non-scientific interests that motivate the other side and how these distort their understanding of the truth.

Many NGOs, amongst other groups, insist that GM is a technology that swells the profits of rich multinationals at the expense of the world's poor, and that the governments of wealthier nations support their local multinationals and their technologies out of economic self-interest. Its advocates, in turn, accuse the NGOs of

BOX 23.2 Golden Rice in the crossfire

By the time researchers Potrykus and Beyer developed their technique for producing Golden Rice – developed to alleviate vitamin A deficiency and blindness in the many millions afflicted in developing countries – the biotechnology industry had become a powerful force in seed production, controlling much of the technology required to produce it.

Needing a partner experienced in international product development, Potrykus and Beyer originally turned to the Swiss agrochemical company Zeneca (now Syngenta), and did a deal whereby the rice would be freely licensed to farmers whose annual turnover was less than US$ 10,000, but would be commercially licensed to large-scale industrial farmers. Poor farmers in developing nations would benefit, but so too would the company through licensing seed to commercial producers. Subsequently Syngenta gave up control so as to avoid any accusations of it not being a humanitarian project. The company now has no commercial interest and does not expect any return or income, although it retains the patents to prevent these humanitarian varieties being sold by others.

There has been resistance to genetically modified crops from non-governmental organisations throughout, so unfortunately Potrykus, despite his good intentions, has been caught in the crossfire of the conflict between the biotechnology industry and its critics. However, the latter have themselves been charged with opposing the humanitarian aims of the project.

manufacturing crises in order to raise money. Or say that they have some sort of misplaced idealism about the nature of food and farming, and an ill-defined sense of what is in the public interest.

Once we look at the non-scientific bases for the debate, it becomes clear why it cannot be resolved by simple empirical and scientific means.

Asymmetric logic

The opponents of GM foods and crops, in attempting to establish health risks, need to demonstrate concrete examples of health hazard. But they do not need to show that *all* GM foods are dangerous, only that *some* are. GM advocates, on the other hand, want to be able to claim that there is no evidence at all of health risks. A universal claim like this can instantly be falsified if just one instance of health damage results from eating GM food.

> **"Individual GM foods and their safety should be assessed on a case-by-case basis ... it is not possible to make general statements on the safety of all GM foods."**
> *World Health Organization*

It may be, of course, that some GM foods are safe and some are not: both sides are right up to a point. But the only way to ascertain this is by adequate testing – which engenders another controversy. What is adequate? What methods should be used to ascertain GM food safety? The bottom line, for the World Health Organization, is that one cannot categorically say that GM foods are safe. Its 2012 publication *20 Questions on Genetically Modified Foods* states: "Individual GM foods and their safety should be assessed on a case-by-case basis ... it is not possible to make general statements on the safety of all GM foods."

Finding a middle way

If the GM debate is ever to be resolved, probably the best solution is to relocate the discussion to an acceptable middle ground. Here are two attempts to do this.

The UK Government Office for Science

In 2011 the UK Government Office for Science published the results of one of its in-depth Foresight studies: *The Future of Food and Farming – Challenges and Choices for Global Sustainability*. This argued that new technologies such as genetic engineering should not be excluded on ethical or moral grounds. At the same time it does not (over)emphasise the value of GM (or any other innovative technology) at the expense of existing practices – GM is not a panacea for all food production problems. Biotechnology as a whole is highly rated as a means of increasing output, but GM crops are grouped along with cloned livestock and nanotechnology as potential sources of improvement.

The report stresses the value of modern genetics in developing new varieties and breeds of crops but, over 200 pages, it only specifically mentions genetic modification eight times. It suggests that GM is a means of achieving faster or more efficient advances than other methods, but should be used when necessary and appropriate, rather than as the first choice of technique.

The IAASTD

Another important initiative (also discussed in Chapter 22) is the analysis by the International Assessment of Agricultural Knowledge, Science and Technology for Development – IAASTD. Its 2008 report puts biotechnology in a broad context of world agriculture, arguing that it can certainly contribute to agricultural science and knowledge but forms only a part of the solution to world hunger.

Scientific discoveries should not, it suggests, distract us from the social and environmental consequences of using new farming technologies. Managing global agriculture needs to take into account local indigenous knowledge: biotechnology is just one of many contributions to sustainable farming. And it places great emphasis on improving the productivity of small-scale farmers to alleviate poverty and hunger among rural populations. Biotechnology will play its part alongside local knowledge and best practice through developing partnerships between farmers and scientists.

Both the UK Government Office for Science and the International Assessment of Agricultural Knowledge, Science and Technology for Development suggest that while genetic modification can contribute, it only forms part of the solution to world hunger.

The IAASTD report also reminds us that biotechnology is not confined to GM but takes in conventional fermentation, plant and animal breeding techniques, as well as recent advances in tissue culture, irradiation, genomics and marker-assisted breeding and selection. It recognises the controversy over inserting transgenes into plant genomes but is not, in principle, opposed to using GM techniques. Indeed, it acknowledges that both the anti- and pro-GM claims can be true as long as they are not regarded as universally true.

The need to acquire mutual respect

Why is it so important to break down the antagonism and distrust in the GM debate? One strong reason is to avoid throwing out the baby with the bathwater. Genetically engineered foods and crops are just a few of the offerings of modern biotechnology. Even if the health risks posed by GM foods were to prove significant, there are other innovations flowing from biotechnology that can be safely and fruitfully deployed to increase crop yields or nutritional value. Let us not dismiss the whole enterprise out of hand.

If the two opposing forces could take a broad view, stepping aside from their different positions to discuss all points of view sympathetically, they might find common ground and end up realising the best of both their worlds.

They live after all on the same planet, one that faces significant problems. Exploring diverse, even conflicting evidence and listening to other viewpoints is arguably the best, if not the only way to resolve them.

RESEARCH, DISCUSSION
AND ESSAY TOPICS

- Briefly summarise the arguments for and against genetically modified crops and what you feel about the arguments.
- Public perception of genetically modified crops has been on a rollercoaster in Europe. Is it on the up or downward track at the moment and how will it go in the future?
- Taking the European Commission's 2010 report *Europeans and Biotechnology in 2010: Winds of Change?* and using pages 36–44 as your guide (see Further Reading), design a questionnaire to collect opinion about genetically modified food and give it to the members of your group or class, record their responses and write them up as a short report.
- The media has been central to the debate about genetically modified crops. Has it been fair and balanced in its coverage? If not, why not?
- How much does the general public know about the fundamentals of science? Is it important?
- What does the term "natural" mean to people generally and what does it mean scientifically?
- What are the risks of genetically modified crops that people talk about? Are they real?
- There is risk in every human activity but this always has to be balanced against the benefit of any particular activity.
- Non-governmental organisations such as Greenpeace and Friends of the Earth not only evaluate genetic modification technology from a scientific perspective but look more widely. What do they look at?
- The debate about genetically modified crops and food is often described as "the blind talking to the deaf". Can these two worlds be reconciled in the interests of overcoming such problems as poverty, starvation, disease and climate change?

FURTHER READING
AND USEFUL WEBSITES

Alliance for a New Green Revolution in Africa (AGRA).

    http://agra-alliance.org/

Antoniou, M., Robinson, C. and Fagan, J. (2014) *GMO Myths and Truths: An Evidence-based Examination of the Claims made for the Safety and Efficacy of Genetically Modified Crops.*

    http://earthopensource.org/index.php/reports/gmo-myths-and-truths

BASF (originally Badische Anilin- und Soda-Fabrik). *Fortuna.*

    http://basf.com/group/corporate/en/function/conversions:/publish/content/products-and-industries/biotechnology/images/Fortuna_VC.pdf

Bennett, D.J. and Jennings, R.C. (2013) *Successful Agricultural Innovation in Emerging Economies: New Genetic Technologies for Global Food Production.* Cambridge University Press, Cambridge. Chapters 20–25.

Diabetes.co.uk. Human insulin.

    http://www.diabetes.co.uk/insulin/human-insulin.html

EuropaBio (2013) *Pocketguide to GM Crops and Policies.*

    http://www.europabio.org/positions/pocket-guide-gm-crops-and-policies

EuropaBio (2014) *Undue Delays in EU Authorisation of Safe GM Crops.*

    http://www.europabio.org/sites/default/files/position/europabio_undue_delays_update_june_2014_0.pdf

EuropaBio (various dates) Frequently Asked Questions.

    http://www.europabio.org/faq%20

EuropaBio (various dates) Factsheets: Agricultural.

    http://www.europabio.org/filter/agricultural/type/fact%20%20

EuropaBio (various dates) Reports: Agricultural.

    http://www.europabio.org/filter/agricultural/type/report

European Commission (2006). *Europeans and Biotechnology in 2005: Patterns and Trends.*

    http://ec.europa.eu/public_opinion/archives/ebs/ebs_244b_en.pdf

European Commission (2010) *A Decade of EU-Funded GMO Research 2001–2010.*

    ftp://ftp.cordis.europa.eu/pub/fp7/kbbe/docs/a-decade-of-eu-funded-gmo-research_en.pdf

European Commission (2010) *Special Eurobarometer 354: Food-Related Risks.*

    http://www.efsa.europa.eu/en/factsheet/docs/reporten.pdf

European Commission (2010) *Special Eurobarometer: Science and Technology Report.*
http://ec.europa.eu/public_opinion/archives/ebs/ebs_340_en.pdf

European Commission (2010) *Europeans and Biotechnology in 2010: Winds of Change?*
http://ec.europa.eu/research/science-society/document_library/pdf_06/
europeans-biotechnology-in-2010_en.pdf

European Food Safety Authority (EFSA). *2010 Eurobarometer Survey Report on Risk Perception in the EU.*
http://www.efsa.europa.eu/en/riskcommunication/riskperception.htm

gmeducation.org.
http://www.gmeducation.org/

GMO Judy Carman.
http://gmojudycarman.org/

GMO Seralini.
http://www.gmoseralini.org/en/

GM Watch.
http://www.gmwatch.org/

International Assessment of Agricultural Knowledge, Science and Technology for Development (IAASTD). (2008) *Agriculture at a Crossroads: Synthesis Report.*
http://www.unep.org/dewa/agassessment/reports/IAASTD/EN/Agriculture%2
0at%20a%20Crossroads_Synthesis%20Report%20(English).pdf

Ipsos Mori (2014). *Public Attitudes to Science 2014.*
http://www.ipsos-mori.com/researchpublications/researcharchive/
3357/Public-Attitudes-to-Science-2014.aspx

Linking Environment And Farming (LEAF).
http://www.leafuk.org/leaf/home.eb

Monsanto. Roundup Ready System.
http://www.monsanto.com/weedmanagement/pages/roundup-ready-
system.aspx

National Centre for Biotechnology Education. Chymosin.
http://www.ncbe.reading.ac.uk/ncbe/gmfood/chymosin.html

Navdanya International (undated) *The GMO Emperor Has No Clothes: A Global Citizens Report on the State of GMOs – False Promises, Failed Technologies.*
http://www.navdanyainternational.it/images/doc/Full_Report_Rapporto_com
pleto.pdf

Rothamsted Research. Rothamsted GM Wheat Trial.
http://www.rothamsted.ac.uk/our-science/rothamsted-gm-wheat-trial

Smith, J. M. (2003) *Seeds of Deception: Exposing Industry and Government Lies about the Safety of the Genetically Engineered Foods you're Eating.*
http://books.google.co.uk/books/about/Seeds_of_deception.html?id=it9HIOQ 59bkC&redir_esc=y

Smith, J. M. (2007) *Genetic Roulette: The Documented Health Risks of Genetically Engineered Foods.*
http://seedsofdeception.com/shop/genetic-roulette/

The Government Office for Science, London (2011) *The Future of Food and Farming: Challenges and Choices for Global Sustainability.*
https://www.gov.uk/government/uploads/system/uploads/attachment_data/ file/288329/11-546-future-of-food-and-farming-report.pdf

Toxicsoy.org.
http://toxicsoy.org/toxicsoy/greenwash.html

Wikipedia. Árpád Pusztai.
http://en.wikipedia.org/wiki/%C3%81rp%C3%A1d_Pusztai

Wikipedia. Bordeaux mixture.
http://en.wikipedia.org/wiki/Bordeaux_mixture

Wikipedia. Diamond v. Chakrabarty.
http://en.wikipedia.org/wiki/Diamond_v._Chakrabarty

Wikipedia. Dolly (sheep).
http://en.wikipedia.org/wiki/Dolly_(sheep)

Wikipedia. Flavr Savr.
http://en.wikipedia.org/wiki/Flavr_Savr

World Health Organization (2014) *20 Questions on Genetically Modified Foods.*
http://www.who.int/foodsafety/publications/biotech/20questions/en/

GLOSSARY

Amino acids: A group of chemically simple substances that are linked together to make up proteins. Human proteins contain around 20 different amino acids of which nine are "essential" but cannot be made in the liver: instead we obtain them from our food. A good mixed diet will contain them all, but in many poor areas of the world where there is little food choice these essential components are missing. Genetic manipulation of crops to improve the protein composition in food plants is one route to making good these deficiencies.

Antibiotic-resistance marker gene technology: In the first generation of genetically modified crops, **marker genes** of bacterial origin but with resistance to antibiotics were coupled with a gene of interest (that codes for a desirable characteristic) as a way of selecting successfully transformed plant cells. Under this procedure, after the gene transfer has been carried out, the cells are treated with an antibiotic so that only the transformed cells survive, making it possible to identify those that also possess the gene of interest. Although the marker gene serves no purpose after this procedure, it remains part of the genetically modified plant and is virtually impossible to remove. Kanamycin is the antibiotic most commonly used, but it is now being phased out because of concern about the possible development of antibiotic resistance, and the procedure now uses other marker genes that do not require antibiotic selection.

Apomixis: Replacement of normal sexual reproduction in many plants and some animals by asexual reproduction without fertilisation. Apomictically produced offspring are genetically identical to the parent. Apomixis occurs in at least 33 families of flowering plants through many different mechanisms, and has evolved many times from sexually reproducing relatives.

Biodiversity: A broad term. It can mean the existence of a wide variety of *species* of plants, animals and microorganisms within a natural community or habitat. Or it can refer to communities within a particular environment, so-called *ecological diversity*. Then there is *genetic diversity* – wide genetic variation within an individual species – which is important for plant breeders when identifying parent lines with genes for delivering desirable traits.

Bio-economy/bio-based economy: These are terms referring to economic activity based on the use of biotechnology in industrial processes. The term is widely used by government agencies, international organisations and biotechnology companies. (*see also* **Industrial biotechnology**)

Bioinformatics: An important multi-disciplinary field, drawing on computer science, mathematics, engineering, etc., to help store, organise, analyse and retrieve biological data. Software tools have been developed, for example, to help make sense of gene sequence and mutation data from plants and to understand better the links between gene expression and protein synthesis – a key step in determining how crops function.

Biorefinery: A refinery that uses biomass from either waste or specially grown plant materials to produce fuels such as diesel, ethanol and value-added polymer chemicals such as plastics.

Biotechnology: Techniques for applying biological processes to produce desired substances. Not to be confused with genetic modification (GM), which is only one kind of biotechnology. The production of beer, wine, cheese and antibiotics have long relied on the use of fungi (e.g. yeast) and bacteria (e.g. *Escherichia coli*). Now plant scientists are employing modified bacteria or viral gene vectors to introduce novel genes into engineered crops.

C3 plants: Plants in which – during photosynthesis – carbon dioxide is first fixed into a compound containing three carbon atoms. The group includes most broadleaf plants and those that grow in temperate zones. C3 plants, which originated during the Mesozoic and Paleozoic eras (some 100–570 million years ago), still represent approximately 95 per cent of the Earth's plant biomass.

Carson, Rachel: An American marine biologist and conservationist whose writings are credited with launching the global environmental movement. *Silent Spring*, in particular, published in 1962, drew widespread public attention to the environmental risks associated with extensive use of synthetic pesticides. Although *Silent Spring* was met with fierce opposition, it spurred a change in pesticide policy in the USA and around the world.

Cellular imaging: Live cellular imaging is the study of living cells using time-lapse microscopy to obtain a better understanding of their biological functioning by visualising their cellular processes.

Cisgene, cisgenesis: Literally, having the same beginning. This refers to genes that come from the same or a closely related organism, as opposed to **transgenes**, which come from unrelated plants or organisms that could not otherwise be bred by conventional methods.

Club of Rome: The Club of Rome was founded in 1968 as an informal association of independent thinkers from the worlds of politics, business and science – men and women who are interested in contributing in a systemic interdisciplinary and holistic manner to a better world, with a common concern for the future of humanity and the planet. Its aims are to identify the most crucial problems which will determine the future of humanity through integrated and forward-looking analysis; to evaluate alternative scenarios for the future and to assess risks, choices and opportunities; to develop and propose practical solutions to the challenges identified; to communicate the new insights and knowledge derived from this analysis to decision makers in the public and private sectors as well as to the general public; and to stimulate public debate and effective action to improve prospects for the future.

Commodity crops: Crops grown, typically in large volume and at high intensity, specifically for the purpose of sale on the international commodities market (e.g. maize, wheat, rice, soybeans), as opposed to for direct consumption or to a factory for processing.

Companion cropping (intercropping): The planting of different crops close together for pest control, pollination, provision of habitat for beneficial creatures, maximised use of space, and to otherwise increase crop productivity. It is used by farmers and gardeners in both industrialised and developing countries and has been used for many centuries in cottage gardens in England and small-scale farming in Asia and Africa.

Conventional fermentation: The process used in brewing and wine making for the conversion of sugars to alcohol. The same process, followed by distillation, uses starch and sugar components of typically cereal crops (maize, wheat or barley) or sugar crops (cane or beet) to obtain pure ethanol (bioethanol) for use as a transport biofuel.

Cry proteins: Proteins produced by the common soil bacterium *Bacillus thuringiensis* and genetically engineered into crop plants to provide resistance against insect pests. They are toxic to certain insects (e.g. corn borers, corn rootworms, mosquitoes, black flies, army worms, tobacco hornworms, some types of beetles), but are harmless to mammals and most beneficial insects.

DNA, RNA: (*see* **Gene**)

Ehrlich, Paul: An American biologist who became widely known with his controversial book *The Population Bomb*, published in 1968, which predicted serious consequences from population growth in the face of limited resources. Some predictions were perhaps overstated, but Ehrlich's unease about the size of the human population and its impacts on the environment have, generally, been vindicated.

Expression (gene): The process by which information from a gene directs the synthesis of a functional product of the gene. These products are often proteins, but in non-protein-coding genes the product is a functional RNA (e.g. ribosomal and transfer RNA necessary for protein synthesis). Gene expression is necessary for all forms of life – multicellular plants and animals, bacteria and viruses – to generate the macromolecular machinery for life.

Extension services (agricultural): The application of research and new knowledge to agriculture through educating farmers in agricultural and business skills, especially in developing countries. Communication and learning activities carried out for rural farmers, often through government agencies and supported by international development organisations such as the World Bank.

Farnesene: A group of related chemical compounds. One is found in the coating of apples and other fruits, and is responsible for the characteristic green apple odour. Another is released by aphids (green or black fly) as an alarm **pheromone** upon death to warn away other aphids. Several plants, including potato, have been shown to synthesise this pheromone as a natural insect repellent.

First/second-generation: These terms refer, respectively, to a technology in the form in which it is first developed and to the form in which it then later develops, for example, first- and second-generation genetically modified (GM) plants and first- and second-generation biofuels.

Forage: Plant material (mainly plant leaves and stems) eaten by grazing livestock. Historically, the term was applied only to plants eaten by the animals directly as pasture, but it is also used for plants cut for fodder, especially as hay or silage.

Gene, genome, genomics, gene expression, gene discovery: Genes are the molecular units of heredity encoded in a molecule of DNA – the familiar double helix-shaped structure described by Watson and Crick in their historic paper in *Nature* in 1953. They consist of long chains of smaller units called nucleotides (adenine, cytosine, guanine and thiamine, abbreviated to A, C, G and T), the sequences of which determine the gene's function. The total complement of genes, packaged in chromosomes within cells, is the **genome**. When a gene is switched on and active – **expressed** – the information carried by DNA in the form of a chemical code is copied by the formation of another molecule, messenger RNA, which carries the coded message to the protein synthetic machinery in the cell (ribosomes) where it is translated into a protein. That is the function of genes – to make proteins that will carry out a variety of tasks within the organism. In plants, some control growth and height, for example, others insect resistance or yield. (*see also* **Expression**)

Gene flow: Gene flow (or gene migration) is the transfer of genes from one population of closely related plants to another, for example by the transfer of pollen by wind, or in some cases by water or animals, between populations which can interbreed.

Gene therapy: The use of DNA to treat a genetically based disease by delivering therapeutic DNA into a patient's cells to alleviate or cure the disease. The most common form of gene therapy involves using DNA that codes for a functional therapeutic gene to replace a mutated gene that produces a disease or disability.

Genetic modification (or manipulation) (GM) and genetic engineering: All refer to the use of modern biotechnology techniques to change the genes of an organism such as a virus, bacterium, plant or animal. A genetically modified organism (GMO) is any living organism that has been changed using genetic modification.

Genome evolution: The process by which a genome sequence or size changes over time. The study of genome evolution involves several fields of research such as structural analysis of the genome, the study of ancient genomes and the comparison of genomes and the genetic information they contain between different species, genera, families, etc., of living organisms – viruses, bacteria, plants, animals.

Genomics: The study of genes.

Genotype: The genetic make-up or characteristics of a cell, organism or individual, usually with reference to a specific characteristic.

Germplasm: The total hereditary material of plants – in the form of DNA – transmitted to offspring through germ cells and giving rise to succeeding generations. Germplasm banks in the form of seeds have been set up to try to conserve the genetic material which may be lost when older crops are replaced by newer varieties.

GM foods: Genetically modified, genetically engineered, the product of recombinant DNA technology – these terms are pretty well interchangeable. Much of the debate and controversy surrounding novel biotechnology turns on GM crops and foods, but these are not the only form of newly developed crop varieties.

Green Revolution: An important series of research, development and technology transfer initiatives for increasing global agriculture production that began in the late 1940s and largely came to fruition in the 1960s. Norman Borlaug, the Father of the Green Revolution, built on his early success in Mexico by taking a programme of plant breeding, irrigation and financing of agrochemicals to India and other parts of the world, where yields improved dramatically.

Greenhouse gases: Pollutant gases, largely from human activity (anthropogenic impact), that absorb infrared radiation from the sun and thereby contribute to global warming – the enhanced greenhouse effect. Carbon dioxide from car exhausts, power stations and other fossil-fuel sources is the main concern. But other pollutants contribute, namely nitrogen oxides, ozone, methane and chlorofluorocarbons.

Hectare: The standardised metric unit for measuring land – 10,000 square metres. It is used throughout this book, though some people often prefer to use the acre (1 hectare = 2.471 acres).

Homologous gene targeting: The genetic technique in which a gene sequence is exchanged between two similar or identical molecules of DNA (in a genome) to modify a gene. It can be used to delete or add a gene and introduce mutations into the DNA for any gene, regardless of the function or size of the gene.

Horizontal gene transfer: The transfer of genes between organisms, commonly bacteria, other than by conventional sexual or asexual reproduction. Also termed lateral gene transfer, it differs from the transmission of genes from the parental generation to offspring via sexual or asexual reproduction. Horizontal gene transfer has been shown to be an important factor in the evolution of many organisms, and may even be the dominant form of genetic transfer among single-celled organisms.

Hybrid: The offspring of plants that are sexually compatible and hence can inter-breed, and have genomes that are similar or closely related.

Hybrid vigour: Hybrid vigour, or heterosis, is the improved or increased functioning of any biological characteristic in a hybrid offspring by combining the genetic contributions of its parents. This is often observed as greater biomass, speed of development and fertility than in either parent.

Induced systemic resistance: This works by preconditioning a plant's defences against a pathogen (e.g. fungus, bacteria or virus) by prior infection or treatment that induces resistance against a subsequent infection by a pathogen or attack by a parasite.

Industrial biotechnology: Known also as "white biotechnology" (as against "red" for medical biotechnologies and "green" for agricultural biotechnologies), is the application of biotechnology for industrial purposes, including industrial fermentation, which includes the practice of using cells such as microorganisms, or components of cells like enzymes to generate industrially useful products such as chemicals, food and animal feed, detergents, textiles and biofuels. In doing so, biotechnology uses renewable raw materials and may contribute to lowering greenhouse gas emissions and moving away from a petrochemical-based economy. (*see also* **Bio-economy**)

Intercropping: *see* **Companion cropping**

Legumes: Plants in the family Leguminosae, or the fruit or seed of such a plant. Legumes are grown agriculturally, primarily for their food grain seed, for livestock forage and silage, and as soil-enhancing "green manure" because they are capable of fixing nitrogen from the atmosphere in specialised root nodules, which then release the nitrogen to the soil when the plant decays, making it available for other plants. Well-known legumes include alfalfa, clover, peas, beans, lentils, mesquite, carob, soybeans and peanuts.

Linkage drag: The reduction in fitness of the offspring produced by plant breeding due to deleterious genes being introduced together with the beneficial gene or genes during backcrossing.

Lodging: Occurs when the stems of cereal plants cannot support the weight of the plants. All cereal crops such as wheat, rice and barley, and all varieties, are susceptible in varying degrees. Severe lodging is costly due to its effects on grain formation and associated harvesting problems and losses as it takes much more time to harvest a lodged crop than a standing one, if it can be harvested at all.

Low-till agriculture: The planting practice in which disturbance of the soil is kept to a minimum. It results in considerable savings in farmers' time, agricultural machinery, diesel fuel, etc. By reducing ploughing, it also conserves the structure of the top-soil which determines its water-holding capacity and the ease with which plants put down roots, as well as maintaining the carbon storage capacity of the soil. (*see also* **No-till farming**)

Macronutrients/micronutrients: As the terms imply, macronutrients are required in large amounts for maintaining health, micronutrients in small amounts. Macronutrients – protein, carbohydrates and fats – provide the body with energy, while micronutrients – minerals including iron and zinc, and vitamins including A, C, D and the B complex – play a vital role in the body's metabolism and resistance to disease. Both types of nutrients are normally available in a balanced diet.

Malthus, Thomas: British author of an extremely influential book, published in 1789, *An Essay on the Principle of Population*. Malthus feared that continuing population growth in the face of limited resources would lead to hunger and poverty on a grand scale. His ideas influenced the pioneering theorists of evolution by natural selection, Charles Darwin and Alfred Russel Wallace.

Marker genes, marker-assisted selection/breeding: Markers are genes or short sequences of DNA that serve as a tag for another, closely linked gene. In plant breeding, markers are used to map and select genes of interest – those that code for desirable characteristics (traits), more efficiently than traditional selection systems.

Mass spectrometry: A technique now in common use in analytical laboratories for identifying and studying the physical, chemical or biological properties of a great variety of compounds. It is used for determining the elemental composition of a sample, the masses of particles and molecules, and for elucidating the chemical structures of molecules.

Metabolism, metabolic pathway: All the chemical reactions occurring in living organisms. Plants obtain their basic starting material for these reactions from their external environment: carbon dioxide, water and minerals such as nitrogen, phosphorus and potassium. The internal chemistry proceeds by a number of steps – the metabolic pathways – which are facilitated by enzymes as catalysts.

Mitochondrion (*pl.* mitochondria): A specialized subunit found within most of the cells that make up plants, animals, fungi, and many other forms of life (with the exception of largely single-celled organisms such as bacteria). Mitochondria are involved in making energy available to the cell, and other tasks such as signalling, cellular differentiation, the inheritance of certain characteristics, the control of the cell cycle and cell growth and death. Some cells have only a single mitochondrion, whereas others can contain several thousand.

Micronutrient: *see* **Macronutrient**

Modelling: A simulation, usually using a computer, of a real-world phenomenon or system, often for predictive purposes. Weather forecasts are an everyday example. For agriculture, models can be used to forecast production, population growth, environmental impacts and so on. Their reliability depends both on the quality of the mathematical design and the data put into it.

Molecular genomics: The field of genetics that applies recombinant DNA, DNA sequencing and bioinformatics to sequence, assemble and analyse the function and structure of genomes (the complete set of DNA within a single cell of an organism).

Molecular plant breeding: The application of molecular biology techniques in plant breeding, including gene discovery, genetic engineering/modification, genetic transformation and marker-assisted selection. (*see also* **Gene** *and* **Markers**)

Nanoscience, nanotechnology, nanobiotechnology, nanofoods: Nano- (meaning dwarf) science deals with matter at the vanishingly small scale of billionths of a metre. It is now possible to design and build structures at the nanoscale that can be introduced into foods. Examples are nanofilters to remove bacteria from milk without the need for boiling, or sensors to detect pathogens.

New platform: An integrated internet-based facility providing up-to-date techniques for improving plant breeding.

Next-generation sequencing: The technique in which the sequence of a small fragment of DNA is determined from signals emitted as each fragment is re-synthesised from a strand of DNA in parallel manner across millions of reactions. It enables the rapid sequencing of long stretches of DNA making up whole genomes, and produces hundreds of gigabytes of data in a single sequencing run.

Nitrogen fixation: The process by which nitrogen in the atmosphere is converted into ammonia and stored in microorganisms and plants. It is essential for all forms of life because nitrogen is required to synthesise the basic building blocks of plants, animals and other life forms, e.g., nucleotides for DNA and RNA and amino acids for proteins. Therefore nitrogen fixation is essential for agriculture. Microorganisms that can fix nitrogen are prokaryotes – bacteria and archaea (which differ from bacteria in certain characteristics) – called diazotrophs. Some higher plants (especially members of the bean family – *see* **Legumes**) and some animals (termites) have formed associations (symbiosis) with diazotrophs.

No-till farming (NTF): Sometimes called zero tillage or direct planting, this is a method of growing crops that does not disturb the soil through tillage (ploughing, removing weeds, preparing for planting and creating irrigation channels). The effect is to increase the amounts of water and organic nutrients in the soil and decrease erosion. NTF also helps to reduce the amount of diesel used by farm machinery and thereby cut cost and pollution, and helps to maintain the bio-diversity of soil organisms such as microbes, arthropods and earthworms. (*see also* **Low-till agriculture**)

Nuclear transfer: A procedure in which a cell's nucleus is removed and placed into an egg cell with its own nucleus removed so that the genetic information from the donor nucleus controls the resulting cell. Such cells can be induced to form embryos and this process was used to create the Dolly, the cloned sheep.

Orphan crops: Crops that until recently have received little attention from scientific researchers and scant funding for improvement, despite their importance for food security in poorer/developing regions of the world. They are defined as a group of crops that are vital to the economy of developing countries due to their suitability to the agro-ecology and socio-economic conditions, but which remain largely unimproved.

Pathogen: Any disease-causing microorganisms, such as bacteria, viruses, fungi and protozoa, which can invade a plant (or animal), establish themselves and multiply to the detriment of the host.

Pharmacogenomics/pharmacogenetics: While these terms are broadly inter-changeable, pharmacogenomics is the analysis of entire genomes, across groups of individuals, to identify the genetic factors influencing responses to a drug, while pharmacogenetics is the study of an individual's genetic make-up in order to predict responses to a drug and guide prescription.

Phenotype analysis: The analysis of the composite of an organism's observable characteristics or traits such as its structure, development, biochemical or physio-logical properties, fitness and behaviour resulting from the expression of an organism's genes together with the influence of environmental factors, and the interactions between the two.

Pheromone: A chemical secreted or excreted that triggers a social response in members of the same species. There are alarm pheromones, food trail pheromones, sex pheromones, and many others that affect behaviour or physiology. Pheromones are used by single-celled to complex multi-cellular organisms and particularly by insects, while some vertebrates and plants also use them to communicate.

Photosynthesis: The chemical process by which plants synthesise the essential organic compounds of which they are made from carbon dioxide and water, using the energy of sunlight. Since all other forms of life depend directly or indirectly on plants for food, photosynthesis is the basis of life on the planet. It has also been responsible for generating all the oxygen in the atmosphere, as oxygen is released during the process.

Plant-incorporated protectants: Pesticides produced by plants and the genetic material necessary for the plant to produce the substance, for example the pesticidal protein produced by a gene from the soil bacterium *Bacillus thuringiensis* introduced into the plant's genetic material by genetic engineering. The plant then manu-factures the pesticidal protein that controls the pest when it feeds on the plant.

Precautionary principle: The precautionary principle (or precautionary approach) states that if an action or policy is suspected of carrying a risk of causing harm to the public or to the environment, but there is no scientific consensus that the action or policy is harmful, the burden of proof that it is *not* harmful falls on those promoting the action or policy. The general principles of risk management apply:
- proportionality between the measures taken and the chosen level of protection;

- non-discrimination in application of the measures;
- consistency of the measures with similar measures already taken in similar situations or using similar approaches;
- examination of the benefits and costs of action or lack of action;
- review of the measures in the light of scientific developments.

Precursors: In biological processes, substances from which others, usually later in chains of substances, are formed.

Protein, proteome, proteomics: Proteins play a vital role in the functioning of all living matter. They are the workforce within plant cells where they have a variety of roles – as enzymes and structural elements, etc. The full complement of proteins in the cell is the **proteome**, while **proteomics** – the study of the proteome – enables us to identify, characterise, quantify and follow changes in the protein network of the plant cell and thus gain deep insights into the real-time activity of a plant at the level of individual molecules.

Provitamin: A substance with little or no vitamin activity that can be converted by normal metabolic processes into the active vitamin. An example is provitamin A – beta-carotene – the synthesis of which has been genetically engineered into Golden Rice.

Recombinant DNA (rDNA): Genetically engineered DNA prepared by using laboratory methods to insert genes from one species of an organism (or, recently, chemically synthesised DNA) into the cells of an organism of a different species, creating sequences that would not otherwise be found in biological organisms. Such DNA becomes part of the host's genetic make-up and is replicated from one generation to succeeding generations.

R&D: Research and development. In the domain of modern plant biotechnology, this means uncovering new basic scientific knowledge about, for example, genes that confer certain characteristics such as stress or pathogen tolerance and then applying those insights to develop new products or processes that will improve current crops.

Semiochemicals: Chemical substances that carry a message for the purpose of communication between individuals of the same or different species. (*see also* **Pheromone**)

Sequencing: The process of determining the exact nucleotide sequence of a section of DNA – spelling out the individual building blocks of a fragment of DNA and leading to the identification of individual genes. Whole genome sequencing (also known as full, complete or entire genome sequencing) determines the complete DNA sequence of an organism's genome at a single time. The Human Genome Project did this for the whole of our genetic make-up.

Selection pressure: The extent to which an organism – such as a crop plant – with particular characteristics is either favoured or challenged by the demands of the environment in which it is being cultivated. Climate change, for example, is exerting a new set of selective pressures on many crops.

Staple crops: The most commonly consumed foods in the diet of people in a specific region. They vary according to the availability of seed or other planting materials and the topography of the land, type of soil and climate. They are usually cereal grains or starchy root vegetables that can be stored for a long time. The most globally important include rice, maize, wheat and potatoes. Others are barley, oats, rye, buckwheat, cassava, lentils, millet, sorghum, cow pea, soybeans, sweet potato and yam.

Sustainability: In agriculture, the ecosystem-oriented approach to farming, which is sensitive to practices that could cause long-term damage.

Sustainable agricultural intensification: Defined as "producing more output from the same area of land while reducing the negative environmental impacts". Both agricultural and environmental outcomes are pre-eminent under sustainable intensification.

Synthetic biology: The synthesis of complex, biologically based systems with functions that do not exist in nature applied at all levels of biological structures from individual molecules to whole cells, tissues and organisms. A developing field of biology which, in essence, is expected to enable the design of biological systems in a rational and systematic way. What separates synthetic biology from genetic engineering is that, rather than altering an already existing DNA strand, synthetic biology puts these "blocks" together from scratch to build an entirely new strand of DNA which is then placed into a living cell.

Systemic acquired resistance: The resistance response of the whole plant following exposure to a pathogen (anything that can produce a disease).

Systems biology: A biology-based interdisciplinary field that focuses on studying complex interactions in biological systems, and which aims to model and discover the properties of cells, tissues and organisms functioning as a system. These typically involve metabolic networks or cell signalling networks – the complete set of metabolic and physical processes that determine the physiological and biochemical properties of a cell. Systems biology makes heavy use of mathematical and computational models.

Tissue culture: Growing the tissues of plants (or other organisms) in a suitable culture medium containing appropriate nutrients. The technique gives insights into how growth and cellular differentiation are controlled. Breeders are able to use it to regenerate complete plants by vegetative propagation.

Trait, complex trait: Crop traits or characteristics such as herbicide tolerance or insect resistance can be introduced singly or in combination – so-called trait stacking, as with maize or cotton engineered to be both insect-resistant and herbicide-tolerant. Some traits are determined by single genes, others by a number of genes (complex traits) .

Transgene: (*see* **Cisgene**)

Transcriptome: All the RNA molecules produced in one or a population of cells. This reflects the genes being actively expressed at any one time. Transcriptomics or expression profiling is the technique for examining these expression levels during plant growth and development.

Vegetative reproduction (or propagation, multiplication or cloning): A form of asexual reproduction in plants by which new organisms arise from the parent plant without the production of seeds or spores. Natural vegetative propagation is mostly found in herbaceous and woody perennial plants, and typically involves structural modifications of the stem, although any horizontal, underground part of a plant (whether stem, leaf or root) can contribute to vegetative reproduction. Man-made methods of vegetative reproduction are usually enhancements of natural processes, but range from rooting cuttings to grafting and artificial propagation by laboratory tissue culture.

ACRONYMS

AATF   African Agricultural Technology Foundation
ABNE   African Biosafety Network of Expertise
AGRA   Alliance for a New Green Revolution in Africa
AOCC   African Orphan Crops Consortium
AU   African Union
ASSAF   Academy of Sciences of South Africa
BREAD   Basic Research to Enable Agricultural Development
BSE   Bovine spongiform encephalopathy
CBD   Convention on Biological Diversity
Bt   *Bacillus thuringiensis*
DNA   Deoxyribonucleic acid
EFSA   European Food Safety Authority
EIQ   Environmental Impact Quotient
EC   European Commission
EU   European Union
FAO   Food and Agriculture Organization of the United Nations
GEAC   Genetic Engineering Appraisal/Approval Committee
GHI   Global Hunger Index
GM   Genetic modification, genetically modified
GMO   Genetically modified organism
IAASTD   International Assessment of Agricultural Science and Technology
      for Development
ICRAF   World Agroforestry Centre
IP   Intellectual property
IPR   Intellectual property rights
ISAAA   International Service for the Acquisition of Agri-biotech Applications
ISR   Induced systemic resistance
KBBE   Knowledge-based bio-economy
LEAF   Linking Environment And Farming
MAGIC   Multi-parent Advanced Generation InterCross
MAS   Marker-assisted selection
NEPAD   New Partnership for Africa's Development
NGO   Non-governmental organisation

NGS	Next-generation sequencing
NSF	National Science Foundation
NTF	No-till farming
OECD	Organisation for Economic Co-operation and Development
PEER	Partnerships for Enhanced Engagement in Research
PRSV	Papaya ringspot virus
R&D	Research and development
RNA	Ribonucleic acid
SAR	Systemic acquired resistance
SNP	Single nucleotide polymorphism
TILLING	Targeted Induced Local Lesions IN Genomes
UN	United Nations
USAID	US Agency for International Development
USDA	US Department of Agriculture
WHO	Word Health Organization
WTO	World Trade Organization

INDEX